THE THAMES

THE THAMES

England's River

JONATHAN SCHNEER

LITTLE, BROWN

A *Little, Brown* Book

First published in Great Britain in 2005 by Little, Brown

Copyright © 2005 Jonathan Schneer

The moral right of the author has been asserted.

A CIP catalogue record for this book
is available from the British Library.

ISBN 0 316 86139 1

Typeset in Spectrum by M Rules
Printed and bound in Great Britain
by Clays Ltd, St Ives plc

Little, Brown
An imprint of
Time Warner Book Group UK
Brettenham House
Lancaster Place
London WC2E 7EN
www.twbg.co.uk

Contents

Acknowledgements		vii
Preface		ix
Maps		xiii
1	The Reeds of Runnymede	1
2	The River and Liberty	21
3	The Tides of History	43
4	Staging the River	57
5	The River and the Age of Reason	81
6	Water, Air, Earth, Fire	115
7	Dark Waters	136
8	The Earthly Paradise	161
9	River of Fire	194
10	Blue River	217
11	Taming the Thames	240
12	The Thames Transformed	263
	Conclusion: The Thames and the Nation	286
	Notes	292
	Bibliography	308
	Index	325

Acknowledgements

I walked the entire Thames Path (in stages) with an old friend and fellow historian, Chris Clark. What splendid times and talks we had. For much of whatever may be good in this book, Chris is responsible. So are other friends who have helped me to think about it and some of whom have read select chapters: Margot Finn, Catherine Hall, Jim Obelkevich, Ross McKibbin, Michael Barry, Ewen Green, Clare Brant, Paul Monod, Greg Nobles, Andrea Tone and John Tone.

I would like to thank the fellows of Magdalen College, Oxford, for electing me a Visiting Fellow during the summer term of 2002, and the fellows of St John's College, Oxford, for electing me Senior Visiting Research Fellow for the fall term of 2003. The two terms at the Bodleian Library provided by these fellowships were essential. And once again I would like to thank Tania Alexander for offering hospitality in London. Tania has transformed my experience of that wonderful city.

Mark Freedland at St John's College, Oxford, read an early draft of the entire manuscript and generously offered good advice. So did my cousin, John Drucker, and another old friend, David Arathorn. Then when I gave the manuscript to Lara Heimert, my editor at Yale University Press, and to Tim Whiting, my editor at Little, Brown (UK), both read quickly and closely and offered important suggestions for improving it. I would also like to thank the anonymous readers commissioned by Yale Press. Of course any errors that still remain are my responsibility.

Then I want to thank my American agent, Emma Parry, and my English agent, Peter Robinson, both of whom have offered crucial encouragement and advice throughout.

Finally, and as always, thanks to my family, to whom this book is dedicated, for putting up with this latest of my scholarly projects, and especially to my wife, Margaret Hayman, for putting up with me in general.

Preface

*I*t is a mere rivulet compared with the greatest rivers in the world: the Nile in Africa, the Mississippi in North America, the Amazon in South America, the Ganges in India, the Yangtze in China, to name only a few. It is shorter and less impressive than the Danube, the Rhine, the Loire or the Seine in Europe; it is not even the longest river in Britain.[1] Yet who would deny that the Thames is more an avenue of history than any other waterway, that it is a national river in a way that other rivers are not?

The United States, Brazil, India, and China are geographically too vast for a single river to dominate the national history. Other great rivers may run through more than one country, or form a border between countries: they cannot be national rivers either. The Thames runs through England's heartland, west to east, a main thread through a smallish tapestry, an unavoidable presence physically and psychologically. The Scots have their Clyde, the Welsh their Severn, the Irish their Shannon: Thames may or may not be Britain's river, but indubitably it is England's.

Today one may walk along a path beside the river from its source to the Thames Barrier, perhaps 200 miles of its 220-mile length. I walked it in bits and pieces over the course of about eight months beginning in November 2001. I saw it in all its aspects and seasons: with an early evening sun in May slanting on a dark and lonely river running through empty fields east of Lechlade before Kelmscott; on a bright crisp autumn morning with deepest blue sky over the elegant river front at Maidenhead; on a damp winter's day that greyed the bleak, strangely impressive peninsula jutting into the river where sits the ill-fated Millennium Dome. But one walks the Thames less for the scenery than for the history. Almost every mile brings to mind a historical event or a work of art or literature. At least the miles did that for me. I knew already that I wanted to write about the Thames, but it was while walking the Thames Path that this book began to take shape in my mind.

There are too many books about the Thames to count, and some of them are very good. Most, however, deal with only a part of the river (the Middle Thames, the London Thames, the tidal Thames), or with an aspect of the river's history (pollution, locks, bridges, tunnels, boats, etc.). Others focus upon a relatively short span of time (Victorian Thames, twentieth-century Thames), or upon the experiences of an author who decided to trace the river's course by barge or yacht or canoe or even aeroplane. Then there are the books of photographs. And yet the Thames was there when the first inhabitants arrived, and when they cleared the nearby forests; it saw the Romans in and out, and all the other invaders and conquerors. King John accepted the Magna Carta in a meadow by the Thames; Anne Boleyn spent her last days in the Tower of London overlooking the Thames; King George first heard Handel's *Water Music* in a barge upon the Thames; William Morris and Stanley Spencer and countless other artists and poets celebrated the Thames; German bombers followed the Thames as a pathway to London where they loosed their bombs; half a century later, when Michael Heseltine plotted the revival of Britain's economic links with

Europe, he called his plan 'Thames Gateway'. The Thames runs through the warp and woof of English history. It deserves a book that views it in this light.

Yet there have been few good ones. In 1887 Hilaire Belloc offered a narrative history, eminently readable but now hopelessly dated. Frederick Thacker's three volumes written early in the twentieth century (about 'the stripling Thames', which is the upper part of the river, and about locks on the river, and about the Thames Conservancy, the river's governing body) examine aspects of Thames history over many centuries, but make no attempt to link them with the more general evolution of English society. They are charming and meandering books, like the middle and upper reaches of the river itself, more the work of an antiquarian than a modern scholar. There have been others since, more or less satisfactory.[2] The best of them, and the most recent, is Patrick Wright's *The River: The Thames in Our Time*, which shows how the contemporary river and the people who live near or by it are linked with the historic river and the men and women of earlier times. But his book is personal, anecdotal by design, loosely structured with regard to chronology and geography.

The Thames is as inexhaustible a subject as English history itself. Mention that you are writing a book about the Thames and someone inevitably will cite a work or an event that you have left out. Well, the historian must choose. I have tried to write, roughly in chronological order, about subjects that convey the intertwining of the river's and the country's histories. I have tried to convey their mythic qualities, by which I do not mean that I write about myths, but rather that I try to link my subjects with the ongoing construction of England. At first I thought this meant writing a book about a specific process, the river's connection with the evolution of English identity; but although understandings of the Thames have sometimes contributed to definitions of the nation as a whole, they have not done so always, and they have rarely done so crucially. I have attempted to identify a few of those rare occasions, but usually a river is a river is a river. This is a book about some of the river's shifting meanings and their connections with the national story over many millennia.

Jonathan Schneer
Atlanta, GA
1 July 2004

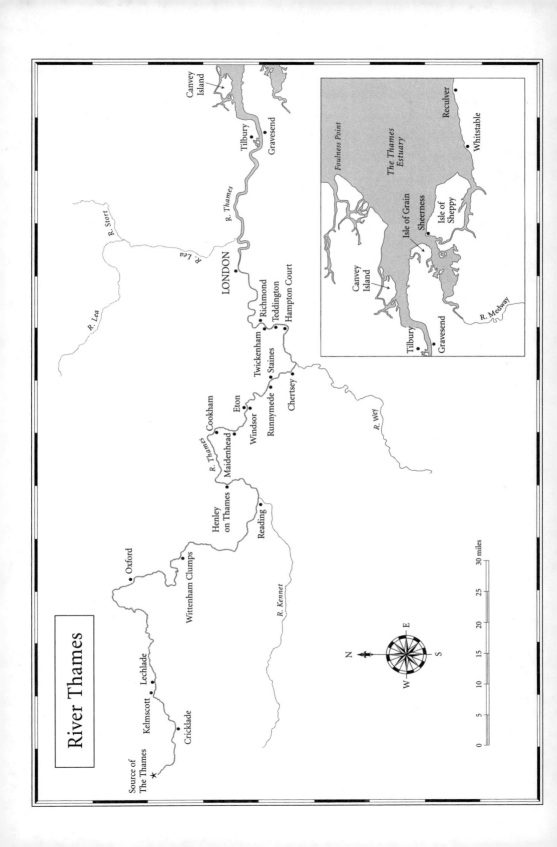

River Thames

Source of The Thames ★

Kelmscott
Lechlade
Cricklade

Oxford
Wittenham Clumps

R. Thames

Henley on Thames
Maidenhead
Cookham
Eton
Windsor
Reading

R. Kennet

Twickenham
Staines
Runnymede
Chertsey

R. Wey

R. Thames

Richmond
Teddington
Hampton Court

LONDON

R. Lea
R. Stort
R. Lea

Tilbury
Gravesend
Canvey Island

R. Thames

N
W   E
S

0   5   10   15   20   25   30 miles

The Thames Estuary

Foulness Point

Canvey Island

Tilbury
Gravesend

R. Medway

Isle of Grain
Sheerness
Isle of Sheppy

Reculver
Whitstable

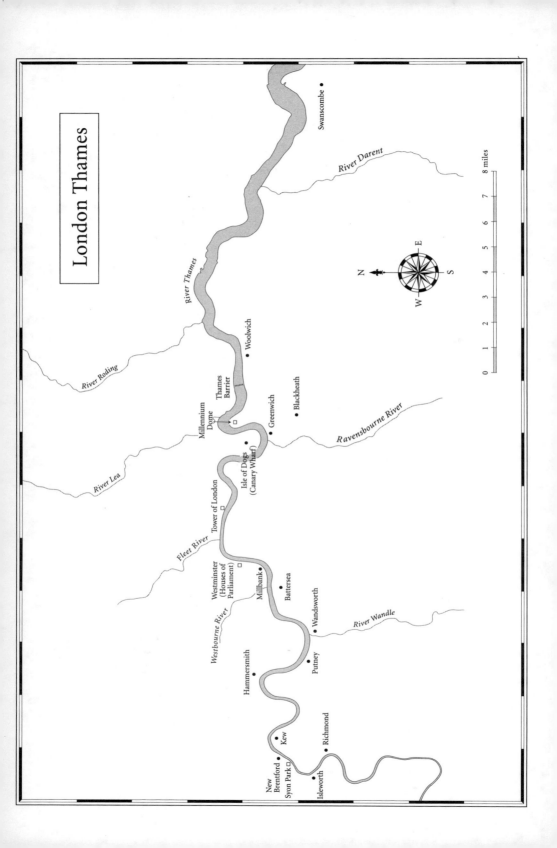

London Thames

Swanscombe

River Darent

River Thames

River Roding

Woolwich

River Lea

Thames Barrier

Millennium Dome

Greenwich

Blackheath

Ravensbourne River

Isle of Dogs (Canary Wharf)

Fleet River

Tower of London

Westbourne River

Westminster (Houses of Parliament)

Millbank

Battersea

Wandsworth

River Wandle

Hammersmith

Putney

Kew

Richmond

New Brentford

Syon Park

Isleworth

N
W   E
S

0 1 2 3 4 5 6 7 8 miles

THE THAMES

1

The Reeds of Runnymede

*T*he sea ends, the river starts, somewhere inside the great, wide, funnel-shaped estuary called the Nore, whose easternmost boundaries we set arbitrarily at Whitstable on the south, and Foulness Point on the north; somewhere within this vast basin at the edge of the Thames where the English fleet used to anchor, sails furled, ropes coiled, taking on supplies and waiting for orders. When the earth and moon line up in a certain conjunction with the sun, a force of gravity pulls the ocean water westward against the east coast of Britain; at the wide aperture of the river Thames, it pulls it inland, into England. It sucks the salt water past the Isle of Sheppey and the Isle of Grain into bays, inlets, coves and channels once known best to smugglers. It draws it past the Medway, where Dutch sailors bearing fire and sword suddenly appeared in 1667, having burst through the rusty chain supposed to block the river. It pulls it past the cemetery of St James's Church in the tiny village of Cooling, where today one may see the thirteen caskets of the Comport family, all dead of 'marsh fever', and where Dickens's creation Pip was supposed, one misty night, to have confronted the terrifying convict Magwitch.

The salty water rolls westwards through a flat, featureless landscape, as if drawn to a great magnet. The river becomes more recognisably a river with banks and mudflats, a wide river, looping towards London. It flows past Canvey Island, devastated in the floods of 1953, when fifty-eight drowned, and water swirled shoulder-deep down the streets and alleys of the town. It flows past Tilbury, where Queen Elizabeth rallied her troops against the Spanish Armada in 1588, past Greenwich and the great Observatory, past Blackheath, where in 1381 the peasant armies of Wat Tyler encamped. Onward it rushes, through London, beneath the Tower of London, St Paul's Cathedral, the Houses of Parliament, past New Brentford where the artist Turner lived as a child with his uncle, forward to suburban Putney, where three hundred and fifty years ago the Levellers and Cromwell debated democracy, and further still, past Twickenham, home to Pope, and past Richmond, home to the poet Spenser. The flood will not turn until it reaches Teddington, 68½ statute miles from the sea.

Begin at the other end. The Thames rises in a field near Trewsbury Mead, south of Cirencester, on the edge of the Cotswold Hills, under a great ash tree. Or it rises in a different field, a few miles distant, near Seven Springs, in the parish of Coberley (although most now say this is the wellspring of the river Churn, which joins the Thames at Cricklade). The source of the Thames has been a matter of dispute. Soon enough, however, the infant Thames is indisputably evident east and south of Trewsbury as a greener line snaking through a green meadow, then as a trickle of water, finally as a narrow stream. Here the countryside is less flat than near the coast, it is dotted with villages of grey slate or golden Cotswold stone, every village containing its church tower and spire to overlook the meandering watercourse.

Past Cricklade and Lechlade the stream gently winds and slowly broadens, through pleasant fields. It passes Kelmscott village - Utopia, William Morris thought it.

> What better place than this then could we find
> By this sweet stream that knows not of the sea,

This little stream whose hamlets scarce have names,
This far-off lonely mother of the Thames.

It runs in twists and turns under ancient bridges, past abandoned priories, lowing cattle, towards Port Meadow, outside Oxford.

And nearer to the river's trembling edge [Shelley wrote]
There grew broad flag flowers, purple pranked with white,
And starry river buds among the sedge,
And floating water-lilies, broad and bright . . .

Gradually it widens, so that racing sculls may glide three abreast up or downstream. It comes to the Wittenham Clumps, strangely shaped little hills overlooking the river, the southern one fortified with earthworks erected by the Atrebates who sought, unavailingly, to oppose the armies of Julius Caesar. It passes Cookham, the village Stanley Spencer celebrated in his famous paintings, and, in a straight stretch lined with poplars on either side, the escarpment that ascends to Cliveden House where Nancy and Waldorf Astor entertained the appeasers, and where a quarter-century later the model Christine Keeler and Harold Macmillan's minister of war, John Profumo, began their scandalous affair. It is no longer a stream but unmistakably a river when it runs through Maidenhead, where Brunel built his famous flat-arched railway bridge and Turner marked the coming of the industrial age in one of his greatest paintings, *Rain, Steam, and Speed.* And it continues to widen as it flows past Eton, and Windsor and on to Teddington Lock, where the fresh water from the west and the salt water from the east finally come together.

Druids prayed to river gods and goddesses along this river; Romans built their villas upon its banks; Christians built their abbeys, their waterwheels and mills. Here clashed Briton and Roman, Saxon and Dane, Saxon and Norman, Cavalier and Roundhead. Here wandered

poet and painter. For thousands of years ships laden with the bounty of
the world have ridden the tide upriver into London; since the sixteenth
century traders, explorers, missionaries, emigrants in search of a better
life, have ridden the ebb tide out towards the sea. The river winds
through England's history, art, literature, even music, as surely as it
winds through the English countryside. 'The Thames is within us,' T.S.
Eliot said. It is 'liquid history', John Burns once famously remarked.
'The Thames is no ordinary waterway,' Winston Churchill agreed. 'It is
the golden thread of our nation's history.'[1]

A golden thread in the tapestry of British history: but the river will still
run when the tapestry has ended, and it runs past where the tapestry
begins. For all that Winston Churchill was a mighty figure his life is but
a flash point when measured against the life of the Thames. All recorded
history marks only an instant in the river's history. The entire span of
human existence marks only a moment more. It brings us only to the
very end of the Tertiary period, between one and two million years ago.
The river was there during the Mesozoic era, when there were no
humans, no hominids at all, nor even mammals.[2]

The blocks of which Britain is composed today date back approximately 400 million years, to the Silurian period of the Palaeozoic era.
They were a tiny part of a massive continent, Gondwanaland, which
over thousands of millennia drifted across even vaster seas, ever north-
ward. Tremendous forces worked over unfathomable periods of time to
modify environments. The sea rose and fell, eroding the land. Glaciers
advanced and retreated. Volcanoes erupted, earthquakes split and tilted
the land. Perhaps 170 million years ago, during the Jurassic period,
something like a proto-Thames river system began to develop. The
fossil record discloses plants characteristic of tropical climates there.
Where the Thames flows today dinosaurs once roamed.

Approximately 15 million years ago Gondwanaland broke in pieces;
Greenland and America separated from Europe. The proto-Thames

occupied the north-west corner of what may be dimly perceived to be the European continent. It tilted from west to east, so that the waters of the proto-Thames flowed in that direction, into a larger river system, a proto-Rhine. On the river bank, near where Trafalgar Square is now located, straight-tusked elephants, hippos, lions, deer, bears and bison replaced the dinosaurs. Archaeologists have discovered the fossil remains of these animals and many others beneath sewer systems and Tube lines.

During the Quaternary, the climate has alternated from warm to cold and back again many times, perhaps fifteen times, perhaps more.[3] In Britain glaciation reached its greatest extent during the Anglian period, perhaps 270,000 years ago. Then great sheets of ice many hundreds of feet thick spread over the land. Probably the glacier blocked the Thames's original easternmost reach, which geologists place near St Albans, in Hertfordshire, pushing it southward in stages to its present channel and estuary; otherwise the river marks the southernmost boundary of the glacier's advance. Another period of glaciation, less extensive, occurred some 70,000 years later, during the Wolstonian stage of the Quaternary. And then again, some 65–70,000 years ago the ice returned to Britain, during the Devensian stage. But the heat and the cold alternated throughout, with ice advancing and retreating, so that there were warmer and colder spells throughout the Anglian, Wolstonian and Devensian stages within the Quaternary, and the reach of the ice was not constant. The glaciers last disappeared from Britain some 10,500 years ago.[4]

If only there was an omniscient historian of the river, she would trace its evolution within the natural world over the thousands of millennia before our earliest ancestors laid eyes upon it; she would consign human history to the last footnote of the last page of the last chapter of her multi-volume study. But we must begin where that omniscient historian would leave off, with the appearance of men and women, or rather creatures like them, exploring the Thames river valley, perhaps half a million years ago, perhaps earlier, for archaeologists have discovered evidence of their presence in East Anglia 200,000 years before that. They would have wandered into this westernmost corner of the European landmass (for Britain was not yet separated from it) in search of game. Their hunting and gathering parties came and went as the climate warmed and cooled over hundreds of millennia; one of these parties eventually established a kind of base on the south bank of a broad river near present-day Swanscombe, just east of what now has become the great city, London. Eventually a member of one of the parties died there. She, for the individual is thought to have been female, left fragments of her skull, and possibly a partial footprint. This would have been some time during the Anglian stage, that is to say perhaps 250,000 years ago. In other words (and here is another reminder of the vast scale with which we are dealing), a quarter of a million years ago, when the Swanscombe woman expired near the banks of the river Thames, the site where she died was already known, perhaps had been known for a quarter of a million years already, by hominids drawn to it in search of game. The river, of course, had been there some 680 times longer than that.

What can we say about the river and its environs where and when the Swanscombe woman died? The Thames itself, with sandy and gravelly banks, was broad there, some thirty miles or so from its estuary, flowing in great loops as it still does towards the sea. The surrounding area consisted of grass-covered mudflats cut by small streams, edged by hazel scrub giving way in turn to oak forests. Over millennia the streams and channels filled with sands and gravels, containing pollens, molluscs, and bones that provide rich records for palaeontologists and environmental historians. We know, therefore, that the Thames and its tributaries teemed with fish; and that animals came to the banks for drink, including elephants, rhinoceroses, horses, deer, aurochs (wild ox), waterfowl and many varieties of bird, to list only a few. During the periods of glaciation, even during their relatively hospitable summer months, the ancestors and descendants of Swanscombe woman would have found an entirely different environment: frozen tundra rather than mudflats, and the animal life to complement it: reindeer, horse, elk, woolly rhinoceros, musk ox and mammoth, among others. But during freezing periods or warm ones the attractions of a river environment were obvious to people who depended upon game and fish for food. At Swanscombe they established their base camp, a proto-settlement, though not yet permanently inhabited. Eventually, however, the site became a kind of factory for the production of stone tools; also an abattoir. Hundreds of stone axes, rough scraping tools and flints have been recovered from it, as well as the bones of countless animals butchered there.

And what can we say about the hominids who lived along the Thames before and at the time of the Swanscombe woman? They most certainly were not, as we are today, *Homo sapiens sapiens*. Our own species first evolved in Africa about 100,000 years ago and did not arrive in Britain for another 50,000 years or more. The hominids who lived near the Thames also predate the stereotypical beetle-browed cavemen whom we call Neanderthals, and who first appeared in Europe only about 120,000 years ago and whom *Homo sapiens sapiens* eventually replaced. The earliest hominids who came to explore and settle in the Thames valley may have been an earlier version of modern man called *Homo sapiens*, or they may have belonged to the more primitive species *Homo erectus*. At any rate, ten times as long ago as the first appearance of modern man in Britain there roamed beside the river creatures (we cannot quite yet call them human), who could shape wood with their stone tools. They wore clothing, otherwise they could not have lived there at all. It is thought that they drove game by starting fires. This all suggests organisation, perhaps even a politics of sorts, although it is entirely irrecoverable now. Over hundreds of millennia they learned to bury their dead, powdering some of them with red ochre, adorning their limbs with ivory bracelets. One has been discovered with the skull of an elephant lying beside it. This suggests something approaching religion. These earliest hominids in Britain are shadowy figures whose culture remains all but unknown, yet we must not underestimate their abilities. The bits of skull left by the Swanscombe woman suggest a cranial capacity of about 1325 cubic centimetres, which is within the range of current humans, although on the small side.

Their earliest artefacts are stone flakes and choppers dating back approximately half a million years. These were superseded by more elaborate stone axes and other implements dating from the Hoxnian interglacial and Devensian phases. Once, perhaps these creatures scavenged for food, but by the time Swanscombe woman died they hunted with wooden spears tipped with bits of sharpened stone or bone or antler or tusk. They pushed far beyond Swanscombe, probing the Thames river valley all the way up to present-day Lechlade, some 20, miles below the source, for there are fragments of stone axes and scraping tools dating from this period scattered along the length of the river. Archaeologists have recovered perhaps a thousand axes and perhaps as many as twelve thousand flakes, cores and other worked pieces of flint and quartzite in Oxfordshire alone. It is true that the further west one travels along the Thames the sparser the archaeological record becomes, and it would seem that the upper reaches of the river were rarely visited before the last ice age (and only intermittently thereafter, right through the Bronze Age), but it is also true that the population of what would become Britain rose and fell in concert with the advance and retreat of the glaciers. It probably correlates as well with the rise and fall of the seas, which sometimes cut Britain off from the mainland entirely. At any rate there are archaeologists and prehistorians who argue that occasionally during the Devensian, and even during the periods that preceded it, south-eastern England and the lower Thames valley could have been fairly densely populated, and that the Swanscombe site was only one of many located along the lower reaches of the river.[5]

Still, the longest chapter in the history of human and proto-human interaction with the Thames, approximately 490,000 out of 500,000 years, is the chapter we can know and write least about. Only with the retreat of the last glacier does the archaeological record become relatively abundant and our knowledge, therefore, relatively detailed.

From the end of the most recent ice age until approximately 5000 years before the dawn of the common era (BCE), however, one still cannot call the record rich. We know that new immigrants appeared, from northern Europe, carrying with them tools and hunting implements more advanced than anything seen before in Britain. They first reached England's southern and eastern coasts, and again the bounty of the Thames drew them. Archaeologists have discovered near the estuary flint microliths, arrowheads, hand axes and temporary hearths, and in the river near Battersea and Wandsworth (south London) harpoons and bone fish-hooks dating from this period. On the southern bank of the Thames, just below its confluence with the river Kennet, archaeologists have recovered microliths of the same period, tiny flint flakes, which would have been attached as barbs to arrows shot from bows. They discovered at the same location, in a shallow hollow, impressions of post-holes where a small hut or shelter must have stood. Further west, at what is today Gatehampton Farm, near the Goring Gap in Oxfordshire, excavations revealed a probable butchery site of the early postglacial period, the earliest so far discovered along this middle stretch of the river.

Near present-day Runnymede, where extensive archaeological excavation has taken place, the pollen records reveal a dense alder forest with few openings. An island grew in the river from alluvial clay deposits. The island attracted some form of human activity, for there are signs of a dug pit to hold a post early in the seventh millennium BCE. Archaeologists and palaeontologists have spent much time at this site. They can tell from fossilised snails and other molluscs how wet the land was; from pollen in soil samples they can identify plants, trees, bushes and flowers and deduce not merely what grew, but in what patterns. Insect fossils, such as dung beetles, suggest the presence of domesticated grazing animals. The carbon dating process can be effectively applied to wood. And, of course, from shards of artefacts and from the bones of butchered animals archaeologists may reconstruct at least some aspects of human behaviour and diet. So we know that at the stretch of river near Runnymede inhabitants practised agriculture during the early postglacial period. They cultivated cereal; they grazed domesticated aurochs in nearby woodlands. By the middle of the fourth millennium BCE the signs of agriculture are more definite. The pollen record, or rather lack of it, suggests clearance of the alder forest. Prehistorians believe that similar clearances were taking place at roughly the same time up and down the Thames valley, converting forest areas to ploughed open land, inadvertently destabilising the river's hydro-ecosystem, rendering its banks vulnerable to erosion, and thus to increased flooding.[6]

All along the river, from near the source to near the mouth, men and women left axe fragments and other tools during this period. For the first time we have clear evidence of river travel, for archaeologists have discovered canoes and paddles dating back between five and ten thousand years. We have evidence, too, of advances in hunting methods. The men of the river valley, who were fond of the meat of red deer, had learned to burn forests so that new forests would grow, so that red deer would come to eat the new growth. They burnt the forests to attract the deer at five-year intervals for hundreds of years.

Again we must be sensitive to the immensity of time with which we deal: life proceeded, along the Thames, on the lines sketched above for approximately five thousand years; a span that more than doubles the number of years elapsed since the rise of ancient Greece.

During these and succeeding millennia the prehistoric people of the Thames river valley gained increasing control over their environment. They learned (no doubt in part from new immigrants who never ceased to arrive) to cultivate cereals and a few vegetables, to domesticate animals, to shelter more effectively and comfortably from the weather.

They used animal skins, grasses and reeds, bark from trees and other natural resources in every manner that human ingenuity could devise, but of this there is now little trace. They grazed pigs in the forests. They also cleared forests, burning them since it was not until the introduction of cheap metal tools that they could cut down trees efficiently. They grazed cattle on the grasslands that replaced the forests. They tilled the ground of the lower river valley with a hoe or digging stick or antler pick, and as a result rain washed the soil into the Thames which therefore shows an increase in the deposition of silt; also of flooding.

We know too that these people buried their chiefs in long barrows. They shaped, decorated and fired clay pots. They engaged in trade along the river and inland. Thus the river had come to play a more complex role in their lives than hitherto. It was no longer merely a magnet for game animals and a source of water. It had become as well an avenue of commerce and communication.

During the late Neolithic and very early Bronze Age humans occupied numerous sites all along the river. Yet their presence was not constant. The pollen record suggests, for instance, that over millennia the forests returned to Runnymede, that agriculture and human activity diminished. This area seems typical of most of pre-Roman Britain in at least one respect: human presence ebbed and flowed. At Runnymede, however, it never disappeared entirely for there is no pollen evidence that the forest canopy ever returned completely. Why men kept the site relatively open is unknown, but here is one hypothesis suggested by archaeologists: the river divided among migrating channels; these left in their wake slow-developing mudflats upon which vegetation grew sparsely if at all, and to which game animals would not have been attracted; the open space on the river, then, may have been maintained by hunters who knew it would attract their prey, forest animals thirsty for river water.

Some 2500 BCE, the evidence indicates renewed occupation of the site at Runnymede. Archaeologists and prehistorians refer to the rise and fall over millennia of Windmill Hill, Beaker, Wessex and Urn cultures. At Runnymede there is evidence of the Beaker culture, shards and fragments of pottery that had once formed beakers, naturally enough. By now apparently local farmers understood the importance of spreading their fields with manure. Irish smiths had learned to smelt metals: copper, bronze and gold. Their presence at Runnymede and elsewhere along the Thames during this period points to the existence of trade routes and to more extensive river travel than ever before. We are, then, light years beyond the rough encampments of Swanscombe woman and her contemporaries, if still light years from the centrally-heated villas and the cities of the Roman occupation.

By the time of the Urn or Deverel–Rimbury culture, perhaps two thousand years BCE, the Runnymede site had become again a centre of activity, in fact of activity much more intense and sophisticated than ever before. There was now a definite settlement stretching back over a hundred metres from the river. Post-holes suggest a cluster of buildings there. During this period the inhabitants of what would one day be England lived in circular houses usually with a diameter of about twenty feet, commonly with a central supporting post and an off-centre hearth.

Residents of the Runnymede site had pushed back the forest so far that grassland now predominated, indicating renewed emphasis on grazing. Hunting would have continued too, but the preferred livestock for meat production was beef and pork. Sheep grazed as well, but were used as much for wool as for food. Dogs had been domesticated; perhaps they herded the sheep. Dairy farming was common. Increased production of grain and cereals, emmer and spelt wheat for instance, demanded more efficient methods of milling and grinding. It is possible that the people who lived at Runnymede grew a few vegetables and herbs, although probably they supplemented meat and cereals mainly with gathered leaves, roots and fruits of wild species. Hazelnuts were popular.

The men and women who lived along the Thames during this period burnt their dead and buried their ashes in urns, which they placed in round mounds known today as tumuli or barrows. They employed spindle-whorls and cylindrical loom weights for weaving. They made extensive use of bronze and may even have worked iron. They wove rushes and sedges into baskets that they may have exported. All these activities would have taken place at Runnymede. Moreover, trade along the river had become more or less regular (similar quay sites have been discovered in Brentford and Wallingford), and would have extended occasionally to Continental Gaul. Archaeologists discovered Continental imports at Runnymede for this period, including a notch-backed bronze razor and a vase-headed pin. Moreover they found at the river's edge parallel rows of vertical stakes, young oak trunks about twenty centimetres in diameter, which must have served as a quay for river traffic.

The river would also have been essential as a link between social groups, of which there were by now a relative multitude strung from the estuary nearly to the source, although settlements remained sparse west of Oxford. To list only a few: we know of excavated settlements along the river at Wallingford, just above the Goring Gap, at Bray, at what is today the Reading Business Park, at Staines, Maidenhead, and Eton Wick; we know that scattered impermanent farm sites dotted the river valley for most of its length; and archaeologists have discovered cemeteries nearer London, at Acton, Sunbury, Yiewsley, Kingston upon Thames and Walton-on-Thames. The river linked them all. It was much more, now, than a source of drink and a magnet for game animals. It was more even than a fledgling highway for travel and trade. It had a social meaning as well.

There is also speculation that the river played a spiritual role in Bronze Age Britain. So much metalwork of this period has been found beneath its waters, or where its waters used to flow, that it seems reasonable to view them as offerings to a supernatural entity, a river god or goddess. Human remains were also being placed or were coming to rest by or in the river. It seems likely, then, that the river held sacred meaning to early Britons, that it had come to represent the spiritual heart of the society growing along its banks.[7]

And so the site at Runnymede appears to have remained, up to the Roman invasion. It was largely untouched by the appearance of new colonists in southern England, named after a rich cemetery in upper Austria, Hallstatt, perhaps a thousand years before the birth of Christ. These invaders introduced iron on a large scale, providing English farmers with cheap tools and weapons, some of which indeed found their way into the Thames. The Hallstatt settlers fortified hilltops, perhaps a defensive measure against further incursions mounted by Marnian chieftains from Champagne. Of these ructions and disruptions there is no trace at Runnymede, nor even of the more successful Belgic invaders from Gaul, who during the century before the birth of Christ brought to England heavy wheeled ploughs that ushered in something approaching modern farming, who turned pots upon wheels, and who built England's first real towns, introduced coinage and feuded bloodily amongst themselves, so that most communities along the river found it necessary to acquire metal weapons. The Catuvellauni established a kingdom of which the river marked a southern boundary, the Atrebates established one for which the river marked its northernmost line. With the Belgae politics in England may be said to finally begin, in the form of tribal rivalries. Yet this is a history not of England but the Thames, and so we may allow these years to slide by. As for Runnymede: 'What say the reeds at Runnymede?' Rudyard Kipling asked in a famous poem. During the century before the Roman intervention in Britain they said little that they had not been saying for a thousand years.[8]

But perhaps the reeds did whisper after all in 55 BCE, not of events taking place at Runnymede itself, but of the Roman triremes sixty miles or more to the east, riding the swell nearly within eyeshot of the estuary. Perhaps a year later, when the triremes returned, they whispered again – of the Belgic/English army, led by Cassivellaunus, which was deployed along the north bank of a river Thames lined with sharpened stakes. The native soldiers tensely awaited the appearance of Caesar's legions. According to one account the Romans sent an Indian elephant across the river first, with a howdah on its back, containing archers and slingers; from this giant and terrifying apparition the Britons fled. Others have written to the contrary, of four thousand charioteers who fell upon Caesar's expeditionary force when it finally crossed the river, but the final result was not different. The Romans routed them – and then returned to Rome. After which – silence for ninety-seven years, until perhaps the reeds whispered of Roman armies once more, a greater force with greater ambitions this time. They were led by the Emperor Claudius and his general, Plautius, and they first appeared only a little east and south of the Thames estuary, at Reculver. In a two-day battle they defeated the Belgic/English chieftain Caratacus, whose troops fought with their backs to another river, the Medway. The armies of Caratacus retreated north and west near to where present-day London is located. It was not more than twenty miles from Runnymede where they crossed the Thames this time, perhaps close to present-day London Bridge. The Romans were temporarily stymied by the marshy ground, in which some lost their lives, but eventually the legionaries crossed too, some over a bridge they constructed of timber, and then the two armies fell upon each other again, and again the Romans triumphed. These battles may be understood as the bloody birth pangs of a new civilisation that would take root in Britain and that would transform the relationship between humanity and the river.

For this time the Romans stayed; the natives could not defeat them, not on the Thames, not anywhere; indeed Caratacus himself was taken prisoner and carried to Rome in chains (where he was allowed to live out his life). The new overlords established administrative and military centres throughout the island, Britain's first real towns, and linked them by a network of straight paved roads. Only the wilder tribes of the

north, the Picts, remained unconquerable. To put an end to their inces-
sant raiding a Roman emperor, Hadrian, directed the construction of a
wall in AD 122. It was 15 feet high, 10 feet thick, 73 miles long, with tur-
rets and fortresses at regular intervals, stretching right across the
country, from the Solway Firth on the west to the mouth of the Tyne
river on the east. This proved effective. So the Romans edged north,
deeper into Scotland, all the way to the very neck of Britain, where
they built a second wall, from the river Clyde to the Firth of Forth.
From this outpost they eventually withdrew, but Hadrian's Wall held for
as long as the Romans held Britain.

And meanwhile, to the south there was rule of law and peace (aside
from one major insurrection led by the warrior queen Boudicca, in AD
60, and several more easily suppressed minor eruptions in later centuries). A fortunate few among the natives, especially in the towns,
enjoyed prosperity and a standard of living that the country would not
see again for more than a thousand years. The majority tilled their fields
much as they had done before. The river Thames ran east–west through
the heart of this more peaceable zone.

And so we know more about it than ever before. The Thames estuary
was probably three kilometres south of its present location; the tide
reached further inland than during the early postglacial period, indeed
all the way to London and perhaps beyond; it did not flow along its
current route, but rather appears to have followed a course that led it
700 metres south of the present-day Southwark waterfront, in a series of
channels interspersed with islands of relatively high ground and the
ever-present mudflats. The marshy areas that had bedevilled the soldiers
of Claudius were ubiquitous. At high tide the river may have been as
much as a kilometre wide just south of Roman London (the Romans
thought it looked like a lake); at low tide it was perhaps 275 metres
wide, as opposed to today when it is a mere 200 metres across.

We do not know how deep the river was, but because it was tidal,
ocean-going ships could sail up it with the stream, anchoring to wait

out ebb tides. Thus over the course of days, they could reach Londinium as it may have been called even before the Romans built upon the earlier, much smaller, much more primitive Belgic settlement at the first place the river could be forded.[9] Londinium grew to be the largest town in Roman Britain, and so we finally have reached the advent of the port of London, although the Romans may not originally have intended it to become a commercial centre at all. But the ships arrived in increasing numbers with cargo for the soldiers and administrators and other Romans posted there, and the cargo had to be unloaded, either at quays to which the vessels tied up, or into lighters in the middle of the stream. Londinium became a major port city precisely because of its location on the river Thames.

Three distinct types of Roman-era ships have been recovered from the Thames at London: flat-bottomed lighters that would have been used only on the river, small coasters that could have sailed both in the river and along the coastal shoreline, and seagoing merchant vessels. In addition it is reasonable to assume that warships moored at Londinium. Moreover, from the quantity of fish bones and oyster shells dating from the period historians have deduced the presence of fishing boats in the port. Probably English fishermen caught sprat near the estuary in fine mesh nets; with hook and line they caught cod and bass nearer to the mouth of the river, and bream where the river and the sea finally met. All would have been carried to London by boat and kept alive during transport in sea-water containers to preserve freshness. Fishermen would also have collected vast quantities of oysters from the waters of the estuary; they were consumed not only in London, but in Rome itself.[10]

During the Roman occupation London exported cattle, hides, corn, slaves and minerals from the hinterlands. It imported vastly more: from local sources, up- and downriver, it accepted daily necessities such as perishables like cheese, meat, poultry, fruit and vegetables; from overseas it took olive oil, grain, wine, salt, preserved fish, glass and ceramics;

also more exotic goods, such as ivory bracelets from North Africa, beads from the Baltic, gold and emeralds from Austria, Egypt, Spain and South Wales. Some of these goods Londoners consumed themselves; others were trans-shipped and sent west up the river in smaller vessels to Egham, Staines, possibly even as far as Lechlade, and then they were distributed along the network of Roman-engineered roads to the rest of the country. No doubt the luxury items were mainly destined for administrators, bureaucrats and military men who, although posted to England, were determined to maintain Roman standards of living, but some must have reached the natives themselves.

The Romans ruled Britain for more than three hundred years, a period only slightly shorter than that which has elapsed since the Glorious Revolution of 1688. 'Imagine him here,' Joseph Conrad has Marlow muse of an early Roman commander in *Heart of Darkness*, 'the very end of the world, a sea the colour of lead, a sky the colour of smoke . . . and going up this river with stores, or orders, or what you like. Sand-banks, marshes, forests, savages, — precious little to eat fit for a civilized man, nothing but Thames water to drink.' To such a man Londinium would have seemed a welcome outpost of civilisation. But we now know that southern England, even before the advent of the Romans, was not quite the wilderness Conrad imagined. And beyond Londinium men like Conrad's Roman commander had soon imposed their own system upon the dark, damp, unknown island.

They imposed it along the river in more than six hundred villas, strung like beads upon a strand as far west as Lechlade, where archaeologists have discovered an oval house enclosure, storage pits, small stock enclosures and pens, within a larger rectilinear enclosure, dating to the earliest days of the occupation. Within decades the Romans had constructed a villa on the site; later they added two masonry buildings and another large domestic building. Less than two kilometres upstream they built another villa, at what is today called Great Lemhill Farm. They erected stone houses nearby at Claydon Pike and at Green Farm.

The archaeologists speculate that this construction programme at Lechlade reflects establishment of a genuine market economy in the area and the introduction of a regular money supply.

At Gatehampton Farm, Goring, Oxfordshire, archaeologists have recovered remains of painted masonry, and tiles for roofing, also tiles for a box flue, a brooch, coins, glass, many shards of pottery and a large and sophisticated corn-drier. There is evidence of a cobbled yard before the building and of an enclosed field system. At the Thames Valley Business Park, just below the confluence of the Thames and Kennet rivers near present-day Reading, they have uncovered examples of Samian ware, a glossy red pottery imported from central and southern France, and of other tableware imported from the Lyons area. They also discovered at this site amphorae of the type usually employed to carry wine from Italy and olive oil from southern Spain. Yet this is said to have been a poor settlement of the period, not to be confused with the more prosperous establishments both up- and downstream which now practically lined the entire river valley.[11]

To take another example: at Beddington, a little south of the Thames and just below Londinium, Romans constructed an elaborate villa on a site that had probably been in use for seven hundred years already, for the post-holes of four round houses point to a much earlier habitation. But the new immigrants operated on a much grander scale. They converted part of a field into a courtyard and constructed masonry buildings including a villa and bathhouse. The villa had painted plaster walls and a clay-tiled roof. The bathhouse had a cold room, warm room and hot room. Six additional structures, including a barn and farm outbuilding, were associated with this estate. During the third century AD the owners added two wings to the villa, one of which had an underground heating system. They also enlarged the bathhouse. The villa had glass windows and tessellated floors.[12]

So much for Conrad's depiction of Roman Britain: two thousand years ago his Roman commanders in fact were beginning to develop some of the economic and social habits with which Britons are still familiar. The Thames remained, as it had for a hundred thousand years, an essential source of water for livestock and people, a source, too, of food in the form of fish. It still expedited travel and all forms of communication, but more crucially than ever before (since the country, including the long Thames valley, was so much more densely settled now). As for Britain's increased prosperity: the river did not make it possible, but certainly facilitated it. Above all the Thames had become the unrivalled artery of something approaching a national commerce. Unlike Hadrian's Wall it would serve its purpose as long as the Roman occupation lasted, and beyond.

2

The River and Liberty

*T*he Thames as an artery of national commerce — but in modern times any major highway is that. The Thames was more significant, even during the Roman era, first because it led from London to the sea, and so had not only immense economic but also strategic military significance; later because it provided a backdrop to, and on rare occasions even played a role in, some of the most notable events in British history. For example the first great victory in the age-old struggle of English barons to limit royal power, and the first historic attempt of English peasants to limit baronial power both took place within view of the river. Just as the Thames wound through the English countryside so it would come to wind through the country's history; so it is wound inextricably into the national fabric.

But consider first the river's military significance. If you walk the length of the Thames today you will see the defensive pillboxes, grim, squat and thick-walled, hollow concrete cubes with slits for machine guns, built during 1940 when Britain was preparing to resist a German invasion. They are strung at irregular intervals along the northern bank of the river, commanding a field of fire across the narrow expanse of water and across the broad flat meadows that lie (usually) beyond the ribbon of river, a reminder that even in the twentieth century hard-headed men and women conceived of the Thames in military terms.

They have done so for thousands of years, at least since the appearance in Britain of the first of a series of organised Continental invaders about 500 BCE. For the interlopers the river was, first, a point of entry into the country, then a highway for military purposes, ultimately a line of defence against new intruders. It marked, too, fifty years before the advent of the Romans, a boundary line between the most recent intruders, competing tribes of Belgic chieftains. When the Romans transformed the river into a primary artery of national commerce by developing the port of London, they only augmented the river's military significance.

As one of the largest marketplaces in Roman Britain, one of the largest ports, indeed one of the largest towns, London's importance to the country as a whole was obvious. Command London and you were close to commanding England. But then you must also command the approaches to London, one of which was the river. The Romans built a series of forts along the southern and eastern coasts. In addition to guarding England's boundaries these structures commanded the approaches to the Thames estuary. And brooding over the estuary itself the Romans constructed a fortress at Reculver, nearly square at 200 yards by 190 yards, with walls 9½ feet thick.

Let us be clear: the city grew because it was located on the river, at the first point where bridging the river was then possible. Because it grew, it became, inevitably, the target of any invading hostile force. A convenient route to the target was by river. Thus the Thames, the cause and source of London's greatness, was also an arrow (albeit an arrow shaped something like a corkscrew) aimed directly at it, which is to say directly at the pulsating heart of the nation itself.

The river acted as a magnet then, upon the Romans as we have seen, and later upon the Saxons (including Angles and Jutes), the Vikings (including Danes and Norwegians), and the Normans. At one time or another, over the course of a thousand years, their raiding parties swept up the twisty channel in stages, round its sweeping bends, aiming ultimately for the great prize, London. When Rome could no longer safeguard her colony England's southern chieftains hired Germanic Saxon armies for protection. This was a big mistake, for the Saxons were not content to play this role. When they seized Thanet, then an island, in about AD 450, they were staking a claim to control of the estuary, and therefore to control of the Thames and of the route to London. But this challenged London's trade, which was her very reason for being. It challenged the English economy. In effect the Saxons were challenging for command of Britain. And, of course, the challenge proved successful in the end.[1]

With the Romans gone and the southern chieftains vanquished, the victorious Saxons settled, intermarried with the natives, and contested for dominance among themselves. Two kingdoms, Wessex and Mercia, came to predominate and eventually the latter was forced to recognise the former as supreme. The upper reaches of the river served as a boundary between them, much as they had divided the Belgic tribes nearly nine hundred years before. Then there appeared a new contingent of invaders from Denmark and Norway. In the year 842 Vikings made their way upriver and plundered London. In the year 850 they did it again; and they wintered that year, as had the Saxons four hundred years before, on the Isle of Thanet at the edge of the Thames estuary. Five years later they were wintering on the Isle of Sheppey, a little further up the Thames and ever nearer to the great city. It took the Anglo-Saxon Alfred, king of Wessex, to defeat (and convert to Christianity) Guthrum the Viking overlord in AD 878. King Alfred rebuilt London, but entrusted it to Ethelred, his son-in-law, an ealdorman of the Mercians, thus making the city into a lynchpin of good relations between the two kingdoms.

Alfred understood that the Thames was not merely an arrow pointing at London, but an arrow pointing outwards as well. It was England's gateway to the sea, to commerce, wealth and power. Under his direction English artisans constructed the country's first great battleships, 'neither after the Frisian design, nor after the Danish', writes his contemporary biographer, the Welshman Asser, 'but as it seemed to him that they could be most serviceable'. Viking warships were up to eighty feet long; they could accommodate seventy people. Alfred built his ships deeper-hulled for stability, which was crucial in hand-to-hand combat; and he built them longer – they may have had room for as many as sixty oars, so that they were faster and could carry more fighting men than the competition.[2] Earlier provincial kings in England had owned fighting ships but Alfred is generally credited with having founded the English navy.[3]

Alfred also strengthened England's inland defences including those along the Thames west of London, at Wallingford, Oxford and Cricklade. He conscripted set numbers of men from these areas. In times of emergency the conscripts were to line the river banks, four men for every 5½ yards, each man able with outstretched arms to touch the outstretched arms of his fellows on either side, a human wall behind the wall of water. Given Alfred's formula for conscripting soldiers the line of men at Oxford would have stretched 2000 yards, and at Cricklade about 1900 yards. Alfred, too, worked out with the defeated Guthrum the borderline that separated the part of England where the law of Wessex prevailed from the part where Viking 'Danelaw' ruled. The boundary was, for part of the way, the river Thames.

Alfred and his heirs ruled uncommonly well for more than a hundred years, until the death of Alfred's great-grandson, Edgar the Peaceable, in 975. They divided the country into shires and the shires into hundreds. They appointed ealdormen to govern these units and shire reeves, or sheriffs, to assist them. They established shire courts and hundred courts. They needed and oversaw development of an efficient royal bureaucracy. They favoured and expedited the growth of towns and commerce and a money economy, although of course the vast majority still laboured on the land, but even here there were significant improvements in technique and efficiency. Most importantly Alfred and his heirs pressed north whenever circumstances permitted, shrinking the territory governed by Danelaw, expanding the territory governed by Anglo-Saxon law. By 954 virtually all England was under their control. For the first time it becomes possible to speak of a united English country.

No wonder the Danes coveted this prosperous, well-run kingdom. From 975, Viking incursions, which had never entirely ceased, grew more ferocious and menacing. Ethelred the Unready, second son of Edgar the Peaceable, tried to buy off the Danes. They took his money and invaded anyway, chasing him to Normandy in 1013. After a period of Danish rule (under Kings Sweyn, Cnut, Harold and Harthacnut in that order) we finally reach the pivot point of English history: the arrival of Duke William the Bastard of Normandy in 1066.

The Thames runs through these years as through all English history. It was still a source of water for agriculture, of drink for man and beast; it remained a highway for travel and commerce. Of course it served other purposes as well: in 1040 Harthacnut exhumed the body of Harold, his unbeloved half-brother and predecessor as king, and dumped it in the river; more pleasantly, Edward the Confessor, last of the Anglo-Saxon kings, nearing the end of his reign ordered construction of a great Abbey at Westminster, hard upon the Thames.

But the military aspect of the river is a constant. Vikings and Saxons waged bloody war on its banks, in London itself in 842, near Reading in the year 871, at Milton Regis near Sittingbourne in 892, at Benfleet in Essex in 893, near London again in 895, indeed at more or less regular intervals right up until 1066. Then the conquering Normans erected a chain of forts and castles to protect London and the river approaches to it. Among them two are of particular interest here: the first built upon a bluff overlooking the river at Windsor, the second located on the rising ground we now call Tower Hill in London. These ominous-looking structures signalled an evolution in the history of the river, which reaches a new stage in its history. Now the Thames becomes enmeshed with the symbolism of English state power and with the struggle for various English liberties.

We know that Romans had occupied the site at Windsor, because archaeologists discovered coins there dating to AD 69; we know that Saxons settled there as well, for the archaeologists have located fourth-century tombs in the vicinity. Saxon monarchs may have held court at a nearby manor house; they certainly used the local forests for hunting, but it was the Normans who grasped most completely the site's strategic significance. That is why they built their forbidding castle there.

In its original form Windsor Castle was made from earth and timber. It stood upon a mound of dirt and chalk excavated by labourers who, under Norman direction, dug a three-sided ditch on the great solitary bluff overlooking the river. No ditch was needed on the fourth side where the ground sloped steeply to the stream below; even the ground to the north of the ditch was rough and perilous. Wooden palisades of sharpened staves, ramparts of stone and earth, and two drawbridges guarding the only entrance to the inner part of the fortress further strengthened the position which, in fact, was to prove impregnable during a siege in the time of King John. Over centuries the primitive structure was expanded and improved. Today it occupies thirteen acres; a thousand years ago a smaller Windsor Castle was enclosed within a larger area, half a hide of land, which is to say within half the amount of land thought to be necessary for a freeman and his dependants to live on, perhaps sixty acres.

That was more than enough. The castle itself dominated the landscape, standing as it did upon the only hill in this part of the Thames valley. One may imagine its early occupants scanning, through arrow slits, the heath and forest of the surrounding countryside, all the way to the hills of Buckinghamshire far to the north. One may imagine, too, the local people gazing up resentfully and fearfully at the grim castle walls of their powerful new overlords. The castle also overlooked the river, the main highway to London. No hostile force could pass along that route. It is not surprising that Norman kings increasingly stayed there, safe, watchful, and fierce.[4]

King John, a great-great-grandson of William the Conqueror, often stayed at Windsor Castle. Born in 1166, he took the throne at the age of thirty-three, acquiesced reluctantly sixteen years later in the famous Magna Carta, which is popularly supposed to be the first declaration of British liberties, died the very next year, in 1216. His was a strife-ridden reign. Even before he became king he conspired against his older brother, Richard the Lion Heart, who had inherited the crown and then immediately embarked upon a crusade to the Middle East. Once crowned himself (Richard had fallen to a French archer while besieging the castle of Chalus, near Limoges, in 1199) John fought a running unsuccessful war against the French king, Philip Augustus, to reassert control over territory in Normandy. He disputed with Pope Innocent III in Rome over the Pope's choice for archbishop of Canterbury, Stephen Langton; with the result that Innocent excommunicated him in 1213. He fought to increase taxes, and to increase efficiency in the collection of taxes, with the result that his own barons rebelled. He was still fighting this civil war when he died, as a consequence of overeating and drinking according to some. Modern historians have found reason to praise John's energy, cunning, military skills and administrative talents, but few would term him a successful monarch overall. Still, it was during John's reign, and in his presence, that events linked the river and the destiny of the nation for ever.

John never ceased to pine for the restoration of English power in Normandy (on his deathbed William the Conqueror had left England to his son William; he left Normandy to another son, Robert Curthose, thus the enduring separation), but the barons of his realm resented

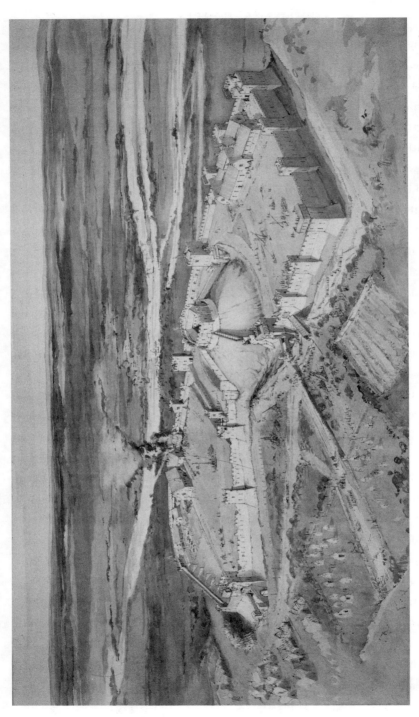

Windsor Castle, overlooking the Thames, c. 1216. One can imagine its early occupants scanning the heath and forest of the surrounding countryside, all the way to the hills of Buckinghamshire far to the north. One can imagine, too, the local people gazing up resentfully and fearfully at the grim castle walls of their powerful new Norman overlords. (Windsor Castle/The Royal Collection © 2004 Her Majesty Queen Elizabeth II)

having to fight and finance the unending and ruinously expensive wars
whose aim was to recover it. The king squeezed them without mercy;
the barons evaded with determination. Eventually both sides appealed
to Pope Innocent as the supreme arbiter of feudal affairs: the barons on
the grounds that John was ignoring a charter of liberties confirmed by
his father, Henry II, in 1154, as well as his own oath to observe good law
and exercise justice; John on the grounds that the barons, his vassals,
owed him unswerving fealty. One would have thought that the Pope
had little reason to love King John, but in fact John had performed an
about-face the previous year, accepting Stephen Langton as archbishop
after all. Perhaps as a result the Pope now counselled John to treat with
the barons, while counselling the barons to submit to their king.

What made John exceptional was the resourcefulness and the ruth-
lessness with which he insisted upon his feudal prerogatives, most of
which he bent to pay for war with France. What made the baronial
resistance exceptional was its organisation, coordination and ambition,
for by now the barons wished to limit kingly power altogether, so that
the monarch himself would be subject to law. The barons rejected
Innocent's counsel. Instead they went to war. John had expected civil
strife for months, but the barons' first act placed him at a disadvantage.
They were strong in the northern counties, and perhaps John believed
that they would first try to strike at him there. Instead they seized
London, with picked men, while the inhabitants were attending mass. It
was a master stroke for all the reasons adduced earlier. Control of
London meant near control of the entire realm. Immediately John had
to negotiate.

Negotiate, but where? John was ensconced at Windsor Castle. For
obvious reasons his opponents would never consent to parley with him
in his own stronghold. They suggested meeting on neutral territory, in
a meadow at Runnymede, on the river, between London and Windsor,
and therefore convenient in a sense. More importantly the barons
judged Runnymede to be safe, not merely in relation to Windsor Castle,

but absolutely. The field they had in mind was large enough for their armed supporters to occupy. Although it was dry, the approach from the south and east was over marshy ground, so soggy that it would require construction of a causeway in the near future. The king's army could not suddenly attack from that direction. The approach from the west was bisected by a stream, another line of defence. In short, if the barons approached from the east, as they would, coming from London, then the king could arrive only from the west, along the river's north bank. 'Runnymede was almost an island' and was, therefore, easily defended, according to one account.[5] Indeed some reports suggest that the negotiations actually took place on a genuine island in the middle of the river, perhaps the one populated by pre-Roman Britons that we noticed in the previous chapter. If so, the geographical consideration is even more apparent: what better place to discuss matters with a hostile figure than one protected on all sides by water, and with opposing forces at opposite ends of a field on the other side of a river? If King John was actually on an island in the middle of the Thames when he accepted the Magna Carta then perhaps this was the first time that the river influenced the course of modern history in a profound sense. This time it did not merely provide a backdrop.

But the river remained in the minds of the negotiators throughout. There was a second document agreed to at Runnymede, one stating that the barons would retain control of London until 15 August, by which time it would be clear whether the king had complied with the provisions of Magna Carta or not. In short, the barons' insurance policy was control of a city of crucial importance to the entire realm, a city which could not be safe unless the men who held it also controlled important reaches of the river upon whose banks it was situated.

Today historians are clear that the Magna Carta was no bill of rights or constitution in the modern sense. It merely laid down rules and limits for the conduct of English kings and proclaimed certain rights and liberties for some of his subjects. King John accepted it because he had to, but always planned to ignore, undermine, and eventually reverse its provisions. John died the next year, however; his nine-year-old son succeeded him as king; and therefore Magna Carta survived and, eventually, prospered. Had John lived, perhaps the charter's most totemic assertion, the supremacy of law over kings, would not have gained purchase in the minds of Englishmen for many years. Most probably the river Thames would not have been indelibly associated with the origins of English law and liberties either. The charter's main features would have been resurrected eventually, of course, but they would have been agreed to somewhere else, not at Runnymede, probably, not on the river at all, perhaps.

This is not to argue that the Thames and liberty were associated in the public mind as soon as the Magna Carta had been approved. But eventually the spectacle (barons and king meeting near the river at Runnymede) and the ultimate meaning of their agreement (limits on kingly power) meshed. When people thought of Magna Carta they thought of it as the root of British liberty, and when they thought of that they thought of the meeting at Runnymede and they thought of the Thames. We may wonder when this perception took hold. It would probably have been whenever British radicals came to see the Magna Carta as a taproot of their own tradition. Only radicals of a certain type would have made the connection, however: not, perhaps, the dry-as-dust lawyers like Sir Edward Coke, who in 1628 discovered in Magna Carta the justification for the Petition of Right against Charles I, but rather the poets, more romantic, who emphasised the link between river and liberty (defined as restraint upon kingly power). In 1642, for example, Sir John Denham wrote 'The Thames from Cooper's Hill'. He believed, as was already common at the time, that the waterway was crucial to England's economy:

> So Thames to London doth at first present
> Those tributes which the neighbouring countries sent . . .

But more to our point, his poem assumes a line linking Thames with Runnymede, with Charter, with England's famous *via media*, in which liberty and order were combined. Standing atop Cooper's Hill, Denham's imagination travelled along the stream to that fabled meadow:

> Here was that Charter seal'd wherein the Crowne
> All markes of Arbitrary power layes downe:
> Tyrant and Slave, those names of hate and feare,
> The happier style of King and subject beare . . .

A century and a half later British poets were still making the same connections: Thames, Runnymede, Magna Carta, and Liberty. It had taken root in the mind of Thomas Love Peacock in 1810, for example, when he wrote 'The Genius of the Thames':

> . . . while Thames shall flow
> That mead shall live in memory
> Where valor on the tented field,
> Triumphant raised his patriot shield,
> The voice of truth to kings revealed
> And broke the chains of tyranny.

By the late nineteenth century the association had entered the common vocabulary, was part of a commonly held myth. Even the humorists understood it. For example, Jerome K. Jerome, when he wrote *Three Men in a Boat* in 1888: 'Slowly the heavy, bright-decked barges leave the shore of Runnymede,' Jerome wrote. 'Slowly against the swift current they work their ponderous way, till, with a low grumble, they grate against the bank of the little island that from this day will bear the name of Magna Charta Island. And King John has stepped upon the shore and . . . a great shout cleaves the air and the great cornerstone in England's temple of liberty has . . . been firmly laid.'[6]

But leave the last word to Rudyard Kipling in 'What Say the Reeds at Runnymede?' written in 1911, as one of the 'Songs' accompanying C.R.L. Fletcher's *A History of England*.

> And still when mob or Monarch lays
> Too rude a hand on English ways,
> The whisper wakes, the shudder plays,
> Across the reeds at Runnymede.
> And Thames, that knows the moods of kings
> And crowds and priests and suchlike things,
> Rolls deep and dreadful as he brings
> Their warning down from Runnymede!

Surely Thames rolled deep and dreadful down from Runnymede in 1381 when kings, crowds and priests once again fought bloodily upon its banks over the meaning of English liberty. And if the river did not wind in and through Wat Tyler's peasant revolt of that year as completely as it did through the making of the Magna Carta in 1215, nevertheless it formed the backdrop to yet another crucial chapter in English history.

Plague, famine, war and taxes ushered in that chapter. Yet for the hundred years preceding it, up until 1307, King John's son, Henry III, and grandson, Edward I, presided over what some consider to have been the 'high summer . . . of medieval civilization'.[7] England's population expanded; social mobility increased. To speak in broad terms, those were years when towns and commerce and prosperity continued to grow, when slavery disappeared (although forms of unfree agricultural labour remained to burden the peasantry), when England finally subdued Wales, though not Scotland. The king's parliaments began to take on something approaching a representative aspect, admitting a few burghers and shire knights when they met, and not just the great magnates. Parliament was becoming crucial to governing the realm. Indeed,

in 1327, a parliament provided constitutional sanction and legitimacy to
the deposition of Edward's incompetent son, Edward II, and his replacement by an exceedingly competent grandson, Edward III who reigned
with great success – at first.

Then, nemesis. It reached England in stages: from the steppes of Asia
to the Crimea with the Mongol army of Kipchak Khan Janiberg, from
the Crimea to the Mediterranean aboard the ships of Genoese merchants, from Continental Europe to the ports of England, inexorable as
a tide – in fact, with the tide – aboard boats bearing grain and wine and
everything else that Englishmen wished to import, but also rats with
fleas that in turn carried the bacillus *Yersina pestis*. This causes bubonic
plague, the Black Death. It appeared in England for the first time in 1348;
it returned in 1361, and 1369, and 1374 and 1379 and on into the next century, eventually killing half of England's pre-plague population.[8] The
Thames was one of many entryways for the terrible disease.

But war was even more endemic than plague during the reign of
Edward III. Like so many English kings before him, he sought unavailingly to conquer Scotland and to establish his rights in France. There too
failure followed his every success, as inevitably as the tides carried boats
with rats to England. At Crécy in 1346 and Poitiers a decade later, he
scored great victories so that he came into possession of vast territories
in France; within twenty years, and after a succession of defeats, all were
gone, except for Calais, Cherbourg, a strip of land around Bordeaux, and
a few Breton harbours. Edward squandered his popularity in England
levying taxes to pay for his failed military campaigns. He squandered his
authority too: for parliament, which aside from the few burghers and
shire knights still meant mainly the barons and the gentry, approved
those taxes only in return for further royal concessions, further devo-
lution of royal power to themselves. Then in 1380 Edward's successor,
his grandson Richard II, capped these disastrous trends by allowing
parliament to levy a particularly onerous poll tax. The barons were
taking advantage of their power to pass on the tax burden to those

below them. There had been head taxes before, but this one took absolutely no account of ability to pay.

The poll tax of 1380 sparked the famous peasants' revolt the following year, although as historians have pointed out, many of the leaders of the uprising were not peasants at all, but rather men of some means who, having survived the plague, had discovered and learned to cherish their much improved bargaining power in a seller's market for goods and services.[9] For them, perhaps, the poll tax, and other laws passed by barons to please themselves (such as fixing wages at pre-plague levels), were cause enough for revolt. But their followers were drawn from all ranks of society below the lords, lawyers and government officials.[10] For this section of the population, roughly an English equivalent of the French Third Estate of 1789, the most recent parliamentary burdens merely capped a long series of provocations and hardships: previous heavy taxes, continuous war with France and Scotland, the remaining and much-hated obligations of serfdom, and, of course, the social crisis engendered by the terrible plague which, of itself, prompted millenarian fantasies of a world turned upside down. To all these must be added alienation from a Church whose officials seemed as grasping as any baron, and whose hypocrisy was more manifest. Nor was this deep-seated rebellious spirit limited only to agricultural districts. In London, St Albans, Bury St Edmunds, possibly in Canterbury and Cambridge, there were townsmen who also resented taxes and feudal restrictions, and who likewise dreamed of a day when the first should be last and the last should be first and who were as capable as their country cousins of decisive action when they thought the day had dawned.

So the explosion when it came was tremendous for having been so long pent up and so deeply and widely desired. It was a clap of thunder and like all thunderclaps it lasted only for a moment, relatively speaking. But the flash of lightning that accompanied it illuminates late medieval south-eastern England where the insurrection was based, including the black flowing ribbon of water running through it, the Thames, upon whose banks much of the action would take place.

The first step of the great revolt was to refuse to pay when tax collectors arrived. On 30 May, at Brentwood in Essex, an angry crowd sent the taxmen packing. The second step was to resist the justices whom the government sent to try tax evaders. When the Chief Justice of the Court of Common Pleas likewise appeared in agricultural Kent the hostile crowd ran him out of town. Then the resistance turned violent. Protesters cut off the heads of government informers. Elsewhere they attacked monasteries; they sacked manor houses. Some jumped to the conclusion that power lay now with the people. At Bocking on 2 June a crowd of rebels vowed to 'have no law in England except only they themselves moved to be ordained',[11] a breathtaking expression of democratic sentiment for the period, one that would only gain long-lasting purchase in the country three hundred years later during the Civil War between Puritans and Cavaliers.

The flame in Bocking was not extinguished immediately, however; indeed for a period it grew hotter. In Canterbury a radical priest, John Ball, preached not merely political but social democracy.

> When Adam dalf and Eve spanned,
> Wo was thanne a gentilman?

Ball had little use for gentlemen. 'What can they show or what reason can they give why they should be more masters than ourselves?' he asked the poor men and women of his flock.[12] For posing such questions Ball had been excommunicated; for continuing to preach he had been imprisoned during the 1360s. Now, on the loose again, he made common cause with the tax resisters. It was a formidable combination. From Brentwood, Billericay and Colchester in Essex, from Canterbury, Rochester and Maidstone in Kent, they converged upon London, adding to their ranks and destroying the symbols of their oppression along the way. These included estates of tax collectors, manor houses of the king's councillors, and documents pertaining to peasants' feudal status and obligations. They halted only before the very gates of London, on the fields of Blackheath overlooking the river Thames.

The Thames was to witness some of the revolt's most violent and indelible scenes. A contingent of rebels led by Abel Ker crossed and recrossed the river, first to encourage supporters in Barking, then to confer with sympathisers in Dartford.[13] From that riverside village a group led by Robert Cave marched downstream to Gravesend where they demolished manor houses and burnt the records of their serfdom. From Blackheath, another contingent of rebels marched upriver to Southwark, where they stormed a jail and released its prisoners, then on to Lambeth where they pulled down Lambeth Palace.

Fifty miles upriver the King was taking his ease at Windsor Castle. He sent messages to the rebels encamped at Blackheath, asking what they wanted. The reply reached Windsor on 11 June: 'To save him from his treacherous advisers.' Richard II was only fourteen years old in 1381. He had only recently taken over from a regency council. Naturally enough the rebels blamed their grievances on it, not on him, and especially on its most prominent members: his uncle, the duke of Lancaster, John of Gaunt, richest and most powerful man in the kingdom; his guardian, his mother Joan of Kent, one of Lancaster's favourites; his treasurer, Sir Robert Hales; and the archbishop of Canterbury, Simon Sudbury. Now these advisers persuaded the young king to confer with his rebellious subjects. On 12 June they followed that trail of history, the winding river Thames, down from Windsor Castle to the Tower of London. And early on the morning of 13 June, Richard and a small party were out on the river again, headed for Blackheath. Of course they travelled by water, out of reach of the rebels. But they travelled within earshot, and somewhere between Rotherhithe and Greenwich they heard enough to give them pause. The rebels might want to save the king from his ministers; but only God could save the ministers from the rebels. Richard's party decided to turn the barge around and return to the Tower.

Parley between king and subjects having failed to materialise, the sub-jects took matters into their own hands. They would have stormed London, except there was no need. The men from Blackheath marched upon London Bridge, and the alderman in charge opened it to them. They swarmed across, taking time first to burn to the ground a brothel owned by the Lord Mayor, William Walworth, a member of the king's party whom they particularly detested. And so, surmounting the Thames they finally entered the city. They tore down the prisons and liberated prisoners, they went after, and killed when they caught them, the lawyers and judges and others associated with the legal system that had enforced the hated tax records and manorial rolls and charters, which also, when they came upon them, they destroyed. But the climax of this extraordi-nary outburst was a symbolic act, not additional murder. It occurred on the Strand, hard by the Thames, where John of Gaunt's great Savoy Palace was located. (John of Gaunt himself had fled to Scotland.) First the rebels emptied it of gold and silver plate, jewellery, fine clothing and the like. All this stuff they scorned to keep for themselves, but rather dumped into the river. Then they burnt the place to the ground.

In one of the more dramatic scenes to occur within sight of a river that had already seen its share and would in future see many more, the young king ascended to a turret of the Tower of London late that after-noon. He looked out over what, centuries later, would become St Katharine's Dock, and beyond to the wide rolling stream. Beneath him milled thousands of rebels, many bloodstained, but few satisfied that their work was done. To the west he would have seen the smoke and fire of the Savoy Palace and of lesser buildings that likewise had been put to the torch. Perhaps young Richard was moved to ask again what his sub-jects wanted, for we know that looking up from the river bank at the remote figure high above them they issued two demands. These were: the surrender of additional 'traitors', by which was meant the king's councillors, blood-curdling enough; and freedom from serfdom, by which they meant social revolution.

No detailed plan of the new society envisaged by the rebels has come down to us, but historians have cobbled together bits and pieces of evidence to provide an outline: they wanted England with no intermediaries between people and monarch (or monarchs, for they may have intended regional monarchies) and no intermediaries between people and archbishop (whom they thought should be one of their own leaders, perhaps Wat Tyler, perhaps John Ball). Thus: no lords, or rather every man a lord; and no priests, or rather every man a priest. Add to this more specific demands put forth at various points: equality before the law; confiscation and redistribution of ecclesiastical property; a ceiling on rents not to exceed fourpence. The rebels even demanded inclusion in 'the community of the realm', which is to say inclusion within what later generations would call the 'political nation' – in other words a voice in parliament. The peasant rebellion of 1381 takes its place as a great democratic upheaval, albeit one that flashed briefly and bloodily across England and then was gone.

On Friday 14 June, Richard rode out after all, to Mile End, east of London, for words with the champions of this radical vision. In 1215 the barons had insisted that King John meet them on neutral ground, Runnymede; in 1381 it appears to have been the king, Richard, and his advisers, who demanded a meeting on neutral territory. They wanted to get the rebels out of London. At Mile End, Richard finally came face to face with the most important leader of the insurrection, Wat Tyler, about whom very little is known, except that he came from Kent, and before the rebellion fixed tiles to roofs for a living. Tyler enunciated the revolutionary demands. The king appears to have accepted them, and to have signed a document so attesting. Perhaps this was a delaying tactic, since it is inconceivable that he sincerely accepted the revolution that the rebels were proposing. When Tyler demanded the heads of remaining 'traitors', Richard answered that he would give them, so long as their guilt had been legally established.

Possibly the rebels took this for carte blanche. At any rate they rushed back to London where the orgy of violence recommenced. They massed before the gates to the Tower of London. So threatening did they appear that the gatekeeper let them in. When they found the king's mother, Joan of Kent, they terrorised her, but let her live. Not so lucky were Richard's two great advisers, Sudbury and Hales. The rebels killed them both and put their heads on pikes which they set at the entrance to London Bridge. Then back into the streets, especially those near the river. They pulled thirty-five Flemings from their riverside houses, and beheaded them all, perhaps because Flemish weavers enjoyed legal privileges that Englishmen did not, possibly merely because they were foreign: for when they were done with the Flemings they went after Lombards and 'other aliens'. Altogether they slaughtered about one hundred and fifty people that day.

Saturday 15 June saw the climax of the rebellion. Again the king rode from the Tower to parley with his subjects, this time at Smithfield, a great meadow beyond the city walls. The royal party occupied its eastern end; the rebels, in their thousands, massed to the west. It was like Runnymede again, though not right by the river and this time without a happy ending for the opponents of arbitrary power. Tyler cantered across the field on a small horse, incautiously alone. He dismounted and made some gesture of obeisance, half kneeling, but then took the king's hand. 'We shall be good comrades,' he is reported to have said. Again he rehearsed the revolutionary demands, and again Richard accepted them, this time with the vague qualification that they must be consistent with 'the regality of his crown', whatever that may have meant. Tyler, as he remounted, called for beer, perhaps in celebration. A member of the king's retinue, unable to restrain his contempt, uttered some offensive remark. Tyler drew his dagger. But he was alone, surrounded by the king's men. The Lord Mayor, Walworth, pronounced him under arrest. Tyler resisted. He ripped at Walworth with the dagger, but to no effect, the mayor wore armour. Tyler, however, had no such protection. Within seconds the royalists had sliced him to ribbons. He

King Richard II and his council on a boat in the Thames; Wat Tyler's rebel army on the shore. (Engraving from Froissart's *Chronicles*, from an etching by Harris/Mary Evans Picture Library)

made it halfway back across the field before falling from his horse. Whether he died then, or later that day, is uncertain. In any event Walworth eventually took possession of the corpse and hacked off the head.

The end of the tale is quickly told. Leaderless the rebellion faded and failed. There could be no such thing as a non-hierarchical England in the late Plantagenet period, or perhaps ever. 'You wretches, detestable on land and sea; you who seek equality with lords are unworthy to live,' Richard informed the remnants of Wat Tyler's army at Waltham on 22 June. 'Rustics you were and rustics you are still; you will remain in bondage not as before but incomparably harsher.' Here, one suspects, is the authentic royal point of view. Within weeks it was almost as if the great insurrection had never been. Wat Tyler's head, which had replaced Archbishop Sudbury's on a spike at the entrance to London Bridge, and which glared down upon anyone wishing to cross the great river, remained as a reminder: of the dream; of what happened to dreamers. It was one thing for lords to seek limitations on royal power, it was quite another for the lower orders to question the lords. The Thames would roll for many a year before that vision was aired again.

3

The Tides of History

*H*istorians have written that Magna Carta marks the emergence of an English nation aware of itself *as* a nation, at least in the sense that most English people now acknowledged themselves to be subjects of an English king. The Peasants' Revolt of 1381 offers additional evidence, since really the followers of Wat Tyler and John Ball were appealing to the crown to arbitrate between two contending national forces. It is finally possible, then, to begin to speak of national traditions, and of a national history.

Through that history the Thames runs gleaming. It practically bisects the foundation event, the struggle between crown and baronage in 1215; it provides the backdrop to 1381. When the barons imprisoned Richard II in the Thames-side Tower of London in 1399 they brought this particular phase of their continuing struggle with the monarchy to an end. They replaced the feckless Richard with a king whose policies, especially with regard to taxation, they hoped would prove less inimical to their own interests. This was Richard's cousin, the son of John of Gaunt, Henry Bolingbroke, now become Henry IV.

Here were the origins of the terrible see-saw conflict between the rival Plantagenet houses of York and Lancaster for the throne of England. For nearly a hundred years the rival factions decimated each other. As the river had seen the conflict in, so it practically saw the conflict out, for the infamous murder in 1483 of the two young princes, the direct heirs of Edward IV, also occurred within the Tower of London, with the Thames still lapping at its walls. Two short years later Henry Tudor ended the War of the Roses, defeating and killing Richard III.

From 1485 until 1625 six successive monarchs, five Tudors and one Stuart, dominated the baronage and the country as never before. So powerful was the monarchy that it dared to break with Rome and to launch a national church, and, over decades, to successfully face down the English Catholics, who secretly maintained the old traditions and some of whom were prepared to fight to restore them. During this period England finally abandoned the fantasy that it could ever rule France; it defeated the great Armada of Catholic Spain, whose king had hoped to bring the apostate country back within the one true fold; it resolved the disputes with Scotland by crowning a Scottish monarch, James VI, to be king of England too. It sponsored the series of explorations that would lead to the foundation of the modern world's greatest empire. As always, the Thames was there.

Consider again the river as it runs through London. Looming above it only five minutes' walk east from London Bridge stands that other great Norman fortress on the waterway after Windsor, the grey, grim Tower of London. We have seen it already, in an uncharacteristic light, as the momentary refuge of young Richard II and his advisers during the peasant rebellion of 1381, and, again atypically, as the high, unreachable platform from which the child king addressed the questing, terrifying mob below. But, as we have also seen, the Tower of London did not prove a refuge for long, and in fact we are more accustomed to think of it as a prison. In that role the ominous structure cast a long dark shadow, and not least during the years when Tudors and Stuarts ruled England.[1]

Its original walls were put up within a year of the arrival of William the Conqueror in England in 1066. It was meant to overawe the London population, to guard the river approach to the greatest city in the realm, to secure the Conqueror's position within the country as a whole. William built the first tower, called the White Tower, within the angle of the old wall that had protected Roman London, but his successors added additional structures and protective walls over the course of centuries. During the reign of King John's older brother, Richard the Lion Heart, workers erected a new line of defence to the west, including a structure now called the Bell Tower. During the reign of Henry III, masons put up more buildings, and toward the end of the thirteenth century, during the reign of Henry's son, Edward, they added an outer wall. Now the vast, intimidating complex was complete.

To enter the completed Tower of London from the landward side one had to cross three drawbridges, two of them at right angles, designed to deter men rushing with long battering rams. The inner defences were probably insurmountable, for checkpoints, portcullises, and heavy drop-gates in the arches would have defeated all intruders. Yet it was not the entrance to the north, on the landward side, that came to loom largest in the public imagination, but rather the entrance on the river side, the one that had to be passed through by boat, through the gate called Traitor's Gate.

It was a wide gate, sixty feet, surmounted by a fine flat arch of jointed and 'joggled' masonry. Once through it, and with the opening to the river barred again, the visitor would see the high outer wall towering behind him and in front the even higher inner wall, soaring to forty feet, while to either side cross-walls loomed. Rank, colourless Thames water lapped at the stairs leading up and into the Tower complex.

From the river to the gate, from the gate to the steps, from the steps to the Tower, from the Tower to the scaffold: the Thames bore England's tragic heroes and heroines to the very edge of their destinies. Sir Thomas More, who opposed Henry VIII's break with Rome, glided along the black water through the Traitor's Gate after his trial in 1534; Anne Boleyn, for whom the break had been made, so that Henry could marry her after obtaining the divorce which Pope Clement VII would not sanction, trailed More in a black barge two years later. Queen Catherine Howard entered the Tower by Traitor's Gate in 1542. She was Anne Boleyn's cousin, and her successor as wife to the fickle, dangerous Henry, and likewise the victim of trumped-up charges of infidelity; she knew what her own fate would be, and practised for it by placing her head on a makeshift chopping block in her prison cell the night before her execution. And twelve years later young Elizabeth, daughter of Anne Boleyn, niece of Catherine Howard, condemned by her sister Queen Mary to imprisonment in the Tower. Elizabeth is supposed to have cried out when she stepped from the boat that had brought her through the grim portal: 'Here landeth as true a subject, being prisoner, as ever landed at these stairs.' Atypically, she lived to celebrate her release and, upon the death of Mary, to revisit the Tower immediately after her own coronation as the queen of England. This time she arrived on the official royal barge, which was bedecked with tapestries, attended by musicians, manned by forty oarsmen. She never returned again.

But it was not only during the years of Tudor rule that the Tower served as royal prison of choice. James I conceived it that way too. For all the Tudor accomplishments, he ruled an England where neither the royal succession nor the religious settlement were completely secure, and where the crown always felt financially vulnerable. Now the Tower and the Thames touch these great themes of early seventeenth-century British history. For if the river led inside the Traitor's Gate it led out of it as well and eastward through the marshy flats to the sea. In part the Thames enters our historic consciousness as the swift-flowing river upon whose current some of Britain's greatest or most notorious or most romantic men and women staked their lives, hoping to ride it to freedom, hoping to escape from the Tower and from England altogether.

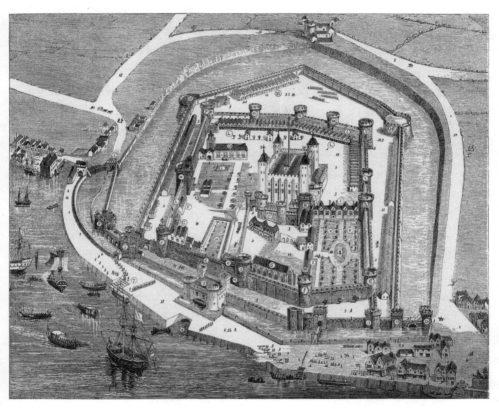

A bird's eye view of the Tower of London during the reign of Queen Elizabeth I. (Tower of London/Mary Evans Picture Library)

For Lady Arbella Stuart the Tower certainly loomed large; and the enticing, fatal Thames wound round her life and choked it at the decisive moment.[2] She was the orphaned daughter of Elizabeth Cavendish (herself the daughter of the legendary Bess of Hardwick, four times married, countess of Lennox and Shrewsbury, richest woman in England) and Charles Stuart. And she was therefore the niece of Mary Queen of Scots, whose brother-in-law Charles Stuart had been. So she was cousin to Mary's son, James VI of Scotland, who succeeded Queen Elizabeth in 1603 as King James I of England. More to the point, she was the great-granddaughter of Henry VII's eldest child, Margaret Tudor, and her second husband, Archibald Douglas, and therefore in line for the throne, only one step behind James, who was the great-grandson of Margaret Tudor by her first marriage to James IV of Scotland. Had James I died without heirs she would likely have inherited the throne. Intrigue followed her wherever she went, because more powerful personalities wanted her for a cat's-paw. Once queen she might have proven a difficult cat's-paw, however.

Meanwhile Protestantism in England rested on foundations that, while firm, were not unshakeable. First Queen Elizabeth and later James I understood that the young Arbella could not help being the (possibly unwitting) magnet for discontented Catholics hoping for a policy of greater toleration or even for restoration of their faith as the primary one in England. She was not Catholic, but perhaps only an indifferent Protestant. In any event, both monarchs kept her under close watch and in a dependent position. Between them they confiscated her entire inheritance. Elizabeth meanly gave her £200 a year; James, when he became king, was more generous, but the allowance he arranged had strings: Arbella felt obliged to move to court where life was more expensive and where she was more dependent upon his favour than ever.

Arbella Stuart had no burning desire to see the restoration of Catholicism to England and she may or may not have nourished royal ambitions. But she certainly wished for independence and that seemed farther off than ever, even though she was now an adult. Marriage would have meant financial independence at the least, assuming her husband had wealth. It would have meant, therefore, the possibility of a fuller life for her. Even if her husband was not wealthy, Arbella hoped the crown would restore her patrimony as a wedding gift, emancipating her from its dubious largesse. In 1602, the year before Queen Elizabeth died, Arbella proposed to Edward Seymour, great-great-grandson of Mary Tudor, Henry VII's youngest daughter, therefore himself an heir to the throne, though a more distant one than Arbella. As a couple, however, they would have had a powerful claim. Would it have proved more powerful than that of the son of Mary Queen of Scots? In any event Elizabeth prohibited their union.

A wiser woman than Arbella Stuart might have sought for a husband among less exalted personages thereafter, for surely James would be more jealous of his newly acquired throne than the aged Elizabeth had been on his behalf. Nevertheless, in late 1609 or early 1610, Arbella, aged thirty-four, proposed again, to a man almost equally unacceptable from the Crown's point of view. Her eye had fallen upon Edward Seymour's younger brother William, twelve years her junior. The younger brother does not appear to have been enthusiastic, but he did not say no. In fact, eventually he said yes. At midnight on 21 June 1610, he and a servant and his cousin, Edward Rodney, rowed to Greenwich Palace, down the coiling river, which now enters the story like the fatal skein it proved to be, if not for him personally then for Arbella and all her aspirations. At the palace, in Arbella's rooms, he married her.

James, when he learned of the wedding, was enraged. He was to tell the bishop of Durham that the marriage was an 'Indignitie' that damaged his honour. He said later to Arbella that, like Eve, she 'had etne of the forbidne trie'. But the king's honour and the woman's transgression aside, it seems clear enough that, whatever her intentions, Arbella Stuart married to William Seymour constituted a combination more threatening to the throne, a more credible alternative royalty, than

Arbella single ever could be. The king's response, then, was predictable. He sent young Seymour to the Tower. He decreed a kind of house arrest for his troublesome cousin under the guard of Sir Thomas Parry in Lambeth.

Seymour may not have entered the Tower of London by way of Traitor's Gate, but his lodging in St Thomas's Tower was immediately above it, so that quite possibly he could see from his window the river and boats passing up- and downstream. He could dream of the river's route to freedom. Meanwhile Arbella was practically within hailing distance on the other side of the Thames and a bit to the west. Probably she made the crossing to see her husband often, for his imprisonment was loose and he was allowed the 'liberty of the Tower', but eventually someone reported to the king. Now James decreed a kind of banishment for her, to the north country, under the aegis of the bishop of Durham.

If, for Arbella, marriage had been before only a means to greater independence and a fuller life, it seems to have come to mean something deeper. She had fallen in love with her husband. Separation was insupportable to her. Travelling north against her will, she either fell sick or feigned illness. Perhaps surprisingly James granted permission for her to stay a month in East Barnet to recuperate. There the desperate plan was hatched, or to that location was conveyed a desperate plan hatched by wealthy supporters including her Catholic aunt the countess of Shrewsbury. Was the ultimate goal merely reunion of the unhappy couple, or was it the creation of a court sympathetic to Catholicism in exile, an alternative to the court of Protestant King James? At any rate, men had been bought, horses and boats arranged, for a double escape. The couple would fly together to France.

What happened next was in some ways the most piquant and touching part of the tragic romance now unwinding, if romance it was. On the afternoon of Monday 3 June 1611, Arbella put on a man's russet boots, hose, doublet, wig, plumed black hat and cloak, and fixed a rapier to her belt. She told the wife of her chaplain that she was returning to

the Tower in disguise to see her husband one last time before heading
for exile in Durham. Dressed as a man, with a gentleman servant,
William Markham, to accompany her, she walked a mile and a half to
an inn where another loyal retainer provided horses. The small party
then galloped not for the Tower, but rather for a different point of rendezvous altogether, another inn, this one fronting the river Thames
past the Tower at Blackwall, where Arbella expected to meet her husband. Waiting boats would then carry them downriver to Leigh where
they would transfer to a hired French barque that would convey them
to Calais.

But William Seymour did not make the rendezvous. His own escape
depended upon the appearance of a hay carter's wagon and horse at the
door to St Thomas's Tower. Unaccountably this was delayed for several
hours. When it finally arrived Seymour donned his own disguise, black
wig, false beard, shabby hat. He slipped from his rooms and took his
place at the carter's seat on the wagon, while the carter hid beneath
bales of hay at the rear. Seymour directed the horse through the various
guarded archways to the great Iron Gate on the river where his cousin
Edward Rodney, the very friend who had witnessed his wedding to
Arbella at Greenwich, now waited with a boat. Knowing they were
behind schedule they rowed directly for Leigh, skipping the inn at
Blackwall. Even so they were too late.

The river itself had a role to play in this sad affair. It was not merely
a stream that had carried Seymour to Arbella's rooms at Greenwich, a
stream down which the doomed couple hoped now to flee together.
The Thames below London is a tidal river that oarsmen must work
with and not against. Had the hay carter appeared as scheduled
Seymour would have arrived at Blackwall by 6 p.m., in plenty of time
for the party to catch the ebb tide and ride it to the estuary. At 8 p.m.,
with Seymour nowhere in sight, however, Arbella's group had to depart
without him. Two hours late, they had nearly lost the tide, and as a
result it took most of the night for her hired oarsmen to row to Leigh.

Even there, on the north bank of the Thames and still some miles from the open sea, the tide remained important. Timing was all. The captain of the French ship insisted that they set sail immediately, although Seymour still had not appeared. In fact at that moment he and Rodney were upstream, struggling in their turn to row against the incoming current. Eventually they made it to Leigh, but hours after Arbella's ship had cast off for France.

Even now all might have been saved. Arbella's ship arrived off the coast of the port city of Calais as intended. Seymour and his cousin persuaded the master of a hoy at Leigh to ferry them across the Channel for £40, an enormous sum. A storm came up and blew them off course so that they did not land at Calais but rather Ostend. Still both vessels had successfully crossed over. And then, a fatal mistake: Arbella's ship did not put in to port. Rather it cruised back and forth off shore, presumably hoping to catch sight of the ferry carrying Seymour.

In the meantime the effort to return them both to captivity had been launched. Edward Rodney had alerted Seymour's younger brother, Francis, to the escape plan in a letter. This arrived sooner than had been intended, which is to say early on the morning after William fled the Tower. Francis took the document to the king immediately. Naturally James wished desperately to recapture the pair. He loosed the human bloodhounds. They quickly traced the fugitives' steps: along the river to Blackwall; down the river to Leigh; out of the estuary and across the Channel to Calais. The government machine functioned swiftly and smoothly. A British naval vessel spotted Arbella's barque, beating to and fro before the port. It gave chase, fired upon the slower ship, and forced it to come about. A boarding party arrested Arbella Stuart and her entire entourage, and brought them back to London.

Thus Arbella Stuart too finally entered the Tower of London. She was never to have a moment of freedom again and died four years later on 25 September 1615. Shortly thereafter William Seymour returned to England. He had waited out his wife's life in safety and comfort on the

Continent, secured a royal pardon once she was dead, and crossed over to England. There he prospered, making a second, uncontroversial marriage. He died in 1660.

Sir Walter Raleigh also became well acquainted with the Tower of London, and possibly with Arbella Stuart, who arrived during the seventh year of his imprisonment. James I shut him up in 1604, ostensibly because Raleigh was implicated in Catholic intrigue against the Crown, in reality probably because the king just did not like him very much. For twelve long years Raleigh languished there, if languished is the right word to describe the condition of a man who, though denied his liberty, managed to write a *History of the World* and numerous political pamphlets, books and poems, whilst carrying on business, and entertaining friends and relations practically whenever he wished, including his wife who had bought a house nearby. Raleigh, who was attended by servants during his imprisonment, set up a small laboratory in a henhouse attached to the grounds, in which he conducted experiments; he concocted a cure-all 'cordial' in this laboratory that even Queen Anne swore by. He became friends with the earl of Northumberland, whom James sent to the Tower after another Catholic intrigue, the Gunpowder Plot of 1605; he was friendly too with another scientist, Thomas Hariot, likewise indirectly implicated in the Gunpowder Plot. The trio represented as glittering an array of scientific talent as could be found under a single roof anywhere in England at that time, including the colleges of Oxford and Cambridge. Walter Warner, another scientist, entered the Tower of his own free will, and stayed to further his education. Perhaps life at the Tower with Raleigh, Northumberland and Hariot compared favourably with life at Oxbridge in certain respects then.

Of course Raleigh, the erstwhile sea dog, chafed, however, and jumped at the chance to escape: not over the walls in the dark of night, but as the result of a Faustian bargain with James I, who in 1616 was short of money, and who let him out because the former buccaneer promised to bring back gold from a mine he thought existed near the Orinoco river in Guyana. It was a delicate mission, since the Spaniards in Guyana would object, and James contemplated an anti-French treaty with Spain. It was expensive, paid for by Raleigh himself, who sold off his entire fortune to equip it. It was plagued by bad luck: storms, sickness, feckless deputies and a crew that was generally unreliable. And it was tragic: for it led to the death of Raleigh's son, Wat, in a skirmish with the Spaniards that could and should have been avoided. Upon learning of this catastrophe Raleigh wrote to his wife, 'God knows I never knew what sorrow meant till now. Comfort your heart dearest Bess, I shall sorrow for us both.' Empty-handed, hopes dashed, promises unrealised and unrealisable, he was deeper in the king's ill graces than ever before, if that were possible. Return to England meant imprisonment again, and almost certain death. He returned anyway. Once having arrived in Plymouth he could easily have escaped on a French vessel to France. He took the road for London. Once in London the French ambassador offered him the means for escape yet again. Sir Walter turned him down. He would prefer to escape in an English vessel, he said. Why, if he intended to flee the country, he had not done so from the comparative safety of Plymouth remains unclear. Raleigh's biographers believe their subject was muddled and sadly diminished during this stage of his life.

On the night of 9 August 1618 Raleigh donned a false beard and made his way to Tower dock, literally beneath the very battlements behind which he had been imprisoned. Days earlier he had discussed his plans with his servants, Hart and Cottrell. They had passed them along to others, who passed them on again. In this manner the government got wind of them too.

Since his return to England, Raleigh had been under loose arrest, supervised by a distant cousin, Vice Admiral Sir Lewis Stukeley, whom the government kept abreast of the escape plan. For some reason Raleigh crossed paths with Stukeley that fateful August night, and confided in him as well, further evidence of his deterioration, since even the most understanding jailer cannot countenance jailbreak unless he stands somehow to profit from it, which Stukeley patently did not. When Stukeley offered to accompany Raleigh downriver as far as the coast, alarm bells should have sounded, but if they did Sir Walter did not hear them. Together the two men boarded a wherry arranged by a genuinely loyal friend, Captain King. The hired crew cast off, rowing east, towards freedom. We may imagine Raleigh's emotions at this point, with the swift current bearing him past the dark Tower, away from the lights of London, into the black night and, he must have hoped, towards a bright dawn. How many times before had he sailed down this river seeking the sea, adventure and freedom?

But there was a large vessel shadowing them. And worse: it now became apparent that Raleigh had left it too late. Already the tide was beginning to turn. The great sailor, the last of the Elizabethan sea dogs, could not even bring his boat to Gravesend. He instructed the crew of hired oarsmen to turn about and head back for Greenwich. As they floundered in the middle of the river, pointed neither east nor west, the boat that had followed hailed them in the name of the king. At last Raleigh knew he had been betrayed, but not how or by whom. He handed to 'Sir Judas' Stukeley, as he would be known ever after, a valise containing his few remaining valuables and keepsakes. He had hoped with these to begin anew in another country.

And so, under escort, Walter Raleigh rode the broad Thames back upriver toward the Tower again. He was executed days later.[3]

Did the Thames's tides alter the course of British history? They certainly put paid to the rendezvous so carefully planned for 3 June 1611, and with it to the spectre haunting Elizabethan and early Stuart England of a Stuart–Seymour alternative court temporarily located in France, and perhaps openly sympathetic to Catholic aspirations. The tides certainly thwarted Sir Walter Raleigh also. Who knows what further contribution the last great Elizabethan might have made? But even if the river did not by itself alter history it entered it, entered the popular mind, as part and parcel of the tale of the nation. King John at Runnymede, Wat Tyler at Blackheath, Arbella Stuart, the doomed romantic heroine broken on the wheel of unrequited love and ill fortune, Thomas More, Anne Boleyn and the other prisoners who exited the Tower and life via the Traitor's Gate, all met their fates on or by or with the Thames. The river joins the story of British history, becomes inseparable from it.

4

Staging the River

*W*hen Henry Tudor defeated Richard III he gripped the monarchy for himself and his descendants with a strong, unyielding hand, but this is more apparent today with historical hindsight than it was at the time. In fact from 1485 to 1689 the royal succession never seemed entirely safe. It was menaced first by Yorkist pretenders, then Catholic barons, then Protestant barons, then ambitious dukes and earls among others. During the reign of Charles I, who took the crown in 1625, the great crisis of seventeenth-century British history finally broke. It had been gathering like a vast black storm cloud for a hundred years, ever since Henry VIII severed connections with Rome. Now there was much lightning and thunder: civil and religious strife, social and political turmoil, war and revolution. For almost three quarters of a century, the Stuart monarchy, indeed the monarchy as an institution, was in more or less dire peril.

Conditions of dynastic instability help to highlight yet another meaning of the Thames. Not for the first time, but more visibly during these tumultuous years than ever before, representatives of every social class employed the river as a sort of flowing stage. Upon it they could strike a pose, deliver a message, drive home a point. Moreover, using the river in this way they contributed to an ongoing process we have already witnessed, linking the river ever more profoundly with the national story.

Think back to the early years of the Tudor monarchy. Henry VIII had often rowed secretly at night from Whitehall to Greenwich to woo Anne Boleyn. But the river was more deeply entwined than this in their relationship. It made possible one of the greatest spectacles of Henry's reign, for when he arranged for Anne Boleyn to be crowned his queen, on 1 June 1533 at Westminster Abbey, she travelled there by stages, and first of all by water from Greenwich to the Tower of London (an ominous enough portent, given her tragic end, but who was to know it on that bright and shining day?).

On the sunny morning of 29 May 1533 fifty barges of the twelve London livery companies, decorated with flags, banners and bunting draped with gold foil, packed with musicians and cannons, and accompanied by many smaller vessels, set out against the tide from Billingsgate for Greenwich. The Lord Mayor of London's barge, hung with cloth of gold and silver, displayed thirty-six shields showing the coats of arms of the Tudors and the Boleyns. Ahead ran a wherry carrying various mechanical monsters including a dragon that could be made to breathe fire; also 'wild men' to set off fireworks. A second wherry followed, sporting a great representation of Anne's principal badge, a crowned white falcon, perched on red and white roses growing from a golden tree stump on a hill, surrounded by 'virgins singing and playing sweetly'.

Anne came down to the river bank to greet this colourful and cacophonous flotilla when it reached Greenwich early in the afternoon. Then she boarded her own lavishly decorated barge, accompanied by the most important ladies of the court. All were sumptuously attired, Anne in cloth of gold. Additional barges drew up to serve other courtiers; still more came for the king, his guard, royal trumpets and minstrels. Together the two parties, Lord Mayor's and Crown's, composed an armada of more than three hundred vessels, large and small. Speeded by the tide they made their way briskly upstream into the sun, towards the Tower, at something like seven knots, past a long line of anchored sea-going ships that saluted with firing cannon. And when they reached the Tower the gunners there 'loosed their ordnance', a thunderous welcome.[1]

Perhaps in this instance the Thames was nothing more than a watery platform, expeditiously placed to facilitate an extravagant spectacle on a red-letter day. Perhaps, however, the spectacle had a deeper meaning. Henry's abandonment of his first wife, his breach with Rome, these were not popular among his subjects or in the wider world. But England's king would wed the woman of his choice, and publicly celebrate their wedding, in the teeth of the opposition, whether foreign or domestic. Does not the spectacular water procession hint at this defiant attitude? For Henry perhaps the Thames was a tool convenient to hand. And then the episode itself: splendid as spectacle but poignant for what it fails to disclose about the eventual fate of Anne Boleyn, it associates the river with a great British tragedy, and thus ever more closely with the nation's history.

For we all know the terrible denouement, in which again the river figures prominently. Only three years later, on 2 May 1536 Anne Boleyn appeared once more on a barge to cross the Thames. The route was the same, from Greenwich to the Tower, but this time the passage boded ill. Anne was the victim of a conspiracy engineered by the king's adviser Thomas Cromwell, who understood that his master wanted to be rid of his wife altogether, for failing, as had the wife who preceded her, to provide him with a male heir. Already the executioner stood waiting in the wings, honing his axe. Thus two journeys on the river bracket Anne Boleyn's short reign as queen. The river limns her singular tragedy. The nation could not view the picture without being aware of the frame.

And so throughout the centuries: Elizabeth I travelled by water from Greenwich to the Tower to celebrate her own ascension to the throne in 1558, as we have seen. When she died in 1603 her coffin was placed upon a black-draped barge in the dead of night, and transported, in a row with other draped barges, downstream from Richmond to Whitehall, a gloomy torch-lit procession. The poet William Camden wrote:

> The Queen was brought by water to White-hall,
> At every stroake the oars did tears let fall . . .

As with Anne Boleyn, so with her daughter: the river indicates the boundaries of her reign.

More commonly the monarchy claimed the stage to celebrate a joyous event; when it did so the monarch's subjects, bit players, had a role to play upon the Thames as well. They must demonstrate their loyalty, love, and affection. Thus, when on the last day of May in 1610 James I proclaimed his son Henry to be the Prince of Wales, the king's subjects knew what was expected of them, and 'all the worshipfull Companies of the Cittie were readie in their Bardges upon the water, with their Streamers and Ensignes gloriously displayed, Drommes, Trumpets, fifes and other Musickes attending on them . . .'[2]

Henry did not live to inherit the throne, but his younger brother Charles did. Finally the storm cloud burst. Charles's policies, his sympathy for Catholicism, led to civil war. Once again the river provides a backdrop to great events: from the execution of Charles's most formidable servant, the earl of Strafford, before two hundred thousand people on Tower Hill; to the great debates at Putney about representative democracy; to the king's own execution outside the banqueting-house at Whitehall. A great moment in the history of the Thames occurred when the revolutionary Sir Thomas Fairfax, newly appointed constable of the Tower of London, came to view the Magna Carta. 'This is that which we have fought for, and by God's help we must maintain,' he breathed reverently, standing in a room that overlooked the Thames, indicating the document that had been worked out in a field by the same river.[3]

In 1660 the Stuart family regained the throne. Almost immediately Charles II, son of Charles I, sought to make use of the river as his ancestors had done. He planned to travel by royal barge down the Thames, from Hampton Court to Whitehall with his bride, Catherine of Braganza, on 23 August 1662. On 29 July someone from the court contacted the Lord Mayor of London, who in turn issued instructions to the twelve great livery companies of the City: the king 'expects such demonstracion of affection from this Cittie as hath bin vsual upon so greate & solemne occasione'. It seems obvious that Charles wanted more than merely to please and impress Catherine of Braganza. He wished to reassert Stuart legitimacy, and to elicit the reaction that his uncle, the Prince of Wales, had received in 1610; he wished to do as other kings had done, such as Henry VIII when celebrating his marriage to Anne Boleyn. One only hopes that, during her triumphal progress upon the river in 1662, Catherine did not recall what Anne Boleyn's celebratory journey on the Thames had presaged some 125 years earlier.

The people of London certainly played their part in this drama. In fact, on the appointed day the City outdid itself on Charles's behalf. According to the great seventeenth-century diarist John Evelyn, *Aqua Triumphalis*, as the extravaganza was termed, had been 'the most magnificent Triumph ever floted on the Thames, considering the innumerable number of boates & Vessels, dressd and adornd with all imaginable Pomp: but above all, the Thrones, Arches, Pageants & other representations, stately barges of the Lord Major & Companies, with various Inventions, musique, & Peales of Ordnance both from the vessels and shore'. Ten thousand boats (in Samuel Pepys's estimation) came out that day, so that the river all but disappeared from view, except for a narrow channel in the middle left open for the king whose own barge, grandest of all, was hung with crimson damask and bore a canopy of cloth of gold supported by Corinthian pillars themselves wreathed with ribbons and garlands of flowers. Nevertheless Mr Pepys's attention wandered. 'That which pleased me best,' he confided to his diary, 'was that my Lady Castlemaine stood over against us upon a piece of White Hall, where I glutted myself with looking on her.'[4]

Somewhere 'between Chelsey and Pox-hall' (Vauxhall?), as the king's barge glided past them, Thames watermen, who earned their living ferrying passengers along the river, declared their loyalty to the king, just as he had hoped they would. They sang in three parts: 'Let sadness flie Boyes, flie; The King and Queen draw nigh . . .' The seamen made similar declaration further downstream, but being used to running aloft along a ship's rigging, they also were able to throw 'themselves into severall Antik postures and dances'. A little further on, the river itself was made to salaam. 'Divinest pair!' it exclaimed to the royal couple, or rather the actor personifying Isis, 'Lady of the Western Meadowes and Wife to THAM', exclaimed, as reported by John Tatham, Gent, in his *True Relation of the Honourable the City of Londons Entertaining Their Sacred Majesties Upon the River of Thames* . . .

Divinest pair! . . . Isis (to meet
Your unmatch'd loves) kisses your Sacred feet . . .

Not even Henry VIII had received this sort of gooey declaration. But Isis's protestation of allegiance and subordination merely represented a variation upon a theme, the association of royalty and river, and loyalty and river; of river and nation. Only this time Thames was made to spell it out.

We may still hear the echoes of royalty's most famous water procession of all, although they evoke not the blaring trumpets announcing the arrival of Anne Boleyn at the Tower of London before coronation day, or the overdone protestations of fealty to newly restored Charles II, but rather soft summer nights on London's river when there were fields and pastures on either side past Westminster, and royalty was taking its ease. But then it was a different era: the country had passed through and beyond the civil war; the permanence of monarchy was assured by the settlement of 1689, which had established once and for all that King and Parliament ruled jointly. The echoes we may hear today reflect this less troubled period. They are in turn cheerful, stately, gentle, and finally unmistakably English.

Although bits and pieces of the work had been performed on the river as much as two years earlier and its original conception cannot be traced, the first presentation of Handel's great composition *Water Music*, performed largely as it has come down to us, took place on the night of 17 July 1717, on a barge carrying the king and a circle of his friends, gliding upon the Thames somewhere between Lambeth and Chelsea.[5] Handel had lived in England for five years by then, having first been granted leave and later dismissed from his duties as Kapellmeister to the Elector of Hanover. He received £200 a year from Queen Anne. Conveniently for Handel, when she died it was the very same Elector of Hanover who succeeded to the English throne, and who renewed his connection with the great composer. George I, as he now was styled, enjoyed water processions along the Thames. In addition, during the summer of 1717, he may have wished to divert attention from a growing rift with his son, the Prince of Wales and future King George II, by sponsoring a series of public events, including a lavish party on the river. Thus, perhaps, the immediate inspiration for this initial performance of the *Water Music* (the piece was commissioned by a German diplomat, Baron Kilmanseck, but he was acting for the king).

To quote the *Daily Courant* of 19 July,

On Wednesday Evening at about 8, the King took Water at Whitehall in an open Barge, wherein were also the Dutchess of Bolton, the

Dutchess of Newcastle, the Countess of Godolphin, Madam
Kilmanseck and the Earl of Orkney. And went up the River towards
Chelsea. Many other Barges with Persons of Quality attended, and so
great a Number of Boats, that the whole River in a manner was cover'd; a City Company's Barge was employ'd for the Musick, wherein
were 50 Instruments of all sorts, who play'd all the Way from
Lambeth . . . the finest Symphonies compos'd express for this
Occasion by Mr. Hendel [sic]; which his Majesty liked so well that he
caus'd it to be plaid over three times in the going and returning. At
Eleven his Majesty went a-shore at Chelsea where a Supper was
prepar'd, and then there was another very fine Consort of Musick,
which lasted till 2; after which his majesty came again into his Barge
and return'd the same Way, the Musick continuing to play till he
landed.

It is a joyous composition, as all who have listened will attest. It makes
particularly striking use of trumpets that would have pealed clearly in
the night-time air, though there are also softer, more limpid movements led by strings and flutes, almost like kisses and caresses on a sweet
summer evening. Handel's introduction of French horns in the F-major
suite would have produced a certain thrill, because Georgian listeners
were barely acquainted with that instrument. One may imagine the
high spirits of those privileged to hear the *Water Music* played for the first
time that night on the Thames.

    It is perhaps a little odd that an expatriate German composer wrote,
for a transplanted German monarch, music that seems today so quintessentially English, that was first performed in so very English a setting,
and several of whose dance movements, the 'Hornpipes', refer specifically to English sailor jigs.[6] But then Handel anglicised his name (from
Händel), abandoned Italian opera to write oratorios in English, and
became eventually an English subject. So much did Englishness
and the *Water Music* become intertwined, in fact, that in 1940 during

England's gravest crisis, Humphrey Jennings opened his great film *Words for Battle* with a passage from Handel's composition, in order to inspire viewers to resist – Germany, the country of origin of King George. Thus was the Thames, or perhaps more accurately a folk-memory, a popular image of the Thames, covered over with barges including the king's own 'shallop', and accompanied by the greatest music ever composed for an alfresco concert, conscripted on behalf of the nation and of liberty.[7]

During the Tudor years England had grown into one of the world's greatest trading nations: dynastic uncertainties and civil war notwithstanding it remained so. London, advantageously located on the broad curving waterway whose outlet was perfectly placed for the flourishing Baltic and growing Atlantic trades, reaped the reward. By the midpoint of Elizabeth's reign it was England's most important and busiest port.[8] Here were located the headquarters of the country's greatest traders organised in Merchant Adventurers' and East India and Russia Companies; and in the twelve great livery companies of the City of London: haberdashers, vintners, cloth-workers, and the like. These merchant princes, like royalty itself, also commanded processions upon the Thames.

From 1453 until the middle of the nineteenth century the best-known and grandest of the London merchants' processions were sponsored by the livery companies on the annual occasion of the investiture of the Lord Mayor (always chosen from among their ranks). On the day of St Simon and Jude, 28 October, the mayor elect would receive his insignia of office at the Guildhall. On 29 October he would travel, by water, from the City to Westminster. His barge, sixty to eighty feet in length, elaborately decorated and with a canopy to protect him from the elements, would be rowed by nine oarsmen per side. It would be followed by barges representing the eleven other great City companies, all of them similarly shaped and sized, and equally decked out. At

Canaletto's depiction of a mid-eighteenth-century Lord Mayor's procession on the river. (Canaletto (Giovanni Antonio Canal) (1697–1768)/© Yale Centre for British Art, Paul Mellon Collection/Bridgeman Art Library)

Westminster the Lord Mayor would take his oath before one of the Crown's judges at the Exchequer. On his return journey, again by barge, the festivities would begin: salutes of guns, pageants and living tableaux representing ships, islands, temples, bowers.

During the Elizabethan years, when the country was at death grips with Catholic Spain, the Lord Mayor's processions could not but reflect current tensions and passions: in the 1585 procession, for example, the Thames, figured as a nymph, offers its fishes and waterways for the benefit of the City, while the City declares its love and loyalty for the queen:

> Then let me live to carol of her name,
> That she may ever live and never die.
> Her sacred shrine set in the House of Fame
> Consecrate to eternal memory . . .[9]

In later years, however, the spectacle reverted to its original purpose: advertisement and glorification of the City merchants and of the river that made their riches and those of London and England possible.

A typical example: in 1634 the cloth-maker Sir Robert Parkhurst was chosen Lord Mayor. Returning from Westminster by water, after having sworn the customary oath, he came upon a great barge filled with 'commodities that marchants and others that are free of the Company of Clothworkers doe receive from foreigne parts by sea'. Actors representing Thetis and Thamesis sat in the prow of this barge. Thetis spoke to the Lord Mayor:

> I every twelve houres, by this Child of mine,
> Do send you silks and velvets, oyle, and wine,
> Gold, silver, Jewels, fish, salt, sundry spices,
> Fine and coarse linen, drugs of divers prices:
> What every Realme or climate can produce,
> I see it safe transported for your use.

> Thus from the bosome of the Deepe my floods
>
> (By Thames) doe every Tyde send up your goods . . .

Here the river does not so much symbolise the nation as symbolically feed it (which means it is as necessary to the nation as ever); the river is linked explicitly with prosperity, with London, the world's great entre-pôt, and with the merchants who dominated it.

This was a theme that resonated so long as London remained a great port. 'Thames . . . thy faire bosome is the worlds Exchange,' Sir John Denham wrote in 1642; and Dryden in 1666:

> The silver Thames, her own domestic flood,
>
> Shall bear her vessels like a sweeping train . . .

And Thomas Love Peacock, half a century later:

> . . . oh Thames! . . .
>
> For thee Golcondian diamonds shine;
>
> For thee, amid the dreary mine,
>
> The patient sufferers toil;
>
> Thy sailors roam, a dauntless host
>
> From northern seas to India's coast,
>
> And bear the richest stores they boast
>
> To bless their native soil.[10]

Long after the Lord Mayor's water processions had been discontinued artists persisted in making similar statements on canvas. Here we will mention only George Vicat Cole's *The Pool of London* painted in 1888. When William Gladstone saw this work he wrote, 'The picture seemed to speak and to say "You see here the summit of the commerce of all the world."'[11] But as we know, it was the Thames that made commercial London possible.

When William Gladstone saw this work, he wrote, 'The picture seemed to speak and to say, "You see here the summit of the commerce of all the world."' (*The Pool of London*, George Vicat Cole (1833–93)/The Trustees of the Chantrey Bequest 1888/Tate, London 2004)

The river as a stage for royals during an era of dynastic instability, and as a stage for Londoners intent upon demonstrating their loyalty to the Crown; the river as a stage for London merchants during the era when England rose to be a great commercial power, and the river as *sine qua non* of English prosperity. There was a more democratic river too. Very occasionally, perhaps two or three times in a century, crowds of Londoners would appropriate the Thames to hold one of the famous frost fairs. Now the flowing stage hardens because the river has frozen, and the actors who strut upon its glassy surface are less interested in making a statement than in making money and having a good time. But there was something dark and worrying, even menacing, about those icy carnivals too.[12]

Frost fairs occurred when the river froze solid enough to support not merely the occasional individual tentatively venturing out to test the ice, but hundreds or even thousands of men, women and children at a time. During frost fairs the Thames watermen, unable to ply their normal trade ferrying passengers across and along the river, would convert their boats into makeshift sleds, and push or pull customers in them.

Or they would erect tents, often nothing more than blankets resting upon a frame made from crossed oars, but with a fire inside and a vent for smoke, and from these primitive shops they would sell food and drink. Soon enough, however, hackney coachmen from the London streets drove their horses out onto the ice to compete for customers, and London traders set up booths and stalls in competition with the watermen's. Entire streets developed, lined with primitive shops in which nearly anything could be purchased: all kinds of food and drink, both hot and cold, plus 'Earthen Wares, Brass, Copper, Tinn and Iron, Toys and Trifles'. Barbers set up shop. Printers brought their presses out onto the ice. For the majority frost fairs provided a spectacle and amusement to rival anything mounted by kings or Lord Mayors. All sorts of entertainments took place on the frozen river: games, gambling, races, rides, even hunts; and everything was for sale. Only for the watermen, who could no longer ply their trade and earn their customary living, were frost fairs less than an unmixed blessing.

Frost fairs have disappeared not because of global warming but because the old London Bridge was pulled down in 1831. The old bridge, made of stone and timbers, with towers (both for ornament and military defence), houses, shops, even a chapel on it, and the famous entrance with heads of traitors impaled upon iron spikes, was the main entrance into London from the south, and indeed the only structure to span the London Thames until construction of Westminster Bridge in 1750. It crossed the river upon a series of nineteen relatively narrow arches. These rested on piers driven deep into the river bed. 'Starlings', large timber casings designed to fend off river

Rowlandson's impression of Thames watermen competing for custom.
(*Miseries of London – The Thames at Wapping*, Thomas Rowlandson (1756–1827)/
Guildhall Library, Corporation of London/Bridgeman Art Library)

debris and traffic, protected the piers. Over the years the 'starlings' were extended, thus narrowing the arches further, which meant in turn that the river was concentrated into ever-fiercer torrents as it passed beneath the bridge. At ebb tide the water rushed through so violently that it became dangerous sport, even life-threatening sport, to 'shoot' the bridge – that is to pass under by boat. In winter, if the weather turned really cold and stayed that way, chunks of ice would lodge against the 'starlings', and eventually block up the arches altogether. Then the Thames above London Bridge could freeze solid enough to support a frost fair.

We do not know how many frost fairs took place before the old bridge was torn down in 1831. The Thames froze many times before that date, and horses and carriages ran over it, and yet no frost fair was established. Perhaps the earliest fair upon the river took place in AD 695 when, according to one historian, 'The Thames was frozen for six weeks and booths built upon it.' It would seem, however, that the first really notable frost fair took place in 1564, when boys played football in the middle of the frozen stream and Queen Elizabeth, attended by her lords and ladies, went frequently upon it to 'shoot at marks'. From that year until the last fair upon the ice in 1814, there were nine bona fide frost fairs in all. Of these the frost fair of 1683 seems to have been the biggest and to have lasted longest.[13] When it was over one who had seen it wrote:

> When maids grow modest, ye dissenting crew
> Become all loyal, the falsehearted true,
> Then you may probably, and not till then,
> Expect in England such a frost again.[14]

After a typical autumn in which frosts alternated with mild weather, a hard and unrelenting freeze began in mid-December 1683, so that by Christmas ice along the banks of the Thames was strong enough to

When chunks of ice blocked the archways beneath London Bridge (see far end of lower print), the river to the west stood still and froze. Watermen, whose customers could now walk across, erected tents and sold food and drink from them. With the replacement of old London Bridge by a new one with wider arches, the river continues to flow, no matter how cold. 'Frost Fairs' have dissapeared. [pic 1] (*Thames Frost Fair*/Historical Picture Archive/Corbis) [Pic 2] (*Frost Fair on the Thames*, formerly attributed to Jan Wyck (1640–1700) *c.* 1685, English School/© Yale Center for British Art/Bridgeman Art Library)

support 'some thousands of people', although a channel of water yet remained in the middle of the stream. Watermen, bereft of their usual customers and desperate for a source of revenue, began erecting booths along the margins and selling food and drink in them. By 5 January the stream in the middle had frozen too, and a coach and six drove across. Now the booths and stalls appeared in two parallel rows stretching nearly from bank to bank. A temporary thaw in mid-January drove them off, but after three days the cold returned, the river froze completely, and the lines of booths returned. In the end the frost fair extended roughly from London Bridge all the way to Vauxhall, in several lines with clusters of booths along the way and, at the centre, the original double row, called 'Temple', or 'Blanket', or 'Freezeland', or 'Broad' Street. It bisected the river from the foot of Temple Stairs across to the Old King's Barge House. The frost fair of 1683–4 would last until the second week of February.

For the majority, frost fairs were winter festivals, made more special because, occurring perhaps once in a generation, they were so rare. The frozen Thames was a curiosity. People imagined fish suspended in the ice beneath their feet, bewildered and fearful.

> Up o're the Ceiling we great Thunder hear
> Which strikes the very Sturgeon into fear.
> Both Carts and Coaches with their ratling Wheels,
> Great noise of Men and Horses trampling heels.[15]

And then sliding on the glassy surface was fun.

> It was really curious for to see
> Both old and young so full of glee . . .[16]

So they came to the river in throngs, many thousands of them, with money, if they had any, in their pockets. Down to the river, too, came the men and women who hoped to separate these easy marks from their hard-earned shillings and pence.

'People of all quallityes and ages as has hardly ever been seene before' walked out upon the river during the frost fair of 1683–4. From the king and members of his family, who on one occasion had their names printed on a small ticket as a remembrance (this was a popular thing to do), all the way down to the poorest apprentice, the frost fair proved a magnet, not once, but often. Even the very poorest could at least warm themselves in one of the booths, where there were fires to mull wine, or to boil water for hot chocolate and coffee, or to roast meats, bake pies, gingerbread and pancakes.

> The prentices starv'd, at home, for want of coals,
> To catch them a heat do flock thither in shoals . . .[17]

Imagine the colourful scene, made sharper by the clean winter air of pre-industrial London: the white snow, clear ice, gaily coloured flags and banners advertising the hundred booths and stalls; the hawkers, coster-mongers, skaters, bowlers, fiddlers, men on stilts; the sliding chairs 'and other devices such as were made of sailing Boats, Charriots and Carrow-Whimbles . . .' There were puppet shows, horse races, bear and bull baiting, even a fox let loose to be chased by hounds and hunters (and, according to some accounts, by King Charles II). A butcher roasted an entire ox upon the ice. A showman displayed a menagerie of 'pleasant monkey[s]'. Sword-swallowers and fire-eaters amazed their audiences; the latter also by treading upon glowing coals.

Many found magic and enchantment on the ice-bound river.

> There is such whimsies on the frozen ice,
> Make some believe the Thames a Paridice . . .[18]

Two hundred and fifty years later the fabulous scene was recreated, and embellished, in Virginia Woolf's *Orlando*. 'Frozen roses fell in showers when the Queen and her ladies walked abroad,' Woolf wrote of a frost fair set in Stuart London. 'Coloured balloons hovered motionless in the air. Here and there burnt vast bonfires of cedar and oak wood lavishly salted, so that the flames were of green, orange, and purple fire. But however fiercely they burnt, the heat was not enough to melt the ice which, though of singular transparency, was yet of the hardness of steel.'

It is at the frost fair that the young Orlando (in his male phase) experiences disappointment in love for the first time. He sees his beloved Princess Marousha Stanilovska Dagmar Natasha Iliana Romanovitch with another man, and it breaks his heart. Orlando's finer feelings notwithstanding, however, promiscuity and sexual licence were constitutive elements of the frost fair.

> And some do say a giddy senseless ass
> May on the Thames be furnished with a lass.

Some of the tents were brothels. Watermen complained of whores plying their trade inside hackney coaches on the ice.

> Maids there have bin said
> To lose Maiden-head
> And Sparks from full Pockets gone empty to Bed.[19]

A bawdy humour prevailed (although attention to metre did not):

> . . . the gay Damsel try'd
> (As oft she had done in the Country) to slide
> In the way lay a stump
> That with a dam'd thump,
> She broke both her Shoostrings and crippl'd her rump.

The heat of her Buttocks made such a great thaw
She had lief to have drowned the man of the Law.[20]

In 1683 more than one surviving puritan was scandalised. John Evelyn disapprovingly refers to the frost fair as 'a bacchanalian triumph'. The London Nonconformist Roger Morrice wrote in his diary in early February, 'All manner of debauchery upon the Thames continued upon the Lord's Day and Monday, the 3 and 4 of this instant.'

Meanwhile the London watermen strove, without much success, to earn a living. When the river froze and hackney coach drivers came out on the new white highway to compete for customers whom otherwise they could never have approached, and when traders set up booths and stalls offering far better fare than watermen ever could, the men who rowed upon the river for a living faced not merely unemployment but starvation. For them, frost fairs were calamities. The watermen appealed as a body to the Court of Aldermen and the Lord Mayor: 'Divers others who have no relation to the river interfere with [us] and deprive [us] of this meanes of [our] support.' Men who belonged to the Watermen's Company were 'free of the river', they claimed, while tradesmen and coach drivers should stay off. They meant by this that watermen held monopoly rights to certain types of river trade by custom, if not by statute law. Here was a straightforward clash between the old-fashioned belief in reciprocal obligations linking individuals with society, as understood by the watermen, and the ethos of individualism and competition just emerging at the close of the seventeenth century, and advocated by the tradesmen and coach drivers. The watermen had their sympathisers:

O Scullers I pity your fate of Extreams
Each Land-man is now become free of the Thames . . .[21]

wrote one, but even in 1684 there could be only a single outcome. The tradesmen's stalls did not come down; the coachmen continued to carry passengers upon the ice. The watermen barely managed to fend off an attempt by the Water Bailiff to tax their little booths.

There was nothing exhilarating or liberating about frost fairs so far as the Thames watermen were concerned, then, and yet there is, in the frost fairs, at least an element of the French charivari, the ritualised carnival when rich and poor exchanged places, if only for a day. For some the world literally turned upside down at the Thames frost fair.

> . . . the country squire
> does stand and admire
> At the wondrous conjunction of water and fire;
> Straight comes an arch wag, a young son of a whore,
> And lays the squire's head where his heels were before.[22]

Certainly there was an atmosphere conducive to freedom and licence at the frost fairs, it was what made them so popular, it was what drew people to them, and it was in part what so worried the prudes like Roger Morrice. But the occasion was double-edged. A hint of menace, of class antagonism, the possibility of 'rough music', as English social historians have termed it, might underlie the boisterous ambience as well. One doubts that 'sons of whores' were accustomed to knocking down respectable gentlemen with impunity elsewhere in London.

The frost fair reversed nature. The weather was unnaturally cold: it froze flowing water, imprisoned fast-moving boats in ice and allowed men to walk upon the stream. One poet thought the temperatures that made frost fairs possible even reversed the order of heaven and hell:

> Call fire a Pleasure henceforth, not Doom!
> A fever is become a Wish. We sit,
> And think fall'n angels have one Benefit.[23]

Frost fairs were not simple festivals if they produced sympathy for the devil. They were charivaris in the most profound sense of all.

And, by their very nature, they were short-lived; they would disappear when the weather warmed. 'A Day, nay an Hour, may dissolve our whole community, and make the merriest of us all look grave,' wrote one who had pulled a printing press out on to the ice.[24] Treading on the frozen river provided, therefore, a frisson of danger. The miniature city erected literally upon the Thames was doomed, as everyone knew. But then so was London doomed, and so was everything and everyone else doomed in the long run. Frost fairs compressed history. In this sense they were best understood not as spectacles, nor even as charivaris, but as grim reminders of mortality.

> And now the stragling sprite is once more com
> To visit mortals and foretel their doom.[25]

Frost fairs cautioned lazy, comfortable, humanity to mend its ways.

> Y' are plagu'd now with Ice, 'cause you love to back-slide:
> Methinks it should warn you to alter your station,
> For y' have hitherto built on a slippery foundation.[26]

One 'poetical-historical-philosophical' London astrologer who styled himself 'Icedore Frostiface, of Freeseland' wrote, after a frost fair in 1740, 'It is observable that when any Frost has happened remarkably severe, it hath soon been followed by some extraordinary Revolution, Change or Event.' Recalling the great fair of 1683–4 he observed, 'This was but a Year before that gracious and merry Monarch King Charles II . . . was taken out of the World in a very suspicious Manner; after which came in a Deluge of Popery and arbitrary Power.' Even the hard frost of 1708–9, he reminded readers, 'was followed by a great Scarcity of Provisions; the memorable Sermon, Trial and Peregrination of Dr. Sacheverl; the

Disgrace of the Duke of Marlborough and the rest of Queen Anne's Ministry; Fears of the Pretender, &c.'

Frost fairs, then, offer a microcosm of English society during a particular historical era, in part simply because all classes were present in a restricted space during a short period of time, in part because they reveal if only for an instant the nature of relations between those classes. They were, in fact, abbreviated, focused versions of the larger society, but with a democratic twist. The Thames, frozen like glass, holds up a mirror and reflects – England.

5

The River and the Age of Reason

Some two hundred years ago, in May 1797, Britain was engaged in a life and death struggle with revolutionary France and her allies Spain and Holland. Her own Continental allies had fallen by the wayside. In those desperate times everything hinged upon England's navy, whose main job was to keep the French fleet bottled up in Brest, the Spanish in Cadiz, and the Dutch in the estuary of the river Texel. Let these enemy ships break the blockade and invasion loomed. So the British fleet beat ceaselessly back and forth, up and down the Channel. It formed a line that must not be breached.

But every ship's crew had to rest on occasion, had to put in to an English port for replenishment. One of their sanctuaries was an anchorage called the Nore at the very mouth of the Thames, just east of its confluence with the river Medway, some forty miles from London. Marshy, muddy land on either side partially shelters the basin formed by the confluence of the two rivers, as they open out here into the English Channel. Two hundred years ago this was desolate territory, best known to smugglers and seabirds. The wide Nore itself, however, was a glorious sight in sunlight and good weather when dozens of anchored vessels commonly rode the glossy swells, and merchantmen, sloops, barges, coasters in full sail passed either to or from the greatest port in the world.

The Isle of Sheppey (not really an island) forms a portion of the Nore's southern rim; and perched on the north-western tip of this protrusion of land jutting into the estuary is the fishing village Sheerness, drab and unlovely, built upon silt and mud reclaimed from the water by the great retaining wall of an ugly fortress.[1] In the spring of 1797, in this unprepossessing village, and upon the waters of the estuary it overlooked, an extraordinary sequence of events occurred, one of the most interesting, potentially historic, and ultimately tragic of the time, namely a daring experiment in self-government, the sailors' revolt known as the mutiny at the Nore. British seamen seized control of their ships. They had been pushed to the bounds of endurance and beyond by the atrocious conditions and the brutal discipline of the Royal Navy; they were inspired by the republican and 'levelling' ideals of an era called today 'the Age of Reason'. For a period of weeks they, not the British government, controlled the gateway to London, and a good part of the King's Royal Navy as well – and this while the nation was at death grips with France.

What did they do with their new-found power? It does not detract from the story to answer this question in a few lines: the immediate achievements of the mutinous sailors were few; their rebellion ended in failure; most of the leaders paid with their lives. Nevertheless, even if only for what it *might* have accomplished, the mutiny at the Nore is among the most thrilling and sad of all the chapters in the long history of England's river. During the 'Age of Reason' in Britain, as during all other ages, the Thames is present, in this case it is even central, to critical events and the national mood.

Imagine the Nore in the spring of 1797 with perhaps a dozen ships bobbing at anchor, most belonging to the Royal Navy's North Sea Fleet.

Sheerness, drab and unlovely, reclaimed from the sea by the great retaining wall of an ugly fortress. Site of the sailors' mutiny of 1797. (*Coast of Sheerness*/ Historical Picture Archive/CORBIS)

They had been patrolling the French and Dutch coasts; now they were taking on water and supplies at the wide end of the river Thames. Their crews were scrubbing decks, stitching sails, making repairs. When given shore leave they frequented the rough taverns and pubs of Sheerness.

The ships at the Nore represented a microcosm of the navy as a whole. Some were well officered and captained, with crews relatively well treated. Too many, however, suffered under the rule of despots whose subjects feared and despised them. One, the *Director*, was commanded by the infamous Captain William Bligh, the very man who, in 1789, had driven his crew aboard the *Bounty* to mutiny. Such captains, and there were many, enforced discipline with an instrument of terror called the cat-o'-nine-tails. A single blow from this great whip will knock down a standing man; two blows will split one inch-by-one inch pinewood. The 'cat' will easily break a man's skin and often his ribs; nevertheless on some ships its use was practically routine.

But then, for the men of the lower decks, most aspects of navy life were atrocious in 1797. For sustenance they received nearly inedible food;[2] they drank filthy water. They earned nineteen shillings per lunar month, wages that had not risen since 1652, but payment was usually in arrears. Pensions (£7 p.a.) were derisory. Moreover, when a British ship took a foreign prize and the prize money was divided among the crew, the sailors received tiny shares in comparison with the officers, shares hardly worth the trouble spent and danger endured. They depended upon ships' doctors who possessed variable skills, and many of whom were dishonest, carrying on a black market in medicines and bandages and instruments. But the doctors were only imitating officers and captains who frequently fiddled their ship's books. Pursers were equally corrupt: they purchased supplies on land at the standard measurement, sixteen ounces to the pound, but sold them to sailors aboard ship at fourteen ounces to the pound.

Worst of all, about half the men serving in the Royal Navy in 1797 had been 'pressed', which is to say kidnapped, either by official gangs that scoured Britain's ports for able-bodied men, or by the navy itself, which stole them at sword- or gunpoint from merchant and fishing boats (not always even British; Americans were pressed into the British navy too[3]) as they approached England's home waters. Seamen hated impressment and the forced labour that was its result at a time when unfree labour was disappearing in Britain. It accorded ill with cherished if vaguely defined ideals about the rights of 'free-born Englishmen'. The contradiction seemed all the greater during a war fought against France, ostensibly on behalf of freedom and English liberties.[4]

The sailors were not docile men. If an opportunity to desert presented itself, many took it (though so many were recaptured that one historian writes of 'a revolving door effect'[5]). If an appeal to the Admiralty Board seemed likely to bear fruit, then sailors appealed. This required the surreptitious composition and circulation of a letter, not easy matters in a ship's close quarters. But it could be done, and we may imagine hardbitten men, gathered deep in a ship's hold at night, ears cocked for an officer's tread, painfully composing by candlelight the petition they hoped would move the hearts of distant and forbidding figures in London. 'We are nockt about so that we do not no what to do,' wrote the men of the *Winchelsea* to the Admiralty Board in 1793. 'We hope your Lordships will be so kind to us and grant us a new commander or a new ship, for the Captin is one of the most barbarous and one of the most unhuman officers that ever a sect of unfortunate men eaver had the disagreeable misfortune of being with,' wrote the crew of the *Shannon* during the same year.[6] Desperate circumstances called forth more desperate measures. In 1794 seamen driven to breaking point aboard the *Culloden* sailing in the Mediterranean turned against their officers. But the Mediterranean is practically an inland sea; there was no escape from it. So the leaders of the mutiny surrendered as soon as they were promised amnesty. The promise was a lie: all were hanged from the yardarm.

It is not coincidental that the tempo of protests aboard ship increased during the 1790s, and for two reasons. First, during the war with France the navy's manpower demands had become so heavy that every local- ity in the country was forced by law to supply a number of sailors based upon population estimates. These 'quota men', many of whom resented being forced to serve, were often older, more independent, better edu- cated, and less amenable to discipline than the recruits of the past. Some had accepted a bounty (or the promise of a bounty) from the government as payment for joining, usually to settle debts. Such men usually came from the 'very classes most attracted to the Democratic Movement'.[7]

Second, protest was increasing on land too during this period. These were years when the English radical tradition received a French infusion of Jacobin ideas, egalitarian and democratic; when 'Corresponding Societies' ensured that such ideas were discussed and pondered every- where in Britain that men could read; when Tom Paine's *The Rights of Man* sold 200,000 copies; when Irish dissidents, led by Wolfe Tone, linked up with their English counterparts, and with France, and eventually fomented insurrection. These were also the years of industrial revolu- tion, of agricultural enclosure, of the slow but inexorable eradication of what historians have termed the moral (or traditional pre-capitalist) economy. They were, in short, years of social and political ferment and protest in which British sailors inevitably took part. In fact certain English revolutionaries believed the seamen had a critical role to play in overthrowing the monarchy and establishing a democratic republic.[8]

In 1797 it did indeed seem for a time that they would play it, and an important focus of their activity was the Nore, at the estuary of England's river, the Thames. Here took place the mutiny referred to ear- lier. It seemed to threaten the foundations of the British government. Upon the river already recognised as a cradle of British history desper- ate men laid plans to rock the ship of state.

The roots of their organisation are to be discovered, probably, among ships anchored at Spithead off Portsmouth, close to the Isle of Wight, where the Channel Fleet was accustomed to shelter. Clandestine meetings took place there in late 1796 and early 1797, and a letter was composed demanding improvements in pay, pensions, food and treatment. The Board of the Admiralty ignored it. The sailors then dispatched a petition to Parliament itself. They did not wait for Parliament to act, however; rather they seized control of all the ships at Spithead belonging to the Royal Navy. The Admiralty Board could not ignore them now. In fact it considered the action of the seamen at Spithead to be 'the most awful crisis that these kingdoms ever saw'.[9]

And so it could have become, if the seamen had let it. They saw their act not as rebellion, however, but as industrial action, and they never asked for more than the Admiralty could afford to give them. Instead they printed and distributed their petition to Parliament, so that the populace would understand how moderate it was. They publicly stated that they would make no further claims 'in order to convince the nation at large that we know when to cease to ask, as well as to begin'.[10] They ordered unpopular officers ashore, not as a measure of vengeance, but in order to eliminate the possibility of friction between them and men unaccustomed to wielding the whip hand (though later they would not have them back). And when, faced with this adamantine determination, the government finally acceded to their demands and brought before Parliament the necessary bills and insisted upon their passage, the leaders remembered the fate of mutineers aboard the *Culloden* three years previously, and would not return the ships to the control of the officers until they had received the king's pardon as well, and all participants had seen copies of the proclamation with their own eyes.

But a strike in the navy subverts, if only for a day and no matter how carefully limited, those principles of discipline and subordination upon which all armed forces, except for guerrilla armies, are based. The men of Spithead had squared the circle; they had engaged in mutiny, but persuaded the public and themselves that it was merely a labour dispute. They had not persuaded the government or the Admiralty, however. And if sailors anchored elsewhere, at the Nore for example, contemplated emulating their brothers at Spithead, they would have need of the same iron discipline and wise leadership. Otherwise they were sure to find waiting for them the hangman's noose and the terrible whip that their lordships were accustomed to employ against troublemakers. But the combination of discipline and wisdom displayed at Spithead was rare, as rare on the Thames in 1797 as anywhere else at any time.

And the men of the Nore did contemplate emulating their brothers. How could they not when they suffered from the same conditions and were living through the same revolutionary period? Again we may imagine the secret conclaves amidships, the whispered planning sessions, the fearful glances over shoulders, but this time a new element too, perhaps, namely optimism, since those participating knew that they were part of a larger movement. They decided to seize control of their ships on Friday morning, 12 May, when their captains would all be aboard a single vessel, the *Inflexible*, forming a naval court martial to judge a Captain Savage who had lost his ship. We now know that the Spithead mutiny would end three days later, on 15 May, and that the men of the Nore would have shared in most of the benefits it produced, gaining results without incurring risk. Instead they took a braver, nobler, more generous, ambitious and dangerous route. They were to suffer for it.

On the appointed morning the men of the *Sandwich*, anchored off Sheerness at the mouth of England's river, gave the signal for action, three great cheers. The sound could have died on the water, and the mutiny with it. Instead the men of the *Director*, Captain Bligh's own vessel, and then of nearly every other ship of the line and frigate anchored at the Nore answered with tremendous cheering of their own, an unprecedented explosion of pent-up feeling and aspiration. Sailors lining the decks and perched in ships' riggings would have looked at one another with a mixture of incredulity, bravado and giddiness, not quite believing what they had launched. Yet they had done it; the spring was wound up; their strike had begun. The sound reached the court martial aboard the *Inflexible*. Not surprisingly Admiral Buckner adjourned proceedings and sent his captains back to their respective ships to find out what was happening.

We may regard as typical the report of Captain Robert Mosse of the *Sandwich*: 'The people all quiet but had taken command of the ship, planted sentinels with cutlasses both on the decks and gangways, were in possession of the keys of the magazine, store-rooms, etc. . . . [They] demanded and almost instantly seized all the arms, which I am told are lodged in a storeroom below. They are strick in their discipline and look-out, and have a watchful jealousy throughout.'[11] Yet, taking a leaf from their brothers at Spithead, the men of the Nore promised to obey officers' orders so long as they did not threaten their real control of the ships, and to fight their country's enemies should they appear.

On 13 May the sailors' General Committee, representatives from all the striking ships, collected £20 to pay the expenses of a four-man delegation to Portsmouth. The four would confer with leaders at Spithead and report back. Here we come to the first false note struck in the affair at the Nore, for the quartet had been poorly chosen. One took advantage of his liberty to desert altogether, he is never heard from again; another stayed a week in Portsmouth enjoying the comforts of town life, we do not know when he finally returned to his ship at the Nore; the other two were more responsible, but even they did not hurry. Perhaps they thought there was no need, for they arrived at Spithead in time only for the victory celebration on the 15th, and when they spoke with the Spithead leaders they were advised to give up their strike now that the main objectives had been realised. They did not arrive back at the Nore with this message until 19 May, however, by which time events there had already achieved a momentum of their own.

Recall the Thames frost fairs, held on impermanent ice, transient revels, with an element of charivari thrown in. What now was taking place on the Nore was charivari writ large: a world turned upside down, with the last become first and the first last, and with the meek inheriting the earth. Only they were not so meek. Sailors organised great marches through the streets of Sheerness, on one occasion ten thousand strong.[12] They met in the pubs and taverns. Their wives and families flocked to see them. Several sailors travelled up to London, hoping to establish contact with sympathisers. Others fraternised with troops in the garrison. The ships' delegates rowed to daily meetings aboard the *Sandwich* and the *Director*, accompanied by brass bands playing patriotic airs. There was nothing the officers could do about it. It was charivari because it reversed the natural order, and because, as with frost fairs, everyone knew the reversal was temporary.

There was, however, a harsher strain, a note sounding a rougher music, which already distinguishes the action at the Nore from the one at Spithead. The note sounded, for instance, on 17 May, in the treatment meted out to the boatswain of the *Proserpine*, as described by Captain Cunningham of the *Clyde*, who later wrote a tendentious account of the entire affair, *A Narrative of the Occurrences that took place during the Mutiny at the Nore* . . . (London, 1829). The boatswain

> was disfigured with a large swab tied upon each shoulder, a rope round his neck and his hands tied behind him; in this state he was placed in a boat and rowed round the Fleet, with a Drummer by his side occasionally beating the 'Rogue's March'; he was then landed at Sheerness and marched through the Dock Yard and Garrison, guarded by a party of Mutineers; and when they considered him sufficiently punished and degraded they let him loose and left him without farther molestation.[13]

There had been another portent even more ominous. In a strike, unity is all. Each morning the men of every ship gave three cheers, symbolic of their continuing devotion to the cause. But some ships were more devoted than others. When, one morning, the crew of the *San Fiorenzo* did not cheer, militants aboard the *Inflexible* sent a cannon ball through her rigging. *San Fiorenzo* decided to cheer after all.

There was, too, by the time the delegates returned from Spithead, a visible leader of the rebels at the Nore, a quota man only recently assigned to the *Sandwich*, Richard Parker, late of Perth, Scotland. His crewmates had elected him to the General Committee; this body elected him to be their president. Parker claimed later not to have sought or welcomed these positions, but they may have appealed to his vanity, the record is not sufficiently complete and we simply do not know. At any rate his visibility as leader stands in stark contrast with the invisibility of the leaders at Spithead, where the organisers of a dangerous action were canny enough to keep out of the limelight.

We know the bare bones of Parker's background.[14] He was the son of a well-to-do baker and grain merchant of Exeter; he quit school to join the navy; served as a midshipman during the war against the rebellious colonies of America, rising to the status of petty officer in HMS *Mediator* in 1783. When the war ended he shipped as a master's mate to Africa and India. In 1791 he married Ann McHardy, daughter of a Scottish farmer, but the sea still called to him and with the onset of armed conflict against France he rejoined the navy. Then, it would seem, his troubles began. He was discharged from two separate ships 'in consequence of his immoral conduct', according to Captain Cunningham. He may once have led a protest over bad food. In 1793 a first lieutenant of the warship *Resistance* brought him to a court martial. Another captain was willing to take him on as a petty officer, but he became ill and had to be hospitalised. In fact bad health, probably rheumatic fever, dogged Richard Parker.

Bad luck dogged him too. While in hospital he missed an important British naval victory and, since he would have been petty officer, the chance of significant prize money. When he returned to his wife in

Richard Parker, president of the sailors' 'floating republic'. A proud, nervy, perhaps naive figure, and in the end a tragic one. (Hulton Archive/Stringer/ Getty Images)

Scotland he managed to lose whatever fortune he did possess, despite probably having worked as a schoolteacher. In 1797 he entered a debtors' prison in Perth. There he accepted the king's bounty of 20 guineas in order to settle his debts, and agreed in return to re-enter the Royal Navy as a quota man. Yet given his previous troubles with naval authority he cannot have been sanguine. What were his thoughts as the tender transporting him down the Thames from London neared Sheerness? He attempted to throw himself overboard and commit suicide.[15]

Why did the seamen of the Nore choose this man to be their president? He was brave, resourceful, well spoken and literate, as we learn from records of his trial later. Perhaps his literacy counted heavily in his favour. Equally, his former status as an officer must have weighed for him, since the mutinous seamen would have wanted someone who understood officers, knew their tricks, spoke their language. There is some evidence that the sailors thought he was the nephew of a genuine Admiral Parker and this too may have weighed with some. Probably decisive was his past history of rebelliousness including the court martial. Yet there is a darker interpretation of Parker's rise. He appears to have been impulsive, nervy and given to second-guessing himself, not qualifications for leadership of men engaged in a desperate endeavour. But these were not traits that would have disqualified him either, if harder, cagier, mutineers wanted a front man to distract attention from themselves.

From the depths of despair to exaltation; from the lower decks of the *Sandwich* to the presidency of a good portion of the North Sea fleet, equivalent to the position of an admiral, and all in the space of a few days. Parker's ascent was dizzying. It would have turned the head of a stronger man. Almost certainly it turned his. When the remaining two delegates to Spithead returned advising an end to the action at Sheerness, Parker demurred. So did the rest of the General Committee meeting aboard the *Sandwich*. They were glad to receive the higher wages, but the Admiralty had replaced fifty-nine unpopular officers from the ships at Spithead, it had not agreed to replace any at the Nore. No officer should be allowed back, Parker and his allies agreed, without the consent of his crew. Then, the king had pardoned only the Spithead men. The men of the Nore would not end their own strike, delegates stated, until the pardon extended specifically to them. 'Remember the *Culloden*,' some of them cried.

Now the ships anchored at the estuary of England's river had become a microcosm not of England's fleet but of a self-governing nation: every vessel a fledgling state, with its own political parties and points of view, sending representatives to a federal body, the General Committee, led by a well-intentioned if weak president. And there was a royalist court across the sea, as it were, an alternative government waiting in the wings, for many of the legitimate captains, though powerless, remained aboard their ships and met regularly in Sheerness with those unpopular officers who had been forced ashore. No doubt the officers had their agents and spies, seamen who remained loyal to the old order, and who reported to their former superiors on the discussions and resolutions passed on board. This information would have found its way back to the Admiralty in London. We know too that the *San Fiorenzo* already was a reluctant member of this floating republic, as it has been called. So too was Captain Cunningham's *Clyde* a reluctant participant in mutiny. On the other side we are sure that the *Inflexible* and the *Sandwich* and the *Director* provided a core of militants. Perhaps other ships' crews were more evenly divided. Almost every ship transformed into a debating chamber then, but doubtless also into a warren of intrigue, spy and counter-spy, plot and counter-plot; pride and elation on the one hand, whisper, envy, fear on the other.

Meanwhile, the General Committee had issued further demands. These were: regular leave for seamen when their ships returned to shore, pay in arrears to be brought up to date, pressed men to receive two months' pay in advance for purchasing slops from the usurious pursers, prize money to be distributed more equally, the death penalty to be no longer applied to deserters, while those who had deserted in the past receive retroactive pardon, discipline (enforced by the infamous Articles of War) to be moderated. Finally the Committee invited a party from the Admiralty Board to meet with them in Sheerness, as one had done with the leaders of the Spithead mutiny.

None of these were unreasonable demands, Parker must have told himself as he (alone) affixed his signature to the list of grievances. That the seamen at this point were optimistic and high-spirited is evident. They paraded the streets of Sheerness, President Richard Parker at their head. On 20 May they brought Admiral Buckner to the *Sandwich* in a procession of honour through the fleet, although they failed to accord him proper respect when he boarded, an oversight that would be made much of later. The admiral agreed to take the list of further demands to London, but the reply with which he returned a few days later was disappointing. In fact it was a bucket of cold water. The Admiralty would raise pay as it had promised to the men of the Nore as well as Spithead, and would extend the king's pardon to them; but nothing more. And the government had done worse, ordering two regiments of militia into Sheerness garrison. They arrived on 22 May. On that date we may say the charivari officially ended. The old order had reasserted itself.

Here was the first crucial juncture in the Nore mutiny. If the seamen abandoned it at this point they might all, Parker included, have escaped with their lives. No doubt there were some who argued along these lines. But the militants prevailed. They argued that surrender meant defeat, since the men had gained none of their own demands. Perhaps worse still, surrender meant yielding their newly discovered dignity and self-esteem, and the infant democracies that fostered them. Forward motion was the only policy. John Blake, one of the delegates for the *Inflexible*, successfully moved the establishment of a treasury to pay for travel, and for a London lawyer and for the printing of proclamations meant to sway the public. Then it was recalled that eight

President Richard Parker presenting the sailors' demands to Admiral Buckner. President Parker has not removed his hat. For this and for being 'guilty of everything that's bad', he was to hang. (Mezzotint by an unnamed artist, reproduced in 'The King', 19 August 1905, p. 658/Mary Evans Picture Library)

gunboats were moored just off Sheerness, while the government troops were holed up in the fort. Immediately a party of seamen swarmed into town, captured the eight boats, and brought them back to the fleet in midstream. As they passed the fort each gunboat fired a symbolic round in its direction. If the government chose war, then war it would be. But these acts suggest yet again that President Parker was not an intimate of the militants. He had just written to Admiral Buckner that the government's introduction of troops was 'an insult to the peaceable behaviour of the seamen through the fleet at the Nore'.

With their president or without him the advocates of a forward policy sought to enlarge the strike. Halfway up the Thames to London, near Dartford, four warships rode at anchor. And the bulk of the North Sea fleet was stationed at Great Yarmouth. Perhaps their seamen could be induced to join the mutiny at the Nore, just as the men of the Nore had joined the mutiny at Spithead. On 26 May the Committee dispatched a fast cutter to Yarmouth. It dispatched armed longboats up the Thames to Dartford.

So many times this river had borne armed and desperate sailors from its estuary towards the capital, but never before Englishmen with such purposes as these. From one spy or another, however, the government had caught wind of their plans. As the mutineers passed Tilbury fort, its cannon opened fire. So, the seamen must have thought, as the balls and shot splashed the water before and behind, it was war after all. 'You are to take the most vigorous means in your power preventing them on board,' the government had instructed the four ships at Dartford. Nevertheless the men from the Nore managed to board one of them, the *Lancaster*, amidst the 'greatest confusion'. Its captain escaped through a porthole into a waiting skiff. Writes one historian, perhaps a little excitedly: 'The red flag was now flying fifteen miles from the Court of St. James'.[16]

The men of the *Lancaster* said they were willing to join the mutiny. But to reach the fleet at the Nore they must sail downriver and pass the guns at Tilbury. A ship-of-the-line was a larger, slower, much easier target than the low longboats dispatched earlier that day from Sheerness. An index of the militancy now prevailing in the General Committee was its next proposal: they would capture the fort. Imagine the militant sailors, with the guns of the most powerful vessels in the fleet to back them up, demanding this sort of action. Few among the seamen were prepared to stand against them. President Parker was not. He appeared on board the *Iris* and the *Brilliant* and persuaded their crews to take part in the scheme. Then he boarded the *Clyde*, a strange choice given its lukewarm attitude towards the entire project, and endeavoured to enlist its crew as well.

What were his motives? He would later claim that he, and indeed most of the delegates of the General Committee, were continually being pushed by extremists aboard the *Inflexible* to adopt a revolutionary posture in which they did not believe. If so they were walking a very high wire. England was at war and faced invasion. A crucial portion of the fleet was on strike. Had the fort fallen to the mutineers they would have owned the lower Thames. Storming Tilbury certainly seems a revolutionary step. Perhaps for that very reason the men of the *Clyde* would not take it. Writes Captain Cunningham: 'This infamous proposal was received by the people with indignation and instantly rejected; and although Parker made use of many threats to enforce obedience to his orders the people steadily refused compliance.'[17]

There ensued a confused several days during which optimism and determination waxed and waned on both sides. The pace of events was hastening, but so jumbled that it is hard to put them in intelligible order. On the one hand, the government sent reinforcements to the garrison at Sheerness, and into the fortress at Tilbury and even into east London, in case the Nore men should attack the capital itself, while withdrawing troops whose loyalty was questionable. It cut off all supplies to the ships at the Nore. It ordered the arrest of any man from the Nore who ventured on to land. It passed bills in Parliament that gave it an even freer hand to deal with the seamen, and extended its powers to deal with any who befriended them. It considered pulling Admiral Duncan and the remainder of the North Sea fleet back from Yarmouth to attack the rebels, and dispatched Captain Bligh to find out whether it could be done. The message Bligh carried to Duncan read in part: 'The welfare, and almost the existence, of the country may depend upon what is the event of this very important crisis, but till we know what we can look for from your squadron it will be very difficult for us to know how to act.'[18]

From the other side, the action seems less purposive. The General Committee ordered the fleet to draw up into defensive formation, two great arcs across the Nore, with gunboats protecting the flanks. But sailors aboard the *Clyde* complied reluctantly, and only when they realised that if they did not they would have to face the *Inflexible*, which carried twice as many guns. A delegation from the Admiralty arrived in Sheerness not to discuss terms but only to accept surrender. Now, perhaps, we see Parker in his true colours. Calling together the crew of the *Sandwich* he asked them whether they preferred continued defiance or submission. 'Give it up,' many of them cried. But this was impossible. Too many people on too many ships, including the ships with heaviest armament, remained committed to the cause. Still Parker may have thought he had gone some way toward saving his own skin. He had signalled the Admiralty, whose spies knew well enough what was happening on every ship, that he would end the mutiny if he could.

And in fact, Parker's question to the *Sandwich* had helped open the floodgates. Dissension, hitherto lurking beneath the surface everywhere, now came out into the open. Every ship divided into factions. Flags went up and down the masts according to which party was stronger, white for surrender, red for continued defiance. Aboard the *Clyde* and *San Fiorenzo* and five other small ships advocates of caution predominated; aboard the *Director* (Bligh's vessel) and the *Brilliant*, *Iris* and *Grampus* the crews divided and fought it out, and militants proved the stronger. Aboard the *Inflexible* and the *Swan* militants formed the obvious majority. In the end red flags prevailed everywhere.

They were not (even yet) red flags of revolution, however, whatever had been the motives behind the scheme, apparently now abandoned, to attack Tilbury fortress. On the anniversary of the restoration of monarchy to England each vessel, whether moderate or militant, signified its continuing loyalty to the crown by firing a salute. This ceremony was repeated a few days later, on the birthday of George III.

Meanwhile at least two ships contained majorities straining to secede. In the quietest hours of the night, as 29 May became 30 May, the *Clyde* finally made good her long-contemplated escape, drifting silently a good part of the way into Sheerness with the flood tide. Then the next day at dinnertime the *San Fiorenzo* cut loose too, but only after a hair-raising dash through the entire fleet, which raked her with fire, so that much of her rigging was shot away.

And so it see-sawed, up and down, the battle of the flags a victory for the mutineers and a defeat for the government, the loss of the two ships a serious blow to the militants and a boost for their opponents. And then came the next reversal only hours later, when three ships appeared from the north-east. They were the forward line of Duncan's fleet advancing either to support or to suppress the mutiny. Aboard every vessel lying at anchor, and from the heights of the fortress wall in Sheerness, anxious hands brought spyglasses to anxious eyes and trained them upon the distant vessels. They bore the red flags of rebellion. Captain Bligh's mission to Yarmouth had been for naught. Moreover, the three were merely a harbinger: ten more of Duncan's fleet would arrive within a day or two to strengthen the mutiny.

Emboldened by this augmentation of their force, which now numbered twenty-two large and a host of smaller vessels, a greater force than had won many of England's most famous naval battles, the ships' delegates added further demands to the original eight, including that courts martial for accused crewmen be conducted by sailors and marines, not officers, which is to say by a jury of their peers. They decreed that the most obnoxious officers receive their comeuppance, ducking some in nets in the sea until they nearly drowned, tarring and feathering others. Those who were thought to have conspired against the strike received little mercy. A second master, two master's mates, one midshipman and a sergeant of marines, all belonging to the *Monmouth*, one of Duncan's fleet, were tried, found guilty and flogged; the sergeant had his head shaved, the second master had half his head shaved. Aboard the *Sandwich*, seamen made effigies of the prime minister, William Pitt, and his chief ally in Parliament, Henry Dundas, strung them from the yardarm and took potshots at them, leading observers at Sheerness to conclude that two opponents of the mutiny had been executed.

Yet all this was secondary when compared to the next major step. 'Till we have all our Grievances redress'd and till we have the same supply from and communications as usual with the shore we shall consider ourselves masters of Nore Shipping,' the delegates informed the king in a communiqué that was as much threat as petition. They had blockaded the estuary of England's river. A ship could ride the flood tide up to London only with a pass signed 'R. Parker, President of Delegates'. Soon a hundred vessels lay at anchor in the mouth of the Thames. From these the men of the fleet took the food and water denied them by government edict. It was a heady moment for 'the only class of beings in our famed Country of Liberty really *Slaves*', as Captain Thomas Pasley had once called them.[19]

Stopping up the Thames was in fact a breathtaking and a dangerous departure. It was not a mere extension of the strike, although some historians have misinterpreted and minimised it thus. For the moment, a revolutionary moment, the quota men, the pressed sailors, the despised and powerless seamen, controlled access to the world's entrepôt and the nation's capital. The new move suggested that the strike had no real bounds; and a boundless strike is not a simple industrial action. It is, or can become, a revolution.

Now the seamen appealed not merely to the king, but over his head to the nation as a whole. 'Shall we,' they asked their countrymen,

Shall we, who in the battle's sanguinary rage, confound, terrify and subdue your proudest foe, guard your coasts from invasion, your children from slaughter and your lands from pillage – be the footballs and shuttlecocks of a set of tyrants who derive from us alone their honours, their titles and their fortunes? No, the Age of Reason has at length revolved. Long have we been endeavouring to find ourselves men. We now find ourselves so. We will be treated as such.

And, in a message to the Admiralty Board:

The few reasonable Articles we have presented to your Lordships should have been attended to in a respectful Manner, otherwise . . . some others may Pop up their terrific heads, to stare your Lordships in the face. We . . . hope you will take the necessary steps to save your Country from a Civil War, which may end in the ruin of your-selves and Uneasiness of our most gracious Sovereign, to whom we have ever been and will be loyal whilst there is a probability of our Grievances being redress'd.

Note in the first message the implicit reference to what forty years later the Chartists would have called 'the useful classes' who alone created the honours, titles and fortunes of their social superiors. Note in the second message the conditional allegiance to Crown, the threat of civil war and of further 'terrific' demands.

We can guess what these demands might have been: an end to the war with France and a reformed Parliament or even establishment of a democratic republic. Such ideas swirled and whirled among the ships' companies at the Nore, they were common parlance among their most advanced spirits who were reading Tom Paine and in contact with the London Corresponding Society. As one of them, a delegate aboard the *Leopard*, put it, 'The country had been oppressed for these five years; the war had been too long; and now is the time to get ourselves righted.' Delegates representing the *Champion* thought that the French people had 'the only government that understands the rights of man'. There was also a vague reaching towards some different and more humane arrangement of society, nostalgia for a mythical golden era long gone, one that had been governed by a moral economy. An unknown seaman aboard the *Repulse* penned these lines:

> In days of yore, when rich and poor agreed,
> Poor served the rich and the rich the poor relieved.
> No despotic tyrants then the womb produced,
> But, mutual all, each loved and none abused,
> But now how dreadful is the scene reversed;
> We're blest with birth, but with oppression cursed.

This is the view of a man who, quite possibly, has read Rousseau, who cannot see into the future, whose vocabulary does not yet contain the word 'socialism', and who therefore looks to a romanticised past for a better model of society.

So the mutiny at the Nore teetered on a knife's edge: on one side of the blade a daring but limited industrial action; on the other, the militant side, the industrial action transformed into a political strike with vast implications. We have indications, too, how the militants would have attempted to realise them. They had been in touch, again, with the seamen of the fleet at Spithead, some of whom regretted ending their strike. The men of the Nore would sail to Portsmouth and the two fleets would combine forces. Together they would attract the remaining vessels among Duncan's squadron blockading the Dutch. With nearly all Britain's navy at their command, who could say them nay?[20]

At the lower end of the Thames, seamen were debating the greatest questions of the day. Upriver, the commercial classes of London, previously not unsympathetic to the seamen, took great fright. Their income, their fortunes, perhaps even their government and way of life were at stake. When 'three percents' (stocks) fell to 47½, the lowest level on record, they practically stampeded into Prime Minister William Pitt's waiting arms. Many volunteered to fight the rebels. They flocked to Tilbury where ships were being prepared for battle. Private ship owners offered their vessels for the looming confrontation. Others raised money to reward loyal seamen.

The government, too, perceived itself to be engaged in a life-or-death struggle. At Pitt's direction the king declared the seamen to be rebels. Circulars were distributed, proclamations printed, speeches delivered, all carrying the same message, that the striking seamen were engaged in a treasonous act. Fearing that the seamen would sail on London, guns blazing, the Admiralty strengthened river defences, dragged chains across the water, littered the stream with obstacles and debris. At the very edge of the estuary, under cover of darkness, it scuttled the buoys and smashed the beacons that normally guided ships through the banks and shoals, so that the rebellious fleet could not get out. Escape was not rendered absolutely impossible by this manoeuvre, but nearly so, for the ships' pilots would have to rely upon memory and feel to gain the open sea.

It is interesting to note here how physical geography influenced attitudes and events and how, once again, the Thames contributes to the shaping of history, is more than a stage in this instance, becomes a giant if formless character in the great drama. Had the fleet mutinied while it was anchored off the coast, say at Yarmouth, things might have turned out differently. It would not have occurred to delegates, for example, that they could pressure the government by interfering with the trade of London, and therefore they would never have been tempted to blockade the nation's capital, in which case they might have kept the sympathy of the country, as the seamen of Spithead had done. Had the fleet not been anchored in a river the option of escape could not so easily have been closed. In short, had the fleet not anchored in the Thames but somewhere else, the mutiny might have had a different outcome and so might have had history.

But the mutinous ships were, in fact, riding a river, with access to the sea behind them now rendered extremely problematic. Pitt expected them to sail in the only direction open to them, cannons booming. But this was never an option, even for the most militant. In fact, when it came down to it, the majority of seamen shrank even from the plans for making a rendezvous with the men of Portsmouth. Those who had not drawn attention to themselves, which was of course the greater part, could still hope for the king's pardon. Any further act, including flight, was more dangerous for them than capitulation. Why risk anything further?

Too late the militants realised that blockading the river had been a fatal misstep. They had got too far ahead of their base; they had staked their lives on a desperate enterprise now going wrong. With the imposition of the blockade the men of the Nore drew to the very edge of the cliff, peered into the abyss and, while some were enthralled, the majority drew back. This was the division, now plain to all, which eventually broke the movement.

From knife's edge to razor's edge: and the General Committee could not rest there long. Its meetings continued at a fever pitch. The delegates, bowing to the inevitable, suspended the blockade. They rejected the Portsmouth option and decided instead that the fleet would divide into groups: those who wished to surrender would remain at the Nore while their more daring comrades would disperse in varying directions.[21] There remained the matter of negotiating the tricky shoals and channels and currents leading to open sea without buoys and lights to guide them. It could be done, but the pilots did not sympathise with the strike. They would be acting under compulsion. Perhaps, therefore, the denouement was a foregone conclusion. On the morning of 9 June President Parker gave the signal for sailing. Every ship answered, but not a sail unfurled and not a ship moved.

The razor was very sharp now. Delegates met yet again and devised another plan, a sad comedown for the militants who had dared dream of revolution, but not quite yet an admission of defeat. They would accept their new wages obtained for them by the Spithead strike and return to duty, so long as dilapidated and overcrowded ships were repaired or scrapped, objectionable officers permanently excluded, and no one charged with treason. President Parker signed this last petition of the Nore mutiny on 10 June, and entrusted it to Captain John Knight of the *Montagu* who carried it immediately to London.

So they waited for the Admiralty's answer. The militants dared not relax their grip upon the rank and file. The rank and file increasingly resented the militants as the hopelessness of their situation sank in. Each ship a tinderbox, then, tensely waiting on events, crewmen eyeing each other with hatred, fear, maybe even despair now. Two more vessels broke free, the *Leopard* and the *Repulse*. As the latter drew away President Parker rushed to the quarterdeck of the *Sandwich*. His behaviour during the next hour perfectly represents the difficulties facing the militants; also his own dilemmas, and perhaps his shortcomings. First he swore he would send the fleeing ship and its crew to the devil. He was rowed to the *Director* whose great guns could be trained upon the escaping vessel. Once aboard, however, he reversed himself, beseeching the crew not to shoot at brother Englishmen. Then when the *Repulse* ran aground and its crew quite ill-advisedly fired a gun in the general direction of the fleet, Parker, in a rage, reversed again, demanding that the *Director* open fire after all. He rushed to another boat, the *Monmouth*, where he helped work the guns himself. Yet there is evidence that the crews purposely aimed high, and eventually the *Repulse* made a successful getaway.

It was slipping out of control now. Aboard most ships 'dreadful contests' broke out. A bloody battle took place aboard the sloop *Swan*, whose militants drove advocates of surrender overboard and into small boats. When these approached another vessel, *Isis*, they discovered a furious struggle raging there too. Again the militants proved stronger, but only after three died in the fighting and many were wounded. 'Englishmen murdering Englishmen! Our people are all in an uproar,' wrote Joseph Hardy, a junior officer aboard the *Nassau*, formerly of Admiral Duncan's fleet. But the militants were far from having it all their own way. On the morning of 10 June the crew of the *Nassau* refused to hoist the red flag. 'Our boat with a delegate has gone round the North Sea [Duncan's] Fleet to bring them into our way of thinking, that is to have pay & the King's Pardon & return to their duty. They have succeeded with 5 sail of the line already & are going aboard.'[22]

In those ships where the moderates now outnumbered and had outfought militants, they handed control back to officers. These vessels soon were breaking away from the main fleet and heading upriver past Sheerness to Gravesend: first the *Standard*, then the *Agamemnon*, *Nassau*, *Vestal*, even the *Isis*, where previously militants had prevailed in bloody combat; then the *Grampus*, *Champion* and *Brilliant*. Militants aboard these vessels knew what fate awaited them. One, William Wallace, a Scotsman from Ayr, put a bullet through his brain rather than surrender. Others, reading the writing on the wall, tried to escape while they still could. The next day a large boatload of men under full sail outpaced a revenue cutter patrolling near the mouth of the river. Where these particular militants landed and what became of them we do not know.

On the ships still holding out, crewmen believed that the delegates and the Admiralty were negotiating terms. In fact the delegates were simply waiting for word from the Admiralty on the demands carried to London by Captain Knight, and when he returned with their inevitable rejection President Parker had had enough. On the 13th he again called together the crew of the *Sandwich* and put it to them once more: would they prefer to continue the strike or return the ship to the officers? 'To the officers' came the nearly unanimous cry. Later that day, as if trying to show that he had never been militant at all, Parker helped man the capstan so that the *Sandwich*, parliament ship of the Nore mutiny, could hoist anchor and drift into Sheerness.

A few of the larger boats still would not come in, but the mutiny had finished. Aboard the ships still holding out bloody battles broke out yet again. Now they could have but one outcome. Still, some of the militants kept their heads. A party from the *Inflexible* escaped the fleet in a longboat. They rowed to Faversham, stole a small ship and sailed it to Calais. A group from the *Montagu* escaped to Holland. There are reports that men from the *Swan* also managed to get away. The vast majority of militants, however, now faced the prospect of pitiless retribution.

Richard Parker's fall was even more rapid than had been his ascent. After arranging to surrender the *Sandwich*, he surrendered himself. The ship's officers, restored to their former authority, put him into a lieutenant's cabin under guard. When, only a few hours later, the *Sandwich* rode the flood tide into Sheerness harbour, they shackled him hand and foot and took him by longboat into town, and thence by coach to Maidstone jail. There the former president of the fleet sat, without access to lawyer or wife or family or any friend, attempting to prepare for his court martial. The charges: 'For causing and endeavouring to cause mutinous assemblies on board his Majesty's ship *Sandwich*, and others of His Majesty's ships at the Nore on or about the 12th of May last, for disobeying the lawful orders of his superior officers and for treating his officers with disrespect.'

The wheels of justice, if that was what he was about to receive, did not grind slow or fine for Richard Parker, but rather swift and rough. Everything happened in a rush; finesse was necessarily absent. He received less than a week to organise his defence. The trial began on 22 June, he received his sentence on the 26th and died four days later. The prosecutor was his former superior officer, Captain Mosse, of the *Sandwich*. On the 19th Evan Nepean, Secretary to the Admiralty, wrote to Mosse, 'You may prove almost anything you like against him, for he has been guilty of everything that's bad.' Mosse, who did not appreciate Nepean's advice, nevertheless understood what was expected of him: 'the conviction of the villain Parker', which was so certain that 'the place and time of his execution might have been previously settled'.

Still, the erstwhile president fought for his life. He told the court that

> The Delegates insisted on my assuming the situation I appeared in, and it was impossible for me, or any individual under similar circumstances, to have resisted such appointment. As soon as I saw that fatal spirit of the mutiny which prevailed, I immediately thought it my duty and I endeavoured as far as in me lay to stop the further progress of it.

It may well have been the truth, but it was difficult to prove, not least because for much of the mutiny he had certainly *seemed* to be a militant.

One critical point had to do with his conduct during the escape of the *Repulse* and the *Leopard*. He claimed to have opposed shooting at them. 'I saw the guns in the quarterdeck [of the *Director*] cast loose [to shoot at the *Repulse*]. I pointed out the impropriety and cruelty of one brother fighting against another,' which was true. But what of eyewitness accounts that he had helped to point guns and shoot only a little later, vowing to blow the escaping vessels all the way to hell? Parker said they were lies.

'You have been talking a great deal about Hell,' he replied to one who testified against him. 'I wish to know whether you have been promised anything for advancing this hellish account?'

'No sir, I never was promised anything.'

'I will bring witnesses to disprove what this man has said.'

But he never did. He could not, since too many had seen him helping to load the guns. Thus his main line of defence: trying to prove that
'I was obliged to act a part I abominated.'

Charged that he had been disrespectful of officers, he sought to prove
it was not so. True, Admiral Buckner had boarded the *Sandwich* without
receiving proper honours. However, 'I was sorry that it should have
been so, but . . . I was at the time on shore attending a procession.'
Moreover, when he too had boarded the *Sandwich* that day and realised
the situation, he placed himself in danger by attempting to rectify it. He
had ordered the crew to man the yards, a gesture of respect, but he
explained, 'it was signified if it was complied with that the *Inflexible* and
the other ships would fire upon and sink the *Sandwich*'.

It was a brave but doomed performance. Admiral Buckner did not
remember Parker ordering the *Sandwich* to show him due deference but
rather the 'degree of insolence' with which he had behaved; Dr Snipe,
ship's surgeon to the *Sandwich*, recalled that Parker had not removed his
hat while carrying on a discussion with Captain Mosse; Captain Dickson
of *L'Espion* also drew attention to Parker's disrespectful attitude. When
the accused attempted to cross-examine he discovered the cleft stick on
which this part of his defence rested:

'Do you recollect when you came on board with Admiral Buckner
whether I did not go between decks to exhort the men to treat the
Admiral with proper respect as well as to apologize for their not doing
it?'

The problem was that in doing this he had demonstrated his role as
leader of the mutinous crew. The court therefore advised him to with-
draw the question. Parker did so. But then how could he prove his
innocence of this particular charge? He was damned either way. If he
had not understood this before, surely he understood it now.

Yet he grasped at a final straw. Perhaps the court would be moved by
testimony about his role in ending the mutiny. He needed more time to

arrange for the summoning of additional witnesses. '[Captain Pasley] informed him it could not be granted.'

Even if Parker's defence was true, nevertheless he had been the most visible of the mutineers. The Admiralty would make an object lesson of him for that. If it was not true, if he had advocated some of the most militant schemes (and there is much testimony that he did), then the task of his judges was even easier. In the end it took the court only two and a half hours to find him guilty of crimes that are 'as unprecedented as they are wicked, and as ruinous to the navy as to the peace and prosperity of the country. The court doth therefore adjudge him to suffer DEATH.' But by this time Richard Parker cannot have been surprised.[23]

Two days before he was to be hanged he wrote a sad, contradictory, bitter letter to a friend. The Admiralty confiscated this message, whose burden only reiterated the main lines of his defence: that the delegates had sought always to temper the extreme demands of militant seamen. Parker confessed with pride that the plight of the sailors had greatly moved him. He possessed 'a tender sensibility at every species of human woe'. This, he now realised, had clouded his judgement. He had foolishly 'suffered humanity to surmount reason'. Now, as a result, his life and the lives of most of the delegates were forfeit, while the fickle seamen would live to watch them die. 'I ought to have known mankind better.' He concluded: 'Oh, pray for me, that in the last scene I may act my part like a man . . .'

They hanged him on 30 June, from a yardarm aboard the *Sandwich*, still anchored off Sheerness, with the entire fleet surrounding it and the crews all mustered to watch, and scaffolds erected on the land for spectators to climb so that they could see as well. His wife, who had unavailingly petitioned the king for mercy on his behalf, had managed to make the journey from Edinburgh, arriving at the penultimate moment. Could she not see her husband one last time? But the fatal tide that had wrecked Arabella Stuart's dreams and doomed Sir Walter Raleigh, was against her too, rolling in through the Nore and westward up the Thames to London. Twice her hired oarsmen gave up the attempt to row her to the ship. On the third attempt the currents were less strong, the tide finally had begun to ebb, and she drew nigh just in time to see him, in a suit of mourning, hands bound behind him, halter round his neck, hood not yet pulled down over his eyes, atop the platform built specially for the purpose high above and out from the cathead of the *Sandwich*. Then the act itself, his last, and as daring in its way as the first act of mutiny, the cheering aboard the *Sandwich* only six weeks before. He sprang from the cathead 'with great rapidity' before the gunshot signalling for the reeve rope to string him up, so that in the end he had taken his own life. Mrs Parker fainted.[24]

In his last statement to the court President Parker had dared to hope that 'my life will be the only sacrifice'. It was a forlorn wish. By the most recent count over four hundred sailors were tried before courts martial, of whom fifty-two received the death sentence (although possibly as few as thirty-six suffered it), and more than three hundred and fifty received lesser sentences, most involving the cat-o'-nine-tails.[25] They might almost have preferred the fatal penalty. George Scott, of the *Sandwich*, for example, was punished 'with 300 lashes, to be inflicted on board such ships and in such proportion as the Lords Commissioners of the Admiralty should think fit'.

So ended a tragic chapter in the history of the Thames and the nation. The abortive mutiny on the Nore takes its place as part of a great movement for political reform and social amelioration, somewhere between the revolutionary conspiracies of the early English Jacobins and the demonstration that resulted in the 'Peterloo massacre' of 1819. Despite many setbacks it proved an irresistible tide in the end, and to it the sailors had added their mite.

They had added more than a mite to the movement for improvement of conditions within the navy itself. The British sailor of 1797 lived and worked much the way his predecessor did a hundred and fifty years before. This was what provoked his revolt. And if the Admiralty Board

was unmoved by it, and if the general public felt threatened by it, nevertheless in laying bare the unjustifiable inequities and hardships which
were its cause, the sailors planted seeds that bore fruit. England could
not risk such a mutiny again; reform was therefore inevitable: further
pay increases, more equitable distribution of prize money, restricted
use of the dreaded cat-o'-nine-tails, a term of five years beyond which
sailors could not be made to serve against their will, even an end to the
system of impressments. As the two best historians of the mutiny have
written in their joint account, '1797 opens a new era in the organization
of the Royal Navy, or at least marks a turning-point in its history.'[26]

During this critical phase in the unwinding of two great movements
for reform the Thames provided more than a venue. To some the river
itself represented the nation. A London poet rejoicing in the government's victory gave voice to what may have been popular sentiments.
The Thames, he wrote, was Britain's 'Guardian Genius', whom the
sailors had violated and betrayed.

> But with heart-felt Sorrow wounded [wrote Christopher
>   Anstey]
> All aghast and pale She stood:
> Thames her piercing Cries resounded
> Back to Medway's trembling Flood:
>
> 'Tell me, ye, on whom relying
> I the Sea's Dominion hold,
> Why these hostile Flags are flying,
> Tell me true, my Sailors bold.'

Anstey's Thames embodied conservative, law-abiding patriotic values.

> 'To Old England firm and hearty,
> And obedient to her Laws,

Sailors own no other Party,
Than their King and Country's Cause.'

But a great many of the seamen at the Nore would have begged to dis-
agree. At the climax of their strike, they had conceived of the river very
differently. It was a highway leading into London. They could block it
and choke the government; they had the nation by the windpipe, or so
they thought for a time. Then they realised what their opponents knew:
that the river was a bottleneck, and they were in it, and the government
had stopped it, so that they could not escape. They would have done
better to stick to the sea, to have kept out of England's river.

6

Water, Air, Earth, Fire

*O*ne summer evening, almost certainly during 1796, nine or so months before the sailors' mutiny at the Nore, a young man sat painting on the north bank of the Thames at Millbank, close, probably, to where the Tate Gallery (Britain) is now located. The young man sat facing the full moon that had just risen in the east, downriver. He outlined the roofs of the shops and houses in that direction on the opposite shore in greyish purple, capturing the tinge cast by a sun that had already set beneath the horizon. The effect is to suggest that it had been warm that day, and that the evening still retained a vestige of summer heat. He managed to convey also that the night was still and quiet. The water scarcely ripples in his painting. Two small boats glide by from the west, the first with a nearly slack sail. One can almost hear the oars of the second of the two vessels being drawn from the water by the boatman, and the peaceful murmur of water lapping at the near shore. One can almost feel the soft air of the summer evening.

The artist modestly called his painting a 'study', to imply that he still had much to learn about depicting moonlight on canvas, but in fact it is the work of one who already had looked closely not merely at the

moon and sky but also at light and dark and water and air more generally, and who had thought carefully about how to paint them. It is,
too, the work of one who knew the Thames very well, and the boats
that plied it, and the men who laboured on or near it. Perhaps it is not
surprising that the painter of *Moonlight, a Study at Millbank* went on to
become the Thames's foremost interpreter in oil and watercolour. In
1796 he was only twenty-one years old. He stood a mere five feet four
inches tall, he had a prominent chin and over-large nose, but for his
physical imperfections he compensated with a thrusting ambition and
prodigious talent. His name was Joseph Mallord William Turner.

Turner's knowledge of the Thames came from a combination of
close examination and natural connection. He was born and lived his
first decade within four hundred yards of it, in Maiden Lane, between
the western end of Covent Garden and the Strand; he would die
seventy-six years later only a few miles upstream, in Chelsea, just as the
morning sun broke through the clouds and made the river sparkle. As
a child he explored its banks. When he was ten, his parents sent him to
live with his uncle in New Brentford, just north of Kew Bridge. Already
the child amused himself by copying artists' depictions of the Thames
and by colouring printed engravings of it. When he was fifteen, returned
to Maiden Lane, and become a student at the Royal Academy of Art at
Somerset House, he probably painted the first of his views of the Thames
from Richmond Hill. It was a tribute to his teacher, the president of the
Academy, Sir Joshua Reynolds, and it was the view of the river that
Reynolds saw from the back of his country house. In later years Turner's
restless genius led him to wander Europe and the British Isles, sketchpad
or paints and easel always at hand. Time and again, however, he
returned to the English river of his childhood. It was wound round his
soul, crucial to his sense of himself. Many of his paintings reveal a vision
of England in which the river plays a vital role.

When, that summer evening a year before the sailors' mutiny,
Turner painted from nature the Thames by moonlight, English

landscape art rested upon the shoulders of Dutch, Italian and French masters of previous centuries. For a hundred years or more, from the mid-seventeenth century, it had stalled as a kind of displaced portraiture, not of faces but of great houses and their surroundings, or of villages which played the role of country houses in the landscape and *their* surroundings, or, following the lead of the great French landscape painters, Claude and Poussin, of a cultivated, civilised, ordered countryside that was modelled upon an idealised version of the Italian campagna. For more than a hundred years English landscape artists had portrayed their country in classical terms. They flattered the landed class who were their chief clientele, by comparing them to noble Romans. They idealised peasants too. The Roman poet Virgil had written in the *Georgics*:

> O happy, if he knew his happy state!
> The swain, who, free from business and debate,
> Receives his easy food from Nature's hand,
> And just returns of cultivated land!

'Georgic' English landscape painting of the mid-eighteenth century celebrated the ostensibly innocent, amiable agricultural worker and his unproblematic relations with his social superiors. Later in the century English artists added to their georgic art a fascination with 'picturesque' aspects of the landscape: notable rock formations, interesting-looking trees, ivy-covered bridges over streams. When animal and human figures appeared in such works they were likewise depicted as picturesque.

From about the 1750s British landscape painting evolved to reflect artists' interest in 'sublime' aspects of the countryside, noble mountain peaks, wild rushing torrents and waterfalls, precipices, vast billowing seas, dramatic skies; also an interest in history, so that sublime objects in themselves, for example ruined abbeys and castles (but even particularly dramatic historical events), were placed against backgrounds that might also be sublime or picturesque. Turner himself, with a career to make, would paint georgic, picturesque and sublime landscapes in the years following 1797. At the beginning of his career he showed that he could imitate the styles of old masters and surpass them. He made a great reputation painting not only landscapes but also grand classical, biblical, or historical subjects, and contemporary ones in which he sometimes commented upon current events.

But English landscape art at the turn of the eighteenth century was poised for a new departure, and Turner himself would play an important role in carrying it forward. He knew that England's agricultural workers were not always or even usually picturesque, guileless, good-natured rustics who could expect Nature to provide them with easy food. And, as his early painting of the Thames at Millbank already suggested, he was both too conscious of the particularity of his subject to accept the Italian model for ever, and too appreciative of its modest loveliness to maintain an exclusive interest in landscapes that were sublime. And, though he was not unique in this regard, his really close observation of nature and the elements already distinguished him.

By late 1804 Turner had become a member of the governing council of the Royal Academy with a growing reputation for brilliant if unpredictable painting, for attracting wealthy patrons, and also for having a difficult personality. That winter he rented Syon Ferry House overlooking the Thames at Isleworth, not far from New Brentford where he had lived as a child with his uncle. In 1805 Syon Ferry House would become his base for more than a year of exploration along the river, sometimes tramping, but mainly in a small sailing boat with a little cookstove and retractable awning to protect him from the elements. During this period Turner directed his exquisitely tuned sensibility exclusively to the river and its surroundings. He closely and sympathetically observed the men and women who worked near or on it, and he recorded his impressions on sketchpads, canvases and wooden panels. He belonged to a circle of young artists, including William

Delamotte, William Havell, John Linnell, William Mulready and William Henry Hunt, who were interested at this time in painting more closely from nature, and who focused upon the Thames valley. But it was Turner who produced a unique record of it, many dozens of sketches, watercolours and oils, illuminated by his surpassing genius. The sketches he made that year formed the basis of finished paintings for decades to come. Indeed throughout his life he would return to ideas and themes he had developed during that single magically creative year.

One of those themes was that the Thames valley both exemplified and contained within itself the virtues of the nation. The vision was both personal and political. It was personal in this sense: Turner, as he sailed and sketched the river, was also metaphorically cleansing himself, washing away London dirt and troubles. Apparently these were legion. Successful as he was, his elders in the Royal Academy nevertheless thought him rude and arrogant, his manners 'more like those of a *groom* than anything else'.[1] They criticised him for being a bad influence on younger painters. An art critic declared that he had 'debauched the taste of the young artists in this country by the empirical novelty of his style of painting'.[2] Benjamin West, who had replaced Reynolds as president of the Royal Academy, discerned 'imbecility' in his work.[3] But Turner rediscovered in the green Thames valley and on the calm, peaceful river, that is to say in a section of the English countryside whose most important feature was the river Thames, an answer and an antidote to metropolitan carping and backbiting.

He was always attracted to great subjects taken from history and classical literature. At his Syon Ferry House retreat Turner chose for his reading material the works of Virgil, Homer, Plutarch and Ovid among others, for he intended to paint his riverscapes as scenes from classical poetry. His notebooks contain scattered snatches of verse he copied from the great poets suggesting that what he read moved him deeply, and that he identified with certain of their heroes. He listed potential classical scenes for his paintbrush: from Plutarch's *Lives* and from Virgil's *Aeneid*, for example. Nevertheless it was the river, the countryside, changeable nature, which had the more profound effect upon him.

It is not that classical allusions are entirely absent from his works of this period, for they are not, far from it. The first sketches he undertook upon arriving at Isleworth were of a rotunda; later he painted a study in watercolour of Dido and Aeneas; he sketched in pencil a scene from Ovid's *Metamorphoses*, of Mercury before he slays Argus. Nevertheless, aboard his boat and from the edges of the stream Turner sketched trees, river banks, flowers, cows, sheep, and geese for themselves, as he understood them then, in England, on the Thames, in the summer of 1805. His watercolours, many of them painted on the spot, are often all about light on the river, sky, clouds, rainbows, the effects of weather. Man-made objects nestle comfortably in the landscape or against the river bank. Boats float easily upon the river itself. For the most part men and women, even when they are working, exist in harmony with land- and riverscape. They are neither picturesque nor georgic. Turner captures not their individuality but rather the essential nature of their relationship to their surroundings and to each other: in the bend of a fisherman's back, or the gesture of greeting of one friend to another.

In one remarkable watercolour sketch a rainbow arches over the grey-washed paper, the sky before the colourful arc is dark and ominous; clearly a thunderstorm has just taken place. Two figures shelter under a riverside tree, perhaps marvelling at nature's gorgeous display, as a brown-sailed barge slides down the river.

In another sketch a figure waves in recognition, standing on the road leading to the bridge crossing the stream, behind which sits a small house, almost certainly Syon Ferry House. It is late afternoon, sunlight yellows and reddens the far part of the sky and glimmers on a tree at the river's edge. We may imagine that this is the scene Turner daily returned to. It is peaceful. The man who painted it loved the scene, had left behind and forgotten the troubles of London. He was content. In fact, as

One of Turner's watercolour sketches of summer 1805. Man-made objects nestle comfortably in the landscape or against the riverbank. Boats float easily upon the river itself. For the most part men and women, even when they are working, labour in harmony with land and riverscape. (*River Scene with Rainbow*, Joseph Mallord William Turner (1775–1851)/Tate, London 2004)

he worked Turner was being reborn as an artist; he had been baptised, as it were, in the waters of England's river. These paintings and sketches and studies of summer 1805, observes one who has written about Turner with great acuity, are those of 'a man who had found himself'.[4]

So the vision was personal in the sense that Turner portrayed the Thames valley as the antithesis of London, where politicking and intrigue reigned. The reaches of the Thames he had explored and painted were an Arcadia by contrast, a countryside in which Greek gods and goddesses, and the people who worshipped them, might have felt at home, but where also were preserved England's truest values and virtues: the purity of nature, the slow rhythm of country labour, man's organic connection with the countryside, and with the beasts of the field, fish in the river, birds of the sky. He was painting England as he thought it had been and should always be.

The vision was also political because in 1805, as in 1797, England feared, indeed expected, French invasion. Now, however, Napoleon's armies were vaster and more experienced and better armed than the French armies of 1797 had been. They posed the gravest threat to England since the Spanish Armada of 1588. In his watercolours of the Thames valley Turner was picturing what he believed needed and deserved defending from the French. In his mind the river and surrounding countryside stood for the national verities, for England's essential character, indeed for the nation itself.

It is significant, therefore, that his paintings sometimes omitted the opulent riverside villas of the wealthy, even from stretches of the Thames where viewers knew them to be located. This is true, for example, of a painting, *View of Richmond Hill and Bridge*, which Turner renders as a pastoral, the bridge suffused in early morning light, with women bathing a child at the edge of the river and sheep grazing behind. This depiction worried a critic writing for the 1808 *Review of Publications of Art*: 'We are not sure this is right . . . giving a pastoral character to a scene, part of the beauty of which resides in its architectural elegance.'[5] But he did it again, for example in a painting started but never finished, of nearly the same stretch of the Thames. *Men with Horses crossing the River* (c.1805–6) focuses precisely upon simple peasants and their beasts of burden, though without any georgic overtones. There is not a villa or manor house in sight. But perhaps this view of life on the Thames, in which no social hierarchy, or ostentatious display of wealth, or contrast between rich and poor exists, accorded with the vision of England Turner thought most worth portraying and defending.

Increasingly, during the summer and autumn of 1805, his paintings focused upon working men and women. In *Newark Abbey on the Wey* (the Wey is a tributary of the Thames near Chertsey) bargemen prepare a simple meal in fading sunlight, their vessels tied up below a lock and mill. They are oblivious to the ruined abbey behind them. This seems almost too obvious a dig at artists still enamoured of the picturesque in landscape painting.

Increasingly, during the summer and autumn of 1805, Turner's paintings focused upon working men and women. Here bargemen prepare a simple meal, oblivious to the ruined abbey behind them. (*Newark Abbey on the Wey*, J. M. W. Turner/Tate, London 2004)

Here the vision is nearly bleak: the landscape empty, the meagre 'dinner' referred to in the title is perhaps an ironic commentary upon the bountiful wheatfield behind — that belongs not to the harvesters but to the landowner. (*Harvest Dinner*, J. M. W. Turner/Tate, London 2004)

Then, in *Harvest Dinner, Kingston Bank* (first exhibited in 1809), the vision is nearly bleak: the landscape empty, the meagre 'dinner' referred to in the title perhaps an ironic commentary upon the wheat field behind, where farmhands pitch hay into a wagon – for the landowner. Some of Turner's pencil sketches of this period are equally unflinching: of desperate beggars, men disputing in a tavern, an angry blacksmith.

It was not an idealised Thames and surrounding countryside that Turner depicted in such works, then, but rather the real thing. Turner's genius lay, in part, in his unrivalled ability to comprehend and picture both the real and the ideal. He was simultaneously a social realist capable of unflinching portrayals of rural life, a romantic who could picture it as an idyll, and a classicist who peopled the Thames valley with figures taken from Greek and Roman mythology. Taken all in all his Thames valley landscapes suggest what the countryside really meant to him. He shows us a river that was many-sided, contradictory, complex and, in his watercolours at least, quintessentially English.

His return to London from Isleworth took place at about the same time as the birth of Isambard Kingdom Brunel in Portsea, a suburb of Portsmouth, on 9 April 1806. The infant Brunel would also become a great artist of sorts: the most brilliant of mid-Victorian engineers, the architect of delicate filigree suspension bridges, wrought-iron bridges, bridges of brick and masonry that support miraculous, curving arches; of tunnels with ornamented porticoes and of viaducts apparently modelled upon classical designs and upon a genre of painting called the apocalyptic sublime, of magnificent railway sheds with vaulted Tudor-style ceilings. He designed Paddington Station. He designed a series of transatlantic steamships, culminating in the grandiose six-masted, five-funnelled, 692-foot *Great Eastern*. Brunel was to become, too, the chief engineer and planner of the Great Western Railway, which ran two hundred miles, longer than any other mid-Victorian track, in breathtaking straight lines only occasionally broken by graceful gentle curves, all the way from London to Bristol through tunnels of his own engineering and over bridges and viaducts he had designed to maximise the flatness of his track bed, which rises imperceptibly over its course from London to Didcot at the rate of 1 in 1320. This project marked the pinnacle of Brunel's genius; moreover it inspired Turner's masterpiece of 1843, the painting called *Rain, Steam, and Speed – The Great Western Railway*, which pictures a locomotive rushing over Maidenhead Bridge, Brunel's construction. Here is a striking confluence between two geniuses and their great achievements. The point of intersection was precisely the river Thames at Maidenhead.

Brunel was the son of a noted engineer himself, Sir Marc Isambard Brunel, a French refugee, who is principally famous for overseeing construction of the first complete tunnel underneath the Thames. It ran from Rotherhithe on the south bank across to Wapping in east London, and took nearly twenty years to complete, although it was supposed to take only three. Marc Brunel designed the ingenious machine that made excavation of the tunnel possible, the 'Great Shield', in which thirty-six workmen, each protected by a cast iron casing within a giant subdivided frame of parallel cells three levels high, excavated the dirt, sand, mud and clay in front of them a little at a time. Then the 'Great Shield', which looks in pictures a little like a honeycomb, would be jacked forward so they could do it again, while labourers built up the brickwork of the tunnel behind. Sir Marc based this invention upon close observation of the shipworm *Teredo navalis*, which could eat through a boat's most solid timbers while lining with its own excreta the tunnel it thus created.

Brunel senior was only partially responsible for bringing the enormous and dangerous project to a successful conclusion, however. He was an elderly man. His health was not good. In 1827, only two years after his labourers had sunk the tunnel's first shaft at Rotherhithe, he shifted most of the responsibility for completing it to his son, Isambard, now all of twenty-one years of age. It could have been a crushing burden, but the younger man never faltered, despite labour difficulties, financial difficulties, political difficulties, and environmental difficulties including several floods, one of which nearly took his life. The Thames loomed large for I.K. Brunel long before he designed the Maidenhead Bridge for the Great Western Railway.

We know that Brunel and Turner had friends in common later on, but it is possible that the two men crossed paths at this early juncture. In 1827 Turner owned an inn, The Ship and Bladebone, located two hundred yards from what would become the northern entrance to the tunnel in Wapping. A shrewd businessman, he understood that the completed tunnel would add to the value of his property. Perhaps he sought out the figure who had assumed primary responsibility for its construction. At any rate on the evening of 10 November 1827 with the tunnel about half completed, young Brunel staged a sumptuous dinner for fifty associates and acquaintances under one of the tunnel arches, and for 120 workers who dined less magnificently under another arch nearby. The tunnel was brilliantly illuminated by gaslight. A band of the Coldstream Guards entertained the diners. The Turner Bequest contains an unfinished oil painting entitled *A Vaulted Hall*, which is thought to represent this occasion. Conceivably the artist was one of the diners.[6]

With this much-publicised feast Brunel had intended to reassure the public that his tunnel was safe. Only two months later, however, on 12 January 1828 another disastrous flood occurred, this time with the loss of six workmen, and nearly with the loss of Brunel himself. Work on the tunnel ceased for nearly seven years. Once resumed it would not be completed until 1843. If Turner had been commemorating the dinner with the painting perhaps this is why he left it unfinished.

Meanwhile Brunel moved on to Bristol where, among other projects, he provided the design and engineering for a new, improved harbour capable of competing with the port of Liverpool; and for the beautiful Clifton suspension bridge (although he did not live to complete it); and for two ocean-going steamships, the *Great Western* and the (much larger) *Great Britain*. The two vessels were built by the Great Western Steamship Company, which had been established by the Great Western Railway Company. Brunel now had made contact with the employer for which he would create his greatest achievement.

The directors of the Great Western Railway Company planned to build a line that would connect London with Bristol, and with New York City via their own steamships. It was an audacious plan with immense implications for England's economy and society, but then, as will become apparent, the promoters, financiers and engineers of Britain's railway system during this period were more than mere businessmen. They were revolutionaries engaged in transforming their country's economic and social relations.

In March 1833 the company's board of directors appointed the younger Brunel to be their chief engineer. Immediately he dived into every aspect of the project. He prepared the initial survey of terrain and later, preliminary to the start of construction, surveyed it again in minute detail, a painstaking, physically exhausting business. He helped to frame the necessary legislation (since construction of the railway would require an Act of Parliament); he testified before the relevant parliamentary committee; he even engaged in fund raising. Once construction of the railway began he oversaw every detail of the civil engineering: the cuttings, bridges, tunnels, viaducts, sheds, even the London terminus (which became Paddington Station). His drive and stamina already were legendary from his work on the Thames tunnel; but what set the Great Western Railway apart from the outset was Brunel's conception of the project as a whole. He oversaw its every aspect not because he was a glutton for punishment, but because he had conceived a giant integrated scheme, main line, branch lines, stations, signals, steamships, overriding purpose, all in one, and he could not entrust even a part of it to someone else. It was a symbolic victory for Brunel that he completed the first section of track in 1837 just as his steamship was pulling into New York City harbour. The Great Western

Railway was, in fact, Brunel's gigantic and gigantically successful work
of art.

It was distinctive for another reason. Brunel's vision was markedly
modern. Where other railways of the period were meant primarily to
transport goods, his was meant from the first to transport people at
high speed. Therefore he designed it flat: bridges, viaducts, cuttings,
tunnels all calculated to maintain the level railbed; and he designed it
wide: with a broad-gauge track, 7 feet ¼ inch across, as opposed to the
more common narrow gauge of 4 feet 8½ inches. He thought in grand
terms: of a mighty locomotive with enormous wheels, which having
to turn less frequently than smaller wheels would create less friction
on the straight, broad, level rail. Advocates of the cheaper narrower
gauge were outraged, but Brunel was obdurate and, at least initially,
justifiably so. From the first the locomotives on the Great Western
could travel at speeds of sixty miles per hour, or even more. It was only
later that track improvement made the narrow gauge a preferable
choice.

Where the railway crosses the Thames at Maidenhead the river is
about a hundred yards wide and still navigable. There is a small island in
the middle of the stream. The authorities stipulated that Brunel must
not obstruct either the navigable channel or the towpath on the side,
and that he build a bridge high enough to allow sailing vessels with tall
masts to pass beneath. Brunel's challenge was to do so without jeopardising his level railbed, and with only a single pier in the river to sustain
the bridge. His solution was to place the railway on a viaduct approaching and leaving the river, four land arches east of the stream and four
more arches to the west; to leap half the river with a 128-foot span,
landing his pier on the island, and then to leap the same length again to
the western bank, and, most miraculous of all, to do so with a maxi-
mum rise above the river of 24 feet 6 inches and this largely attained by
the viaducts as the land sloped towards the river banks, so that the railway rapidly gained height over the water without forcing the trackbed

upwards to clear the arch.[7] There was no 'hump' to the bridge. Rather the two semi-ellipses, graceful and clean-lined, form the famous 'flat arches', possibly the flattest ever constructed in brick. Advocates of the narrow-gauge railway seized upon them as a means of discrediting the entire railway project. Even Brunel's contractor did not believe the arches would stand and prior to commencing their construction asked to be relieved of his duties, but the young engineer reassured him, possibly by showing him the famous mathematical calculations he had carried out on the foolscap paper alongside his original design sketches of the bridge. He could not show the plans, however, to the myriad of critics who denounced him for hubris and flat-out error.

In fact the Maidenhead Bridge over the Thames proved to be a great feat of engineering, a jewel in the crown of the Great Western Railway. It balanced hundreds of tons of bricks, with the weight of the haunches of the arch being sufficient to support the long arc, and the weight of the crown of the bridge being sufficient to compress the haunches. When it was done the doubters continued to insist that it was faulty and would fall down. They pointed derisively at the wooden scaffolding and centring that reinforced the structure, arguing that these alone held it up. When the contractor began to remove the timbers, and the brickwork in the eastern arch shifted, they crowed with delight. But in fact the contractor had acted prematurely, the cement on that arch had not completely set. Brunel was furious. But the western arch was fine and, once repairs were made to the eastern arch, the bridge proved solid, as it has remained ever since. There is a legend that Brunel left most of the scaffolding up as a joke on his critics. There is another legend that a great storm finally washed the scaffolding away, and that people turned up when the storm was over expecting that the bridge would be gone too. Recent scholarship debunks these myths,[8] but they serve to emphasise the path-breaking nature of Brunel's achievement, and the incredulity, not to say hostility, with which it was greeted.

Brunel built the Great Western in sections: by 1841, in the midst of the greatest of the several Victorian railway manias, it was complete. Mighty engines roared across the English countryside, pulling carriages of passengers or wagons of freight at previously unimaginable speeds. They signified revolution, not merely in transport, but in the economy as well. To some it seemed that the industrial system, even the individual satanic mills, had been rendered mobile and were rushing through the landscape, spewing smoke and steam, exemplifying velocity, destroying the slower traditional way of life. The agricultural labourer put down his spade as he sensed the approach of the apparition and stared.

> First, the shrill whistle, then the distant roar,
> The ascending cloud of steam, the gleaming brass,
> The mighty moving arm; and on amain
> The mass comes thundering like an avalanche o'er
> The quaking earth . . .[9]

The train was unstoppable. It rushed 'through the fields, through the woods, through the corn, through the hay, through the mould, through the clay, through the rock'.[10] It defied nature and vanquished it. The coming of the railway meant the beginning of the end of old England, rural idyllic England, although there were Britons who attempted to adapt their aesthetic to it.[11] As the giant locomotives of the Great Western Railway sped through the Thames valley and across the Maidenhead Bridge they burst and ripped asunder a countryside that Turner had recorded and cherished and celebrated in his paintings and sketches thirty-five years earlier.

Turner had been born in 1775, when the majority of English people lived on the land much as their ancestors had done for many hundred years. In 1805, when he explored the river he sailed and paddled at a few miles per hour; or tramped its banks and towpath at not much greater speed. He was a Londoner born and bred, but exploring the Thames valley that year he had grasped the pace and essence of English pre-industrial rural and village life. Neither Constable nor any other British landscape artist understood them better, or portrayed them with greater skill or sympathy, or yet with a clearer eye. The railway age, however, announced the arrival in England of a swifter pace, vaster scale, more impersonal values. Turner understood. That the Thames was crucial to him personally and to his vision of England we have already seen. During the 1830s and 1840s it remains a central element in his paintings. Only now it appears in works that record the turning of a great wheel, the passing of an age and way of life, and the coming of a new one, of which the Great Western Railway was both symbol and exemplar.

Turner did not lament the passing of every aspect of the old era. Consider his painting, *Burning of the House of Lords and Commons, 16th October, 1834* (first exhibited in 1835), with its terrifying visual juxtapositions: of the fiery red and orange conflagration, blue-black night sky, white Westminster Bridge. The picture, one of several he completed on the subject, records a real event. In it one can just discern within the inferno the towers of Parliament, doomed but still standing. The surface of the river reflects the bright blaze and the dark sky, while forming an impassable barrier between the great mass of onlookers, of whom Turner was one, on the southern bank and the structural symbols of the government on the north.

It is a painting that depicts the end of an era. The great fire seems almost to be devouring the British regime and British history. It is awesome and awful in its intensity. No incendiary had set it, but Turner's painting reminds us of the men who might have wished to: the Thames-side beggars, the angry blacksmith, the men disputing in a tavern, whom he had sketched a quarter-century before, men separated from their government by an unbridgeable gulf that might as well have been a river of fire. Parliament had rarely addressed their concerns. This work may be considered Turner's political testament.

Or consider one of his most famous and beloved oil paintings, *The Fighting Temeraire, tugged to her Last Berth to be broken up, 1838* (first exhibited in 1839). Here the topical political message is presented less overtly, the contradictions between the former and the new age more starkly, and the role of the Thames more centrally. A great ghostly white ship, three-masted, its sails furled, is being pulled upriver, almost like a beautiful, graceful prisoner against its will, by a squat, ugly, brown-black paddle steamer belching smoke and fire. The *Temeraire*, representative of the age when ships depended upon wind and tide, had played an important role in 1805 during the battle of Trafalgar, the year also of Turner's happy exploration of the river. The *Temeraire* had a glorious history, but no place in a modern navy of ironclads and steam-powered boats.

The painting is elegiac, there can be no doubt that Turner mourns the fate of the glorious and erstwhile 'fighting' *Temeraire*, although his attitude towards the ugly tugboat is less clear; he may consider it a mere neutral agent of the times.[12] A dispute among critics over whether the sun is rising or setting on the scene, whether the tug is pulling the three-masted ship to the east or west, does little to settle this matter. Most think the painting shows the sun at dusk, setting upon the *Temeraire*, symbol of a disappearing and better way of life. It is the natural and probably correct interpretation. On the other hand, in fact the tug was pulling the *Temeraire* upriver toward Rotherhithe, and therefore to the west, in which case the sun behind the great ship must be east of it.[13] The orb is not going down but rising. To sailors, a blood-red sky at morning warns of stormy weather ahead. Can this be Turner's forecast of the dawning age? Are the tug and its prisoner riding England's central highway into an elegiac sunset or rather towards Armageddon? In either case it is the Thames that runs through time in Turner's painting, and that carries the *Temeraire*, representative of a dying epoch, to her fate.[14]

The apocalyptic interpretation gains in plausibility when one considers the third of Turner's late great paintings examined here, *Rain, Steam, and Speed — The Great Western Railway* (first exhibited in 1844), in which he addresses most directly the revolution of which I.K. Brunel was herald and agent. Turner would have understood the magnitude of Brunel's achievement engineering the vast Great Western system; he would have been aware of the miraculous flat arches at Maidenhead, spanning his beloved Thames in two great leaps, and of the doubts that they could stand without support from wooden scaffolding. He would have known about the seven-foot-wide broad-gauge track designed for the mighty locomotives that the Great Western Railway Company sent speeding through the countryside at nearly a mile a minute. As will become apparent he shared the widespread feeling that these resembled monstrous dragons, breathing smoke and fire. Surely he would have recognised that the architect of the whole fabulous project was a titan and a genius; he responded with a work of genius of his own.

His painting is dominated by the broad flat bridge resting upon the arch above the river, and by the approaching locomotive, hurtling demonically forward, towards the viewer, red-gold coal box glowing in front, surely as if the great engine was a dragon exhaling fire. It is reminiscent of the tug, which also spewed smoke and flame as it pulled the *Temeraire* towards the viewer and destruction. But the tug had not dominated the earlier painting as the locomotive does *Rain, Steam, and Speed*. The train emerges from a landscape that is indistinct, and from a windswept, rain-swept, sun-swept sky that is yellow, white and grey all at once, so that we can tell there has been a sun-shower. Is it, perhaps as the tug is, a harbinger of doom, or rather of something unknown and perhaps unknowable, as it rushes from the blurred landscape into the vast emptiness of the Atlantic world (for Turner would have known about the Great Western Railway's steamships too)? Or perhaps Turner imagines the railway shooting like an arrow straight for New York City, vaulting the Atlantic Ocean as it does the river Thames at Maidenhead.

Perhaps Turner is saying that the railway has replaced the meandering Thames, *former* gateway into and out of Britain.

It is an extraordinary juxtaposition. But then the entire composition is a study in contrasts. All that is natural in the painting – sky, river, people waving from a boat at the onrushing train, ploughman to the extreme right – is bathed in light, in fact nearly glows with it, as opposed to the darkly ominous acme of modern technology rushing forward and the miraculous but grim, soot-stained work of engineering that supports it. By contrast we can see the old bridge for pedestrians and horse-drawn wagons to the west, light in colour, almost as the *Temeraire* was light. It is a graceful reminder of a bygone era. But there is something almost brutal about the curve of the single visible arch of the railway bridge. And there is nothing graceful about the railway tracks laid upon it: they are straight-ruled, modern, unnatural, pitiless; while just above them and scampering for its life is the famous hare, no longer visible under a century-and-a-half's accretions of dust and dirt. The hare was meant to be a piquant representative of the natural world. It could not escape the onrushing juggernaut.[15]

In the middle of the river one may just make out a small boat, with a figure under an umbrella. He seems to be fishing or, perhaps, sketching. It must be Turner himself, as he was in 1805. But the Thames provides sanctuary from the rush and push of urban life no longer. The Great Western Railway has intruded with a roar.

Perhaps no painter ever before had captured so well a sense of speed, but then the speed of the Great Western locomotive was something new in the world. Perhaps none had captured so well either the rupturing by iron, coal, engineering and technology of a quieter, slower, more natural way of living (we will not say a more gentle and humane way, because Turner was well aware of the drawbacks to rural life during the *ancien régime*), but then this too was a relatively recent development. And Turner captures the sense of it in an instant: not as though he has taken a snapshot by camera, but rather as a momentary impression of the blur of rushing train, freshness of air, coolness of spring shower; in short, rain, steam, and speed.

Turner's great painting succeeds on several levels. It is, first of all, the work of a virtuoso with the paintbrush. Turner had 'out-prodigied all former prodigies', thought William Thackeray, writing in *Fraser's Magazine* for June 1844. 'He has made a picture with real rain, behind which is real sunshine, and you expect a rainbow every minute. Meanwhile there comes a train down upon you, really moving at the rate of fifty miles an hour, and which the reader had best make haste to see, lest it should dash out of the picture . . .'[16]

It is, too, an extraordinary depiction of industrialism's intrusion into old England, expressed not as a lament, although Turner clearly understood what was being lost, but as a fact. It cannot be coincidence that the river runs right through it. For Brunel, doubtless, the Thames presented merely an engineering problem, an obstacle to be overcome like so many others. But for the artist, Turner, it had a deeper meaning. For him the river was a critical component in a painting depicting England as it had been, as it presently was, and as it was in process of becoming. For him, at least, the meanings of the river and of England overlapped.

What Turner did in *Rain, Steam, and Speed* then, was to unite the genius of Brunel, as expressed in the Maidenhead Bridge and Great Western Railway, and a vision of England, represented in part by the river Thames, to suggest a new and deeper understanding of his country, past and present. The locomotive and its train, presented by the painter as symbols of the new age in all its complexity, come rushing and roaring out of the mist and over Maidenhead Bridge to conquer the immemorial river, shooting off towards the new world. Brunel provided the technological expertise; Turner provided the interpretation. The conjunction of river, bridge, and railway in his great work of art marks a significant contribution to evolving conceptions of the national identity.

7

Dark Waters

When the smoke-belching tug pulled Turner's *Fighting Temeraire* on its last journey down the Thames at least it was to the scrapyard. At least this erstwhile ship of the line did not suffer the worst indignity: she never was stripped of her masts and left to rot as a prison hulk by the Plumstead marshes across the river from Woolwich, or further downstream near Chatham, or in some other muddy, mosquito-infested, estuary or port. Not so lucky the *Sandwich*, the *Nassau*, and the *Belliqueux*, former flagships of Admiral Parker's floating republic. Nor were the inmates of the hulks even so fortunate, if that is the word, as sailors in the Royal Navy had been. The possibility of death or injury in battle was spared them. But the miseries with regard to diet, crowding, discipline and labour that the latter endured paled in comparison with those suffered by their contemporaries, convicts and prisoners of war sentenced to imprisonment aboard the dreaded derelict vessels.

The prison hulks reflect the harshness of two historical epochs: the one that inspired proponents of the Age of Reason to advocate revolution, and the one that followed their crushing defeat. In England the former age had seen, for example, the hanging of Richard Parker and the ferocious suppression of his 'floating republic'; the latter witnessed the reaction to full-blown industrialisation: machine-wrecking and the judicial murder by hanging of machine-wreckers; working-class demands for political representation and even more ferocious repression than ever before, as in the 'Peterloo massacre', when sabre-wielding dragoons broke up a demonstration of men, women and children peacefully assembled in a field outside Manchester, killing eleven, injuring hundreds. Only when this black period waned and the reforming spirit grew stronger in Britain did the Thames-bound Bastilles come to seem unnecessarily cruel, so that reformers first agitated to ameliorate conditions on them, and then to abolish them altogether.

The prison hulks first came into use after the War of American Independence, which deprived Britain of a convenient dumping ground for convicted criminals, and before 1786 when the authorities began

The dreary prison hulks upon the Thames were bywords for misery. Dickens, when he saw one, called it 'a wicked Noah's ark'. (*Prison Hulks at the Thames*, Samuel Prout/Mary Evans Picture Library)

transporting convicts to Australia. During the intervening decade British authorities, who faced a growing prison population, realised they could warehouse part of it in ruined ships that were no longer of any other use. Moreover, convicts could be put to constructive work, and where better than upon or by England's river, so crucial to the national economy? 'For the more severe and effectual punishment of atrocious and daring offenders,' reads the relevant portion of the relevant act,

> where any Male Person . . . shall be lawfully convicted of Grand Larceny, or any other Crime, except Petty larceny, for which he shall be liable by Law to be transported to any Parts beyond the Seas, it shall and may be lawful for the court . . . to order and adjudge that such Person . . . shall be punished by being kept on Board Ships or Vessels . . . and by being employed in hard Labour in the raising Sand, Soil, and Gravel from, and cleansing, the River Thames, or any other River Navigable for Ships of Burthen . . .[1]

Among the many shifting meanings of the Thames we have come upon one of the most terrible. For the men condemned to imprisonment in the hulks stationed along the Thames in the late eighteenth and early nineteenth centuries, life upon the river was like hell itself.

The Act received the royal assent in 1776. Six years later 1017 men and boys had been detained in the dilapidated vessels. The number steadily increased, in part because prisoners of war were kept in hulks during the long conflict with France, but at war's end there were 2429 British convicts in them, and at the beginning of 1828 there were 4446 in ten vessels. What had been originally conceived as a temporary expedient was found to be essential. Many convicts bound for Australia were first imprisoned on hulks and set to hard labour on the river. For them, as will be seen, transportation halfway round the world represented a blessed release.

Even the appearance of the hulks was forbidding and terrible. They were blackened by the weather and mud in which many of them lay when the tide was out. Their portholes were barred with iron. They were moored by great rusted chains. No billowing sail softened their grim outline; rather their masts had been chopped down, reduced to squat and ugly stumps. Old spars resembled dismal blackened sticks. 'A wicked Noah's Ark', Dickens remembered one of the Thames hulks when he came to write *Great Expectations* in 1861. The last hulk had been abandoned five years before his book was published, and before that the early and mid-Victorian penchant for utilitarian reform had led to gradually improved conditions on them (one of the first measures was to lighten the weight of prisoners' chains); nevertheless the hulks would live for decades in the public memory as bywords for ugliness, cruelty, brutality and suffering.

During the heyday of the hulks even the toughest men feared and hated them. Yet breakouts were rare, in part because the penalty for failure could be death by hanging. In the early pages of Dickens's novel the author imagines Magwitch, reduced nearly to the state of a wild beast, desperate not to be recaptured.

A fearful man, all in coarse grey, with a great iron on his leg. A man with no hat, and with broken shoes, and with an old rag tied round his head. A man who had been soaked in water, and smothered in mud, and lamed by stones, and cut by flints, and stung by nettles and torn by briars; who limped and shivered, and glared and growled; and whose teeth chattered in his head . . .

So grateful is this poor creature to the boy who helps him that his gratitude becomes the hinge of the novel, although callow Pip is loath to acknowledge it.

We have the remembrances of a villain who really experienced imprisonment aboard a Thames hulk, James Hardy Vaux.[2] A thief, a swindler, an embezzler, a gambler, a cutpurse, a frequenter of low places, he had seen the insides of Coldbath Fields House of Correction, Newgate jail, and more than one watch-house. He had been transported already to Australia, where his incorrigible tendencies to unlawful activity led him into yet another prison at Hawkesbury and to hard labour at Castle Hill. His first sentence of transportation having been remitted he was sent into slavery of a different sort, that is to say into the Royal Navy, but when his vessel put in to London he deserted and quickly resumed his former mode of living. Vaux was, in short, a man who knew hardship and the criminal world. Yet nothing had prepared him for life aboard the hulk aptly named *Retribution*, lying half in mudflats when the tide ebbed, along the reach of river beside Woolwich, east of London. He was conveyed there from Newgate prison early in 1809, having been convicted of thievery yet again. This time he had outdone himself: the charge was 'feloniously stealing . . . a double-rowed brilliant half-hoop ring. . . a diamond ring for hair . . . a rose diamond and ruby ring, with serpent-chased shank . . . and a pearl and amethyst brooch'.

Vaux boarded the derelict vessel. He was put in chains and led between decks. Experienced and hardened though he may have been, he was appalled. 'Of all the shocking scenes I had ever beheld, this was the most distressing . . . Nothing short of a descent to the infernal regions can be at all worthy of a comparison with it.' The *Retribution* was practically bursting, with more than six hundred prisoners. At night they were locked down to sleep below decks in rows of hammocks, one prisoner every twenty inches. Ventilation was 'defective', to use the unsentimental contemporary word. Vaux does not describe this aspect of life, but consider the *Brunswick*, a hulk resting lower down the river at the junction with the Medway, where 460 prisoners were crowded every night into the orlop deck, 125 feet in length, 40 feet at its widest point, and 4 feet 10 inches high. Fourteen barred portholes, each 17 inches square, admitted such air as might find its way inside, but the atmosphere grew so rank by morning that candles would not burn, and guards who removed the hatches gagged, and were in danger of passing out if they tried to enter.[3] Other prisoners slept in decks below the waterline, where the air was cooler, but even more fetid. And apparently in other prison hulks the hammocks were slung in three tiers, one above the other, hard to imagine, let alone endure.

From such overcrowding in close quarters there could be but one result. If one prisoner became ill, nearly all did. Of 632 prisoners admitted to another of the Woolwich hulks, the *Justitia*, between August 1776 and March 1778, 176 sickened and died, a death rate of nearly one in three.[4] In the Woolwich hulks there were outbreaks of dysentery in 1816, small-pox in 1818, typhus in 1821, cholera in 1832. Catarrh, scurvy, scrofula, diarrhoea and tuberculosis, if less immediately deadly, were nearly universal. Vermin were 'ineradicable'. Prisoners would wash their shirts and hang them out to dry on the old spars. They looked, according to one observer, as if they had all been sprinkled with black pepper.

Given the execrable quality of food served aboard ships in the Royal Navy, Vaux's description of the fare aboard the hulks does not surprise:

> The breakfast is invariably boiled barley, of the coarsest kind imagi-nable; and of this the pigs of the hulk come in for a third part, because it is so nauseous that nothing but downright hunger will enable a man to eat it. For supper they have, on banyan days, burgoo, of as good a quality as the barley, and which is similarly disposed of; and on meat days, the water in which the beef was boiled is thickened with barley and forms a mess called 'smiggins', of a more detestable nature than either of the two former.

The beef given prisoners on meat days was usually ox cheek. According to Vaux it came from 'old bulls or cows which have died of age or famine; the least trace of fat is considered a phenomenon'. Vaux once saw the prisoners throw the whole day's supply overboard ('for this offence they were severely flogged'). Bread was 'all crumbs and broken . . . mouldy and green on both sides'. Liquid refreshment consisted of small beer four days a week, and river water. But, as will become apparent below, drinking water drawn from the river anywhere below Hampton Court was increasingly problematic.[5]

In a hard age, the hard labour expected of men sentenced to the hulks was doubly onerous. The earliest hulk convicts helped to build the docks, quays and yards of the Royal Arsenal at Woolwich. Some were sent down the river in lighters to dig mud and transport it back; others dug it again, from the lighters, and threw it into barrows for further distribution. There were no steam engines or piledrivers, so 'a party is continually busied in turning round a machine driving piles to secure the embankment from the rapidity of the tides'. Discipline was brutally enforced. Vaux describes the guards: 'wretches devoid of all feeling; ignorant in the extreme; brutal by nature, and rendered tyrannical and cruel by consciousness of the power they possess . . . They invariably carry a large and ponderous stick, with which, without the smallest provocation, they will fell an unfortunate convict to the ground, and frequently repeat their blows long after the poor sufferer is insensible.' An observer reporting to the *Scots Magazine* in July 1777 noted the terrified aspect of the prisoners: 'they hardly dare speak to each other . . . not an oath is to be heard; and each criminal performs the task assigned to him with industry, and without murmuring.' At the end of the day they returned to the hulk in chains, 'fetters on each leg, with a chain between that ties various, some round their middle, others upright to the throat'.[6]

When a prisoner died, not an uncommon occurrence, 'the breath of life has scarcely escaped his lips, when the bed on which he has lain is ransacked by his fellow prisoners, to find and possess themselves of any trifling articles he may have concealed.' But this was to put it mildly. Prisoners 'would almost fight to see if he [the deceased] had anything about the bed, so that they might take it, flannels or money', reported one inmate. Another claimed to have seen corpses flung on to the floor, in order to more thoroughly search them for hidden booty.[7] Then, if anatomists did not wish to dissect it, the corpse would be placed into 'a handcart which is used to take dung out' and carried to the marshes to be buried. Not surprisingly, the religious service was perfunctory. During the cholera epidemic of 1832, the chaplain at Woolwich, the Rev. Samuel Watson, would wait until half a dozen convicts had died. He did not dare accompany the bodies to the graveside himself. Instead he would read the service from the deck of the hulk, an entire mile away, and drop a white handkerchief as a signal when it was time to lower the coffins into the earth and cover them up.[8] Here on 'a slip of unenclosed land without any defined limits', and in a grave with no permanent marker, the deceased convict would find his final resting place. So the spongy wasteland on the south bank of the Thames opposite Woolwich became a cemetery for some of England's most wretched souls.

Men of every rank and age were imprisoned in the terrible hulks, including boys who were inevitably brutalised and made playthings of by their elders. All were forced to wear prison garb, 'coarse slop clothing'. The struggle for existence dominated, and the weak went to the wall. 'All former friendships or connexions are dissolved,' Vaux observed, 'and a man here will rob his best benefactor, or even messmate, of an article worth one halfpenny.' In his year aboard the *Retribution* he witnessed murder and suicide and innumerable rapes. He so 'ardently longed for the moment which was to release [him] from so miserable an existence' that he greeted his second transportation to Australia with joy.

Meanwhile from London eastwards the river itself was becoming ever more filthy. A flowing stream, especially a broad river, will hide a multitude of sins, will carry them away. What more natural for people who lived along the Thames, then, than to dump their waste into it? Probably the first inhabitants did so. Certainly their descendants did, and continued the practice until comparatively recently.

Upstream, where the population was not too dense, the river showed few ill effects, until the mid-nineteenth century. Downstream the situation was different. As early as 1357 we find Edward III complaining of the 'dung and other filth [that] had accumulated in divers places upon the banks of the river and . . . [of] fumes and other abominable stenches arising therefrom'. The butchers of London who had been throwing the entrails of slaughtered animals into the Thames were forbidden to do so in 1361, because it 'caused sickness among those dwelling in the City'. Eleven years later the river still remained so crowded with noxious matter 'which had been and was daily cast into the channel' that sometimes vessels could not pass.[9] In 1535 Henry VIII attempted a blanket prohibition. No refuse of any sort could be cast into the Thames at all, but the edict did little good. In 1632 John Taylor, 'the Water Poet', wrote of

> Dead Hogges, Dogges, Cats and well flayed Carryon Horses
> Their noysome Corpses soyled the Waters Courses;
> Both Swines and Stable dunge, Beast-guts and Garbage,
> Street-dust, with Gardners weeds and Rotten Herbage.
> And from those Waters filthy putrifaction,
> Our meat and drink were made, which bred Infection.

Taylor's job was to clean the river.

> My selfe and partner, with costs, paines, and travell,
> Saw all made clean from Caryon, Mud and Gravell.
> And now and then was punisht a Delinquent,
> By which good meanes away the filth and stink went.

This was an overly optimistic, not to say a self-promoting, conclusion.

By the mid-Victorian era even some of the reaches of the Thames far to the west of London had grown filthy and putrid. As one parliamentary report put it, 'Fouling of the water by sewage from cities, towns, villages and single houses generally prevails.' At Kingston 'the daily discharge of the sewage of several thousands of persons renders the banks and streams in the vicinity disgusting to the sight and frequently offensive to the smell'. At Windsor the castle sewers overflowed after heavy rains 'and the lawns along the river were strewn with sewage'.[10]

Of course London was much worse. The cutpurse Vaux, banished for a second time to Australia, was probably long dead, and the hulks on which convicts of his generation had suffered were gone; Britain no longer dumped its human refuse into ghost ships on the Thames. But Londoners continued to dump everything else into it. Late in the eighteenth century, even before Vaux's stint in the hulks, there were already 150 London slaughterhouses, a fish market, numerous tanneries, all emptying waste into the river, where it decomposed into such poisonous basic compounds as carbon dioxide and ammonia. The process of decomposition is itself dangerous to life because it removes oxygen from water. Along the river bed and banks east of Tower Bridge, a deposit of organic mud began to take shape, in which hydrogen sulphide was present. This latter is the compound that produces a smell like rotten eggs. It also turns the water black. Then there were, during this early phase of the industrial era, a small number of gasworks scattered along the eastern reaches of the London river whose waste products, discharged into the water, 'were a source of pollutant . . . of a quite exceptional toxicity'.[11] The erection of cement works and other kinds of factories during the pre- and early Victorian eras led to further poisoning of the stream.

And finally, even before the turn of the nineteenth century, there were London's two hundred thousand domestic cesspools. Irregularly emptied by night-soil men, who conveyed their contents to farmers in the nearby countryside, cesspools were always a potential source of disease. If they became too full, their muck might back up into basements, or it might overflow into streets and yards to poison wells, and if left to lie, become a danger to all in the proximity. Ironically, with the introduction during 1810–30 of improved flushing water closets, which used greater quantities of water, the cesspools overflowed more frequently. Eventually rain might wash their muck down the London streets and alleys, and into the city's antiquated sewers, which, if they themselves did not overflow, carried it eventually to the river — already dangerously polluted by factories, slaughterhouses, and such.

We are accustomed, when we imagine mid-Victorian England, to think of the great exhibition at the Crystal Palace, or of the still-young queen and her beloved German husband Albert, or of Tom Brown's schooldays at Rugby, or perhaps of scenes from Dickens's sunny early novels like *The Pickwick Papers*. A less pleasing image is provided by the historians of medicine and sanitary reform: of 250 tons of faecal matter entering the London Thames daily. This was too much for the river simply to absorb or carry away. It flowed downriver with the ebb tide, and back up again as the tide came in. Moreover, a barrier to the returning filth had been inadvertently removed with the demolition of old London Bridge in the early 1830s. The thirteen narrow arches, which had helped make possible the frost fairs, when blocks of ice had choked them so that the river grew still and froze upstream, also had acted as an obstruction to the filth carried westward in warmer weather. Probably until 1832 water above London Bridge was relatively clean and therefore only those who lived east of the Bridge, including the wretched prisoners aboard the Woolwich hulks, drank from its most polluted reaches and suffered the consequences. After 1832, however, nearly all Londoners drank polluted Thames water, and since unregulated private companies supplied it, and since their methods of filtration were still quite rudimentary, the results were predictable. Cholera outbreaks occurred in 1831–2, 1848–9, 1853–4 and 1866, killing more than thirty-six thousand in all. Typhoid killed nearly 1500 per year from 1850–70.[12] Diarrhoea remained a scourge of London infants until the twentieth century.

But, although the reactionary period of the post-Napoleonic wars had ended, an age of reform had not yet truly begun. As always there were countervailing tendencies, witness the abolition of the hulks, but if anything the mid-Victorian period was an age of individualism and laissez-faire economics. The middle classes, enfranchised in 1832 by the first Great Reform Bill, had seen off the working-class Chartist threat once and for all in 1848, and were congratulating themselves on England's apparent immunity from the otherwise near Europe-wide revolutionary movement; they had cemented their own position by abolishing the Corn Laws which had protected British agriculture, enshrining free trade as intrinsic to the natural economic order; they held workers' combinations to be in restraint of trade, likewise any legislation affecting wages and hours (although some bills, protecting women and children, were passed). Their world-view was encapsulated in the title of Samuel Smiles's bestseller *Self Help* (1859). So while they might sympathise with the health reformer Edwin Chadwick when he argued that London's workers would be more productive if they lived in sanitary conditions and drank clean water, as soon as he suggested that government should take responsibility for such measures they turned away. *The Times* accurately reflected their outlook: 'We prefer to take our chance of cholera and the rest than be bullied into health.'[13]

Thus, despite a few ineffective attempts at reform, in 1855 the London Thames remained a repellent mixture of water, toxic chemicals and decomposing matter, as disgusting to the senses as it was dangerous to health. It looked 'an opaque brown fluid' to the scientist Michael Faraday, who on 7 July took a Thames steamer from London Bridge to Hungerford Bridge. Shocked by the condition of the river, he performed an experiment, dropping pieces of moistened white card into the water at intervals. 'Before they had sunk an inch below the surface they were indistinguishable, though the sun shone brightly at the time . . .'[14]

Faraday noted too that the river stank: 'It was the same [smell] as that which now comes up from the gulley holes in the streets.' Victoria and

Albert, who intended a jaunt down the Thames upon a pleasure steamer, made the same discovery. They retreated rapidly from 'the malodorous waters'. Politicians likewise were affected. It was extremely unpleasant to meet in the Houses of Parliament during summer months, when horrible fumes wafted upwards from the turbid stream below their windows. Captain Mangles, Member for Newport, Isle of Wight, thought 'God had given . . . a most magnificent river and they had turned it into the vilest of sewers.' He delivered this judgement in a House of Commons debating chamber whose windows had been draped with sheets soaked in chloride of lime to combat the river's stench. Benjamin Disraeli, who could stomach even the speeches of William Gladstone in that chamber, could not stomach the reeking Thames during the hot dry summer of 1858, the year of the 'Great Stink'. He fled from Parliament, nose buried in a scented handkerchief. He was not alone, for not only did Members find the smell unendurable, but also, not yet understanding the germ theory of disease, they believed the river's 'miasma' threatened their health.

As long ago as 1827 the visionary artist John Martin, friend and some-time rival of J.M.W. Turner, had proposed dispensing with Thames water for drinking purposes altogether in his *Plan for Supplying the Cities of London and Westminster with Pure Water from the River Colne*. This was but the first of a series of proposals devised by the artist-cum-engineer, some of which gained the backing of influential men, including Faraday and Turner himself, but none of which ever was realised. Once Martin decided to dispense with the Colne river and to take London's drinking water from more western reaches of the Thames, however, his plans anticipated in many respects those of Joseph Bazalgette, the man credited with solving the problem in the end. Both Martin and later Bazalgette planned trunk-line sewers accepting the contents of a system of branch-line sewers, the trunk sewers running parallel to the river on either side to be surmounted by public walkways stretching from Hammersmith to Greenwich. At their easternmost points these enormous pipes would spill their noxious contents into the river, but this would be well below the most populated portions of the metropolis. Upstream the water would be safe for drinking.

It was Disraeli who insisted on giving Bazalgette his chance. As Chancellor of the Exchequer in one of Lord Derby's short-lived Conservative administrations (1858–9) he ensured that the Metropolitan Board of Works, created three years previously to provide London with the rudiments of municipal government, should at least have powers and money sufficient to cleanse the portion of the Thames that flowed beneath his windows at the House of Commons. This meant overcoming not merely the objections of private companies that supplied the metropolis with drinking water, but also of those who held that Parliament should not pay for solving local problems at all. Perhaps most significantly it meant overcoming the general spirit of an age that championed small government for its own sake. Nevertheless, more than thirty years after Martin had published his first proposal and four years after he had died, the savvier Bazalgette, now chief engineer of the Metropolitan Board of Works, designed and caused to be built the trunk sewers, the branch sewers (82 miles of them in all), the embankments. These latter actually narrowed the river, speeding the flow of water, and enhancing the 'scouring' effect that helped to keep it clean. Meanwhile downstream, twice every twenty-four hours, at high tide, on either side of the river at Barking and Crossness, two massive apertures permitted the outflow of 75 million gallons of sewage (150 million gallons per day) into the Thames. If there were people who lived nearby and who objected, they were not numerous or powerful enough to do anything about it.

On the clear, moonlit evening of Tuesday 3 September 1878, a paddle steamer called the *Princess Alice* chugged upriver towards London, on the return leg of a day-trip down to the Nore. She had broken the return journey to let off and take on additional passengers at Gravesend, and she was crowded, overcrowded some were to say later, with passengers from every rank of society, but primarily from the lower-middle and working classes. There were more women than men aboard, and many children.

They had flocked to the *Princess Alice* that morning because the summer was nearly over, and it was a fine day after weeks of troubled weather. Down to Sheerness the steamer had carried them, under glorious blue skies, to poke about the town and to wander the shingle off which the mutinous seamen of 1797 had moored. Now, at a quarter to eight in the evening, the water was calm as the *Princess Alice* approached Tripcock Point near Woolwich in the stretch of river called Gallions Reach, close to where the dreaded prison hulks had lain thirty years before. The air was warm. The daylight was waning, but the moon shone brightly and anyway it was not yet dark. A brass band on one of the decks played 'Nancy Lee'. Men and women were dancing.

The *Princess Alice* was nearly 220 feet long, but she was only 20 feet wide, and she had a depth of merely 8 feet 4 inches. In 1873 she had borne the shah of Persia and his retinue to Greenwich in great comfort, but her owners were interested in a more extensive and less socially exclusive clientele. They extended her decks and built 'a towering' saloon above them. The Board of Trade licensed her to carry 336 passengers in winter and 486 in summer; and if 'for river service in smooth water only or on lakes', 899 passengers. No precise number of travellers for 3 September 1878 ever was established, but the steamer, with its shallow draft, its narrow width, its enlarged decks supporting the great saloon, was completely full on that day. She balanced precariously over the water, top-heavy, in danger, some thought, of tipping on to her side. 'Imagine [the circus performer] Blondin on a rope with a sack of coals on his head! Yet the case is parallel,' wrote a correspondent to *The Times* a few days later, after tragedy had struck.[15]

Tripcock Point juts out into the river from the southern bank of the Thames, which makes a great bend here, nearly opposite Woolwich.

The little peninsula effectively screens vessels approaching from opposite directions, if they are hugging the shoreline, as in fact the *Princess
Alice* was, headed upriver to deposit her passengers; and as was the
Bywell Castle, a large propeller-driven steamer headed downstream
towards the estuary. She intended to pick up coals in Newcastle and to
bring them to Egypt. The *Bywell Castle* stretched more than 254 feet in
length, more than 32 feet in breadth, nearly 20 feet in depth. And she
weighed five times more than the *Princess Alice*. But Captain Thomas
Harrison did not see the pleasure steamer until it was too late. Then he
stopped and reversed engines, to no effect at this penultimate juncture,
and ported his helm as he was supposed to under such conditions.
Captain William Grinstead of the *Princess Alice*, however, starboarded
his helm so that both vessels had turned in the same direction.
Grinstead thus ensured a collision, and his own death. When the collier struck the smaller, lighter, overcrowded and overbalanced pleasure
steamer nearly at the starboard paddle, she split her like an eggshell,
and sank her in less than five minutes. The *Bywell Castle* herself was
barely scratched.

There were passengers and crew aboard the pleasure steamer who
saw what was coming. 'Some of the people around us were straining
their eyes and looking ahead in the same direction as the captain,' Henry
Reed, a stationer at 57 Oxford Street, remembered. 'My wife and I
turned to look as the others did; we were then standing at the extreme
point of the deck, looking up the Thames. I saw a large vessel, a screw-
steamer, several lengths ahead, and coming directly towards us.'[16]
Captain Grinstead cried a desperate warning to the oncoming vessel,
'Hoy, hoy. Where are you coming to?' As if that could prevent the immi-
nent catastrophe. Meanwhile, as the *Bywell Castle* loomed dark and
enormous above the *Princess Alice*, 'People were shouting "Stop! Stop!"'[17]
The collier kept on coming. Herbert Augustus Wiele, a young man
whose brother, Claude, was also a passenger and who also survived,
kept his head. 'I ran down the companion ladder and got to the extreme

after part of the boat, and I took off my boots ready to dive,' he reported.[18]

After the collision a few passengers scrambled up the tilting deck to catch hold of ropes thrown down by the crew of the *Bywell Castle*. These fortunate people were able to climb right up to the collier without even getting wet. Much worse off were those trapped inside the *Princess Alice*'s saloon. They struggled unavailingly to open the doors, which onrushing water made too heavy. Days later divers discovered their bodies in a heap by the unopened portals: a soldier, a woman dressed in black silk with a little boy clinging to her neck, 'whose tin trumpet was tangled in her hair', many others.[19]

The vast majority, however, who had been dancing, singing, partying or simply relaxing on deck, milled about panic-stricken for the few minutes after the crash and before the vessel sank. 'Women with babies in their arms, and fathers rushing frantically about with little children.'[20] This was when Herbert Augustus Wiele did actually dive from the doomed steamer. Another man jumped overboard, first having instructed his wife to throw their children in after him. Then the boat went down. He never saw wife and children again.[21] The steamer sank too quickly for the crew to let down even a single lifeboat. When Augustus Wiele dived from the afterdeck he went underwater. 'When I came up from diving the *Princess Alice* was not to be seen.' The catastrophe was so complete in part because it happened so quickly. 'I can compare the *Princess Alice* to nothing else than a cloud,' said Mr Abraham Dennis, master of the *Boetta*, whose crew afterwards pulled in a few who might otherwise have drowned. 'One moment she was there, and the next moment clean gone.'[22]

So: perhaps nine hundred men, women, children, floundering in the Thames, which was twenty-five feet deep at that spot, and with a swift ebb tide pulling downstream. 'I can compare the people to nothing else than a flock of sheep in the water. The river seemed full of

Bywell Castle slamming into the *Princess Alice* on 3 September 1878. More than seven hundred died as a result. (Getty Images)

The fatal scrum in the filthy waters of the Thames as the *Princess Alice* begins to sink. 'I can compare the *Princess Alice* to a cloud,' said one observer. 'One moment she was there and the next moment clean gone.' (Getty Images)

drowning people,' Abraham Dennis continued. Most of them could not swim. They wore no life jackets. The long dresses of the women filled with water, pulling them under. Desperately the crew of the *Bywell Castle* threw into the river wooden staves, barrels, benches, anything that would float, for the floundering hundreds in the water to catch hold of. They threw down more ropes too. Henry Reed, the stationer of Oxford Street, grabbed one and hung on to it for half an hour, his wife clinging to his back, until finally crewmen pulled them to safety. Four or five others clung to the same rope, including 'a woman screaming all the while. I believe she had lost a child.'

But now a sort of desperate scrimmage in the river had begun. 'I laid hold of a piece of wood, which I pushed before me and it kept me up,' reported Mr H. Drew of Old Change. 'I was afraid every moment that some of the poor people would snatch it from me, for I was surrounded by hundreds – men, women and children, struggling for life and shriek- ing in their agony.' 'Ten pounds,' cried a man before he went under for the last time, 'twenty pounds, a hundred pounds for a helping hand.'[23] Local watermen and the masters of coasters who happened to be in the vicinity did their best. 'I immediately launched a boat and rowed to the scene,' explained J.S. Burnitt, captain of the *Elizabeth* of Goole, 'but was nearly swamped by the crowds who, shrieking and drowning, made a last struggle for life, and it was necessary to quench their hopes by knocking them off the sides with the oars. Eleven were dragged in, and a speedy retreat made.'[24]

Something additional was going on in the water, however, which made the disaster even more hellish, and even more complete. Do not forget Bazalgette's great sewerage system, with its outfalls at Barking on the north bank and Crossness (or Belvedere as it was also called) on the south. An hour earlier, while the *Princess Alice* was steaming upstream, the outfalls had loosed their seventy-five million gallons. Then, as 'A Pharmaceutical Chemist' wrote to *The Times*, there was 'projected into the river two continuous columns of decomposed fermenting sewage, hissing like soda water with baneful gases so black that the water [was] stained for miles, and discharging a corrupt charnel house odour . . .'[25] That same afternoon there had been a fire at a Thames Street wharf, and 'enormous quantities of petroleum, turpentine, oil &c. . . . poured into the river from the wharf, and also into the sewers, which have an outlet at . . . Barking', which hardly improved matters.[26] And of course the Thames-side factories had been continuously discharging their poisonous chemical wastes into the river as usual.

'A Pharmaceutical Chemist' pointed out in *The Times* that extremely diluted sewage, 'say one drop in 10,000', induced typhus or other fevers when taken in milk or water. He predicted that concentrated sewage, 'especially when in a state of active decomposition', would be found to be 'a true poison relatively as fatal as prussic acid'. Richard Dover, whose letter to *The Times* appeared on 19 September, added: 'the presence of 1/1,500 of sulphuretted hydrogen [hydrogen sulphide] in the air is instantly fatal to a bird; . . . 1/800th will kill a dog; . . . 1/150th of its volume has killed a horse'. He thought it therefore a cause for 'gratulation' that the few passengers who survived 'were able to save themselves by swimming through the volume of sulphuretted hydrogen that for an hour or more had been pouring out of the elongated cesspools of the Metropolitan Board of Works'. Dr James Loutit, formerly demonstrator of chemistry at Edinburgh, later told the Board of Trade inquiry into the disaster that it would take a man only five minutes to absorb sufficient sulphuretted hydrogen into his system from the foul water to choke to death.[27]

We do not know that this is actually what happened to any of the passengers struggling in the dirty, murky river. But 'both for taste and smell it was something he could hardly describe', one of them told the coroner's inquest afterwards.[28] 'The water was very dreadful and nasty, it was in a very foul state indeed,' reported another.[29] 'A gentleman of well-known name, who was saved from the wreck but lost his wife, owes his preservation to the rejection by his system as

soon as he reached dry land, of all that he had swallowed,' one newspaper put it delicately. Other survivors who did not manage to vomit
the filth they had involuntarily taken in did indeed sicken. One
became paralysed.[30] Others died, for example Mr W.H. Vachel, of
Surbiton, 'who requested to be taken to the house of his friend, Dr.
Lacey, [of] Burrage Road, where he lingered a few days'.[31] No precise
number of survivors who died afterwards on dry land was ever established, since no coroner's inquest was held for them. The Reverend A.
Styleman Herring, in a letter to *The Times* of 16 September, refers to
'sixteen who have since expired and many more . . . in a precarious
state'. Such deaths after shipwrecks in unpolluted waters were rare,
the *Saturday Review* pointed out. Even the august *Times* was moved to
remark that 'the rate of mortality among the saved, regarded as the
mere effect of an immersion in water on a fine summer evening, is
undoubtedly exceedingly large'.[32]

Additional grisly evidence, if such were needed, that the Thames
waters, below Barking and Crossness had become the opposite of a
'healing river' was soon forthcoming. It was noticed that the dresses of
women pulled from the river turned in colour from blue to violet.
More disturbingly, the bodies themselves, even those dragged from
the stream shortly after the accident, had become discoloured and
bloated. The discoloration was natural if distressing, not least if passengers had bruised or injured themselves while struggling to keep
afloat. Some bloating would also have been natural, since bacteria
already present in the bodies of the dead now were engaged in the
process that results in the production of gases. But watermen noticed
that bloated bodies were rising from the depths of the river faster than
usual. 'They are already floating at and near the surface, although the
traditional nine days which watermen believe to be the period after
which a body rises have not elapsed,' *The Times* noted only six days after
the disaster. Moreover the bodies were more bloated than usual. In fact
they swelled to such an extent that normal-size coffins were too small

for them, and special new ones had to be built. Probably this was because the dead bodies contained many more bacteria than usual. And probably this was because the drowning passengers had swallowed the putrid river water.

It was noticed, too, that the recovered bodies were coated in slime. When washed off, it simply reappeared. A new set of bacteria, external this time, were at work upon the corpses, which now began to decompose at a faster rate than normal, indeed so fast that on 9 September, as *The Times* reported, some of them could only be moved in shells or coffins. Presumably lifting them separated the skin from the bones. 'It is remarkable,' the Reverend Herring pointed out in a second letter, 'that the corpses picked up below the fatal spot were the soonest decomposed.'[33] The authorities tried carbolic acid and white crystals of a disinfecting powder. 'But it was impossible to arrest the process of decay.'[34] So revolting was the stench of the corpses and so disgusting was their appearance that the dockers who had been engaged to move them for 7s 6d a day struck for 10s, and the police who stood guard over them were in constant danger of fainting. The authorities ordered extra bottles of smelling salts. Friends and relatives seeking to identify their loved ones, when not overcome by the stench, were frequently stymied by the discoloration, the bloating, and worst of all, the decomposition. They had to rely upon spotting familiar jewellery, or keepsakes or clothing. But the clothing, which had first discoloured, now began to rot, and had to be boiled and saturated with disinfectants. In the end 120 bodies were interred unclaimed and unrecognised.

Of the 900-odd passengers aboard the *Princess Alice* on the night of 3 September 1878, 130 made it to shore, of whom an undetermined number later died from the poisoned waters. The exact number who drowned outright could never be calculated. More than 650 bodies were recovered. Perhaps 130 more were swept out to sea or buried deep in Thames mud. 'The wreck of the *Princess Alice* is the most terrible disaster of the kind which it has ever been our duty to report. There is

nothing like it, nothing approaching it . . .' began *The Times* leader of
5 September. Of thirty-one women belonging to a Bible class, four
survived. Of six college girlfriends on a river jaunt on a sunny day, not
one returned to shore. An entire family of sixteen perished all together.
For days after the disaster newspapers carried paragraphs like the
following: 'A little boy who says his name is Edward Newman, and that
his mother sells sweets, remains unclaimed at the infirmary. Another
boy, about five years old, has been found at a house in Woolwich and
taken to the infirmary. He says that his name is Freddy Lambard.'[35] *The
Times* now began to carry every day in rows of columns a list of the
names of the dead. To the historian it is a grim presaging of the lists of
casualties that the newspaper would print during the First World War.

It was too late for the passengers of the *Princess Alice*, but reform was
finally inevitable. Indeed, with regard to reform, the temper of the times
had begun to change: already a former mayor of Birmingham, a charismatic radical called Joseph Chamberlain, had transfixed England,
bringing street lighting and local transportation and the provision of
water, and even some working-class housing, under municipal control.
He called his experiment in Birmingham 'gas and water socialism', and
it was merely a harbinger. Measured against this yardstick the revisions
carried out upon the Thames immediately after the disaster of 1878
seem unremarkable: rules of the river to be rigidly enforced; ships to display the properly coloured lights in the proper places; those moving
upstream to stay on one side, those moving down to stay on the other;
newly built ships to have bulkheads, watertight compartments, to contain the damage should a ship's hull be breached.

   But more far-reaching measures were under consideration as well. It
had become obvious to all except those made blind by ideology or by
selfishness that the Metropolitan Board of Works must change its
method for disposing of London's sewage. It was by no means clear that
the Board possessed either the will or the means to undertake such

major revision, but in fact, just before being replaced by the better structured and more representative London County Council (another
manifestation of England's reviving appetite for reform), it did implement new methods for cleansing the Thames. Almost as its swansong,
in 1887, it accepted Bazalgette's latest suggestion: to extract solid waste
materials from the great cesspools that fed the outfalls, and to cart
them out to sea in sludge boats. The remaining liquid, having become
infinitely less objectionable than before, could be discharged more or
less safely into the river.

Bazalgette's solution to Thames pollution was hardly a panacea.[36]
But the river was much changed from the days when convicts had been
stranded on it aboard hulks. By the tail end of the Victorian era, Thames
water east of London was cleaner than it had been for a hundred years

The London County Council sludge vessel *Henry Ward* (1923), under
way on the river Thames. (National Maritime Museum, London)

at least, and England's river reflected a sea change taking place in British opinion. As *The Times* might have sniffed disapprovingly, Englishmen no longer preferred to take their chances; they were willing to be 'bullied into health' by government fiat after all.

8

The Earthly Paradise

*T*hen, at the turn of the nineteenth century, there was a Thames running through London that was not at all a kind of hell for convicts rotting aboard hulks. Wordsworth stood on Westminster Bridge early on the morning of 3 September 1802 and gazed upon a drowsy city bisected by a gliding river, and thought the prospect beautiful: 'Earth has not any thing to show more fair,' he began his famous poem,

> Dull would he be of soul who could pass by
> A sight so touching in its majesty . . .

Seventy years later Gustave Doré, who, in his dark and brooding etchings, pictured tramps sleeping under Thames bridges, nevertheless rhapsodised, with Blanchard Jerrold, about the picturesque urban river.[1] Henry James, who was very much aware of 'the sprawling barges, the dead-faced warehouses, the frowsy people, the atmospheric impurities', yet considered the Thames at London to be magnificent. During the summer of 1877 he looked with wonder at the ceaseless flow of commerce upon it, the massive docks, 'the dark hugely piled bridges'.

Taken all in all it reminded him of 'the wealth and power of the British Empire at large'.[2] A second Thames existed in the minds of many, then, and if it was not for all of them clean and good, as it had been for Wordsworth, it was at any rate superb.

Usually, however, when people spoke of this finer Thames, they meant the river west of Teddington Lock, which was the farthest point that the sewage-laden incoming tide could reach. Not that the Thames was free from filth even there, especially when it ran past the biggest towns, Windsor, Reading, and Oxford. Still, throughout the nineteenth century and into the twentieth, it flowed from Oxford to London mainly through a rural countryside of fields and woods, it was a stream from which trout and perch, bleak and chub still could be drawn. Beyond the big towns, sheep and cattle grazed peacefully on its grassy banks, ducks, geese and the regal swan glided serenely across its smooth surface.

And west of Oxford the river remained largely unsullied. It begins gradually to narrow, as we follow it further westward, past tiny villages of stone cottages, and beneath the curving arches of ancient stone bridges, through a landscape that, in the mid- and late-Victorian eras, seemed timeless. The railway had not penetrated here, when William Morris was moved to wonder during the summer of 1867:

> What better place than this then could we find
> By this sweet stream that knows not of the sea
> That guesses not the city's misery,
> This little stream whose hamlets scarce have names,
> This far-off lonely mother of the Thames?

Morris loved this river and surrounding countryside. He thought it an earthly paradise.

William Morris was, of course, Victorian Britain's Renaissance man: a poet and writer of the first rank (he was offered the Poet Laureateship after Tennyson died but turned it down), a leading figure in the arts and crafts movement, a weaver of some of the nineteenth century's finest tapestries, a carver of exquisite woodcuts and stained glass, a designer of gorgeous books, and of wallpaper that is still popular. He was also a social and political activist, who came to occupy perhaps the first place within the pantheon of his country's socialist pioneers; he was a pioneer, too, of historic preservation and environmentalism. He was, we now can see, England's first 'Green'.[3]

William Morris loved the entire Thames, not just its westernmost stretches. Or, rather he loved the London reaches as he imagined them once to have been, during the time of Chaucer.

> Forget six counties overhung with smoke
> Forget the snorting steam and piston stroke,
> Forget the spreading of the hideous town;
> Think rather of the pack-horse on the down,
> And dream of London, small and white and clean,
> The clear Thames bordered by its gardens green . . .

Moreover, he loved these reaches for what they might yet become — even at Barking and Crossness, where in his time, as we know, there were cement factories and massive uncovered cesspools for all the sewage of the metropolis, and where until but recently the awful prison hulks had lain. He saw instead, in his mind's eye, a 'wide green sea of . . . Essex marshland, with the great domed line of the sky, and the sun shining down in one flood of peaceful light over the long distance . . . and the river and the craft passing up and down . . .'[4] For him the Thames was England's national waterway, an avenue of history, reaching deep into his country's past, flowing steadily towards a brighter, better future.

Morris possessed a 'deep love for the earth and the life on it', as he once put it. This passion, it was nothing less, informed his art and politics and mode of living, including his relationship with the Thames. He had a house on its north bank at Hammersmith in west London and, after 1871, another at the river's far rural end, near the border between Oxfordshire and Gloucestershire, in a little village called Kelmscott, and he came to know the Thames between these two locations as few people ever did or could or will.[5]

His love of the river was long-standing. When he went up to Oxford as a student in 1853 he and the young Edward Burne-Jones (who would become his business partner and lifelong friend) tramped the banks of the stream together. More than a decade later, during the summer of 1867, they returned to Oxford and the river for a holiday, accompanied by their families. The two friends, wives and children in tow, renewed their explorations, on foot, and by water: one shining day down to Dorchester and Wittenham Clumps, formerly a Roman encampment, cut ('trenched' as Morris puts it) into two distinct humps by early English farmers. While his companions basked under the sun-filled blue sky in the heat of the summer day, Morris gloried in the ancient associations the landscape evoked, and in the evidences of a natural union between countryside and the hand of man:

> In this sweet field high raised above the Thames
> Beneath the trenched hill of Sinodun
> Amidst sweet dreams of disembodied names
> Abide the setting of the August sun,
> Here where this long ridge tells of days now done;
> This moveless wave wherewith the meadow heaves
> Beneath its clover and its barley-sheaves.
>
> Across the gap made by our English hinds
> Amidst the Roman's handiwork, behold
> Far off the long-roofed church; the shepherd binds
> The withy round the hurdles of his fold,

Down in the foss the riverbed of old,
That through long lapse of time has grown to be
The little grassy valley that you see.

Rest here awhile, not yet the eve is still,
The bees are wandering yet, and you may hear,
The barley mowers on the trenched hill,
The sheep-bells, and the restless changing weir,
All little sounds made musical and clear
Beneath the sky that burning August gives,
While yet the thought of glorious Summer lives.

Another glorious summer, 1880, and Morris had organised a longer expedition on the Thames: all the way from London to Kelmscott in a hired houseboat called the *Ark*, an 'odd' craft, he judged, 'but delightfully like a largish steamer with a small omnibus on board'.[6] One sunny day followed the next on this Thames journey, and Morris, who was again accompanied by friends and family, found delight in each. His spirits soared as soon as the party left behind the 'Cockneyfied' stretches of London's western suburbs. Radical though Morris might be, he was prepared to appreciate aristocratic Eton and even royal Windsor. In Oxford, as one of his companions commented, 'in spite of Mr. Morris's dreadful revolutionary sentiments we slept in the King's Arms'.

High spirits and good humour prevailed. Quips, silly puns and jokes, were the order of the day. At the Magpie Inn in Sunbury, where the travellers arrived for dinner on the first night of their voyage upriver, there was a bad smell. The waiter assured them it was nothing. 'Is it a sewer?' asked one of Morris's friends. 'Yes sir,' said the waiter. 'Quite sure.'

'Here we were,' Morris wrote afterwards to a close friend, 'on the Thames that is the Thames, amidst the down-like country and all Cockneydom left far behind and it *was* jolly.'[7] Happy as he was, Morris loved best, as on that summer day in 1867, the evidence he perceived of organic connection between man and the natural world. He saw that labour, architecture, river and landscape formed a seamless whole. When they did not, he noticed that too. The boat passed Cliveden woods, part of the great Cliveden estate. These were 'much admired by the world in general', Morris admitted, but 'I confess to thinking them rather artificial'. Immediately following, however, came Cookham Lock. No great estate here, no prettified 'lacquey [sic] paradise', but rather 'the real country with cows and sheep and farmhouses, the work-a-day world again'. Morris's spirits rose. 'How beautiful it was.'

At Hurley Lock he spied 'a long barn-like building, two gothic arch-ways and then a Norman church fitting onto it and joined into a quadrangle by other long roofs'. This was Lady Place, originally a monastery. With his friends he scrambled ashore and spent an hour 'in great enjoyment' inspecting the buildings. Further along Morris was pleased to notice the country people 'haymaking on the flat flood-washed spits of ground and islets all about Tadpole; and the hay was gathered on punts and the like'. It was a scene that went to the root of his sensibility.

They travelled 'through a river fuller and fuller of character as we got higher up'. But it was the very last stage of the journey that meant most to him. He had come to love above all else this part of the Thames and surrounding countryside, where his home at Kelmscott was located. They reached it at the end of their sixth day. 'Night fell on us long before we got to Radcot and we fastened a lantern to the prow of our boat,' Morris reported. They succeeded, with some trouble, in manoeuvring the large houseboat through the narrow Radcot Bridge, and then 'Charles was waiting for us with a lantern at our bridge by the corner at 10 p.m., and presently the ancient house had me in its arms again: J. [Jane, his wife] had lighted up all brilliantly, and sweet it all looked you may be sure.'[8]

*

Back in 1867, as the great poet-artist-designer took his ease 'beneath the trenched hill of Sinodun', the politicians in Westminster, at the other end of the river, had just passed the second Great Reform Bill, enfranchising most male urban workers. This, more than any other single Act, facilitated further reform, since politicians must now appeal to a mass electorate; indirectly the second Reform Bill made possible the 'gas and water socialism' of Joseph Chamberlain in Birmingham, and even the improvements that the Metropolitan Board of Works enacted in the aftermath of the wreck of the *Princess Alice*. Morris does not appear to have taken much notice, however; he was not yet political in the conventional sense, but he had always meant his design firm to challenge Victorian philistinism, as he and his partners understood it. The philistinism, Morris eventually concluded, originated in Victorian capitalism. This perception, not quick in coming, and as we shall see not based merely upon cold observation of an economic system, eventually led him into active politics. Nine years after passage of the great Bill, he walked through the door opened by Disraeli in 1867, appealing to the now enfranchised workers to oppose – Disraeli, who was defending Turkish policies in Bulgaria, and rattling the British sabre against Russia.

But it would not be long before Morris grew disillusioned with the Liberals as well: they, after all, were as much implicated in Victorian philistinism as Conservatives were. The breaking point, and not only for Morris, was Gladstone's imperialism in Egypt, the Sudan and Ireland. In 1883 he abandoned the radical Liberals and joined the Democratic Federation. Soon this body would change its name to the Social Democratic Federation (SDF). It formed the main Marxist strand within Britain's re-emerging socialist movement and was, with the Fabian Society and Independent Labour Party, one of pre-war Britain's main socialist bodies. After the First World War its members would provide the nucleus of the British Communist Party.

For the remainder of his days Morris would lead a double life: always engaged in his art; almost always equally engaged in movement politics.

He continued to write; he continued to oversee and design for 'The Firm', as it now was called; for anyone else this would have constituted a more than sufficiently fulfilling life. But also Morris attended meeting after socialist meeting, demonstration after demonstration, march after march. Above all he wrote: articles, pamphlets, books, and poems, all in aid of the cause. Eventually he quit the SDF, in part because Henry Hyndman, its doctrinaire and difficult leader, offended him; with Eleanor Marx and others he helped to form an alternative society, the short-lived Socialist League (which he largely paid for), and when that broke up, he became the leader of a local branch of the League, renamed the Hammersmith Socialist Society. Eventually he was reconciled with Hyndman and rejoined the SDF. He expended so much energy on behalf of the movement that it may have contributed to his early death in 1896. But another of his doctors considered 'the case is this: the disease is simply being William Morris, and having done more work than most ten men'.

Seven years before he died, the London dockers, barely organised, desperately poor, despised by their employers and by craft workers alike as the lowest of the low among casual labourers, struck for a rise: sixpence an hour. Against all odds they won. The dockers' strike of 1889 was the single greatest victory gained by the movement of so-called unskilled workers, the 'New Unionists'. It helped spark throughout the country a tidal wave of organising drives and labour disputes which in turn led to the formation of the socialist Independent Labour Party in 1893 and eventually to the formation of a mass working-class party, the Labour Party, in 1900.

The Thames provided a backdrop to this signal event, as it had done to so many others. Ships lay idle in the world's greatest port while the men who were supposed to load and unload them made their demands. Like the sailors of the Nore parading in Sheerness, although in better order, the dockers marched through the streets of east London insisting on sixpence an hour and other improvements. Morris was not present, but he was on the river too, at his home in Kelmscott village, from which he dispatched his musings on the dispute to *Commonweal*, the Socialist League newspaper. At this stage of his political evolution he thought that strikes diverted workers from the main task, revolution, and so he underestimated the significance of the dockers' action; also he was a long way away from the London docks, in his great grey house under the trees next to the Thames, fifty miles west of Oxford.

But then, for Morris the house at Kelmscott was hardly an observation post even if, as we shall see, it helped to form his world-view. Kelmscott Manor was for William Morris as Syon Ferry House had been for J.M.W. Turner, a Thames-side refuge from the hurly-burly of metropolitan and political life; a place to replenish the soul. It was more: Turner had taken Syon Ferry House for a year or two; Morris, after finding Kelmscott, returned there whenever possible. He could not live without it; he would not, without it, have been able to make his unique contribution to Britain's socialist movement.

He had thought the village in which the house was located a 'most beautiful grey little hamlet', indeed 'heaven on earth', when he first discovered it 'deep down in the country'. But the house itself, 'beautiful and strangely naïf', nestling between river and church, was more dear to him than even the village, if that were possible. He had rented it in May 1871 with his friend, the Pre-Raphaelite Dante Gabriel Rossetti; eventually he bought it outright.[9] He loved the way its own grey walls fit within the grey village, how they seemed almost to grow from the soil, like the tall elm trees that appeared to march in a line from house to stream, and the willows along the river, and the wild flowers of the fields and river bank. He loved the gardens and outbuildings that surrounded it and which contributed an essential quality to the ensemble and made it whole. Perhaps best of all he loved that the 'baby Thames', as he called it in a letter, was near by, just a hundred yards down a dirt track to the little wooden pier and boathouse. He would spend hours on the river fishing whenever he came to Kelmscott.

He loved the house's interior too, 'from the rose covered porch to the strange and quaint garrets amongst the great timbers of the roof, where of old time the tillers and herdsmen of the manor slept'.[10] He loved that, for all its beauty, it was a simple house, and a useful one to those who had lived in it over the generations, and had made their livings from the land. He loved it, he said, 'with a reasonable love'.[11] He claimed to have dreamt of the house long before he ever discovered it. It was where he felt happiest, most content and secure. 'The wind's on the wold,' he wrote in 'For the Bed at Kelmscott',

> And the night is a-cold,
> And Thames runs chill
> Twixt mead and hill,
> But kind and dear
> Is the old house here,
> And my heart is warm
> Midst winter's harm.
> Rest, then and rest,
> And think of the best.

His love of the river merged with his love of the house, village and land-scape, and from this seamless whole he derived a world-view.

If he had mistaken the import of the dock strike in 1889, distant from it as he had been, nevertheless it was in Kelmscott that he plumbed the depths of his socialism and his feeling for the land, and his ideal that every man and woman should live lives infused with beauty and art. He hated Victorian capitalism because he believed that it was based upon ruthless competition and the exploitation of the working class by the employing class, but also, and more precisely, because he believed that it was destroying the countryside, polluting the river, denying art and beauty to the vast majority of Britons. It was, he knew, mere accident of birth that placed him 'on this side of the window . . . and not on the other side, in the empty street, the drink-steeped liquor shops, the foul and degraded lodgings'.[12] Politics and aesthetics and personal experience fused in his mind. The grey house in the ancient hamlet, set beside the clear waters of the Thames, came to occupy the core of his green, red, utopian vision.

'Love for the earth and the life on it.' For Morris, his house and village and environs exemplified how the earth should be loved and lived upon. To walk in the meadows by the river was as close to heaven as Morris could conceive:

> Now sweet, sweet it is through the land to be straying,
> 'Mid the birds and the blossoms and the beasts of the field;
> Love mingles with love and no evil is weighing
> On thy heart or mine, where all sorrow is healed . . .[13]

But what drove Morris, too, was the threat that he perceived in commercial capitalism to earth and the life on it, and more particularly to his earthly paradise alongside the Thames. In his poetry London is the locus of greed, ambition, filth, and ill will. It stands antithetical to Kelmscott. It darkens the river, dirties the sky, and distorts the moon.

> In the midst of the bridge there we stopped and we wondered,
> In London at last, and the moon going down,
> All sullied and red where the mast-wood was sundered
> By the void of the night-mist, the breath of the town.

> On each side lay the City and Thames ran between it
> Dark, struggling, unheard 'neath the wheels and the feet.
> A strange dream it was that we ever had seen it,
> And strange was the hope we had wandered to meet.[14]

The maleficent city's foul breath reaches even to the trees of Morris's rural idyll:

> Hark, the wind in the elm-boughs! From London it bloweth,
> And telleth of gold and of hope and unrest;
> Of power that helps not; of wisdom that knoweth,
> But teacheth not aught of the worst and the best . . .

The city's harsh light colours the Kelmscott night sky. 'Shall we be glad always?' the narrator naively asks his lover in 'The Message of the March Wind', and the answer is full of foreboding.

> Come closer and hearken:
> Three fields further on, as they told me down there
> When the young moon has set, if the March sky should darken,
> We might see from the hill-top the great city's glare.

It is a striking, indeed a terrifying, image.

He sat, one summer day in 1889 not many weeks before the dock strike commenced, under an elm tree amid 'fields and hedges that are as it were one huge nosegay for you', gazing across the river, marvelling at the landscape, and pondering the history of his country, its current plight, and possible futures. Capitalism, that degrading system, had debased the descendants of heroes who, ages past, had carved the famous White Horse into a chalk escarpment which Morris could just see in the distance 'betwixt the elm-boughs'. It had turned them into ungraceful, ungainly, unbeautiful field hands slaving for nine shillings a week. Similarly, Morris warned with almost unendurable prescience, capitalism would degrade the countryside. 'The beauty of the land-scape will be exploited and artificialized for the sake of the villa-dweller's purses where it is striking enough to touch their jaded appetites. In quiet places like this, it will vanish year by year (as indeed it is now doing) under the attacks of the most grovelling commercialism.'

But Britain possessed 'a countryside worth fighting for', and so Britons must fight to 'preserve its peace'. They must replace the system that degraded humanity and landscape with one that respected and nurtured both. For Morris the cooperative commonwealth meant humankind cooperating not simply with one another, but with the land too, nourishing it, replenishing it as well as taking from it. 'Suppose the haymakers were friends working for friends on land which was theirs, as many as were needed, with leisure and hope ahead of them instead of hopeless toil and anxiety . . . ?' It was possible. It could be. Moreover, if Englishmen did not take up this fight to make it so, 'The worst ugliness and vulgarity will be good enough for such sneaks and cowards.'[15]

But he was confident they would take it up, and in his famous utopian novel, *News from Nowhere*, he imagines England after the battle has been won. It is not accidental that the Thames winds through the book as it does through England's history and through Morris's own life and dreams, and that the climax of the book takes place in a thinly disguised Kelmscott, Morris's earthly paradise.

He wrote the book, in part, as a riposte to the American Edward Bellamy's recently published and immensely popular *Looking Backward*, which imagines a future socialist state. Bellamy thought he was describing a utopia, but Morris recoiled from it. He considered Bellamy's socialism to be regimented, mechanical and soulless. No one has ever thought that about the socialist society Morris envisioned in *News from Nowhere*.

The plan of the book is simple and well known. The narrator (unmistakably William Morris himself, although he is called William Guest in the book) awakes one morning to find himself magically transported far into the future, and into a transformed England. Guest's reactions to the new conditions, his conversations about them with the friends he makes, including a beautiful girl, Ellen, whom he comes to love, and finally a dream-like journey with some of these friends up the Thames from Hammersmith to Kelmscott, constitute the core of the book.

The river is at the centre of the core. Guest awakens in Hammersmith on the river. It is a hot summer morning. Immediately he decides to go for a swim. 'How clear the water is,' he remarks, and then begins to notice other changes. There are nets for salmon on the far bank. 'The soap works with their smoke-vomiting chimneys' are gone, 'the engineer's works gone; the lead-works gone; and no sound of riveting and hammering' coming 'down the west wind from Thorneycroft's'. And Hammersmith Bridge has been replaced by something resembling an idealised medieval London Bridge.

> It was of stone arches, splendidly solid, and as graceful as they were strong; high enough also to let ordinary river traffic through easily. Over the parapet showed quaint and fanciful little buildings, which I supposed to be booths and shops, beset with painted and gilded vanes and spirelets. The stone was a little weathered, but showed no marks of the grimy sootiness which I was used to see on every London building more than a year old.

And on both banks of the river he sees a line of very pretty houses looking 'above all comfortable and as if they were, so to say, alive and sympathetic with the life of the dwellers in them'. Between houses and river ran a continuous garden 'in which the flowers were now blooming luxuriantly, and sending delicious waves of summer scent over the eddying stream. Behind the houses I could see great trees rising . . .'

Within a very few pages Morris thus focuses the issues that vexed him most. William Guest cleanses himself of nineteenth-century dirt and fug, no doubt as the author longed to do, in the waters of a revivified Thames. London, too, on the banks of the river, has been reborn: its architecture made functional, simple and beautiful, its air pure, its water sparkling and clean, a habitat for salmon, a source of nourishment and replenishment. The conurbation has been replaced by a series of villages separated by fields and woods. The vast docks, which once had swarmed with the helots of London, were still in use, 'but not so thronged as they once were', and the wretched population of the East End long since dispersed, 'the place being too low and marshy for pleasant dwelling'. This is as far from the threatening, looming city suggested in 'The Message of the March Wind' as may be.

William Guest tours the remade city with a new friend, Dick, who introduces him to more people. They discuss all the contentious issues of Morris's day, for example labour, art, government, love, friendship and family, all happily resolved by 'the great change' (which took place in 1952); they discuss how 'the great change' came about. Morris gives free rein to an imagination informed by Marx, Keats, Ruskin, the Norse myths, the Greek myths, medieval art and literature, and his own experience of the socialist movement, to name only a few. There are generous and beautiful alternatives to dreary, shoddy, selfish, arrogant Victorian England, he insists. But it is a timeless message. The alternatives remain beguiling as ever. Then William Guest's hosts arrange to take him upriver, to witness the annual haymaking festival. The entrancing sequence that follows is a recapitulation of Morris's real-life journey of 1880.

Hampton Court, Runnymede, Eton and Windsor, Cliveden woods: Morris revisits them all in his imagination. At Hampton Court, William Guest and his companions dine in the great hall, which now is open to everyone, free of charge in an era when hospitality is neither bought nor sold. At Runnymede they meet 'the grumbler', who pines for the old days, when there were more and bigger houses on the river. More importantly Guest meets 'the grumbler's' daughter, Ellen, tanned, grey-eyed, tawny-haired, lithe, not so much a Pre-Raphaelite beauty like his wife as a 'good fairy', though possessing 'a wild beauty' of her own; he falls for her at once; later she will join him on his river journey.[16] Eton has become a true centre of learning, open to all who wish to consult its resident scholars. Windsor Castle has become a combination apartment building and museum. As for the stretch of woods below the escarpment at Cliveden: they 'had lost their courtly gamekeeperish trimness, and were as wild and beautiful as need be, though the trees were clearly well seen to'.

And so up the river, William Guest marvelling all the while at England's transformation. He sees that men and women share their labours, taking pleasure and pride in them, and that whether young or old, they are clean-limbed, happy, frank, curious, and kind. There is equality between the sexes. Everywhere the countryside is beautiful and sweet as it ought to be, a great garden, really, made for the pleasure of all, as well as the livelihood of all; the villages they pass are as they ought always to have been, signs of poverty and shabbiness long gone, buildings functional, simple, and handsome. The prose itself is lyrical, as lovely as the landscape it describes.

News from Nowhere also contains striking aperçus and political writing of a high order. 'Don't you find it difficult to imagine the times when this little pretty country was treated by its folk as if it had been an ugly characterless waste,' Ellen asks him, 'with no delicate beauty to be guarded, with no heed taken of the ever fresh pleasure of the recurring seasons, and changeful weather, and diverse quality of the soil and so forth? How could people be so cruel to themselves?' 'And to each other?' William Guest adds.[17]

The climax of the journey and the book is the attainment of Kelmscott. When Guest's party reaches it, as in 1880 at the end of Morris's journey, 'a tall handsome woman with black wavy hair and deep-set grey eyes' greets them. She must be Jane. All William Guest's senses are alert. He can hear 'the cuckoo's song, the sweet strong whistle of the blackbirds, and the ceaseless note of the corn-crake'. He can smell 'waves of fragrance from the flowering clover amidst of the ripe grass'. He can see the gleaming river, coming 'down through a wide meadow on my left, which was grey now with the ripened seeding

Moonlight, A Study at Millbank (1797). Turner modestly called his painting a 'study', to imply that he still had much to learn about depicting moonlight on canvas, but in fact it is the work of one who already had looked closely not merely at the moon and sky but also at light and dark and water and air more generally, and who had thought carefully about how to paint them. (J. M. W. Turner/Tate, London 2004)

The Burning of the House of Lords and Commons, 16th October 1834 (first exhibited 1835). When he painted this, Turner may have had in mind those Britons without political voice or representation who might as well have been separated from Parliament by a river of fire. (J. M. W. Turner/Tate, London 2004)

The Fighting Temeraire Tugged to her Last Berth to be Broken up (first exhibited 1839). Symbol of a disappearing way of life.
(J. M. W. Turner/National Gallery, London/Bridgeman Art Library)

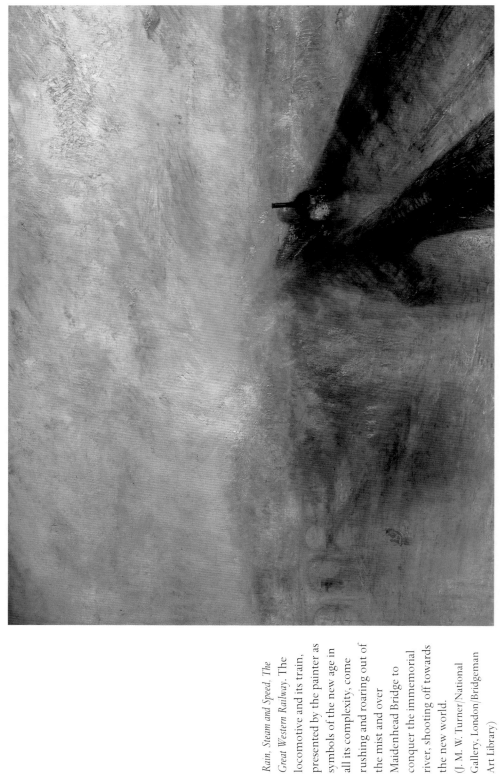

Rain, Steam and Speed, The Great Western Railway. The locomotive and its train, presented by the painter as symbols of the new age in all its complexity, come rushing and roaring out of the mist and over Maidenhead Bridge to conquer the immemorial river, shooting off towards the new world.
(J. M. W. Turner/National Gallery, London/Bridgeman Art Library)

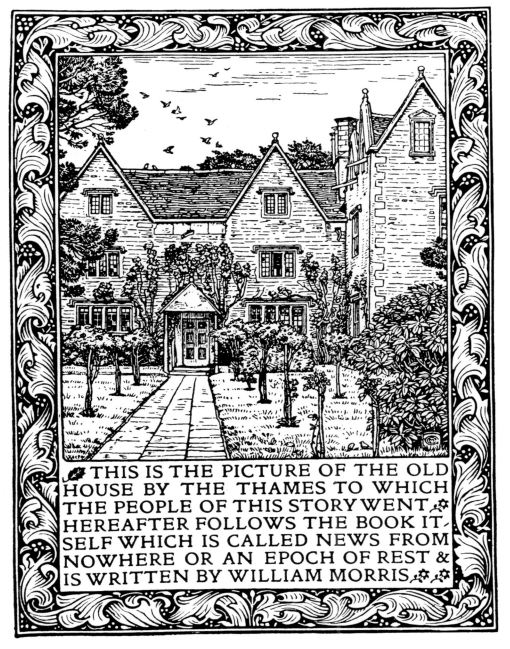

THIS IS THE PICTURE OF THE OLD
HOUSE BY THE THAMES TO WHICH
THE PEOPLE OF THIS STORY WENT.
HEREAFTER FOLLOWS THE BOOK IT-
SELF WHICH IS CALLED NEWS FROM
NOWHERE OR AN EPOCH OF REST &
IS WRITTEN BY WILLIAM MORRIS.

Kelmscott Manor. The East Front of Kelmscott Manor, frontispiece of *News from Nowhere* by William Morris, engraved by W. H. Hooper (woodcut, 1892), drawn by Charles March Gere (1869–1957). (Private Collection/Bridgeman Art Library)

Cookham (1914). An unmistakable English farm landscape. When Spencer painted it he had been reading *English Ballads* 'and feeling a new and personal value of the Englishness of England'. (Tullie House Museum & Art Gallery/Estate of Stanley Spencer © DACS)

Swan Upping at Cookham (1919). The painting, interrupted by the First World War, was originally meant as a paean to Cookham traditions. But look carefully at the water and a viewer will see where Spencer took up the work again. 'Oh no,' the artist exclaimed. 'It is not proper or sensible to expect to paint after such experiences.' (Estate of Stanley Spencer/Tate, London 2004 © DACS)

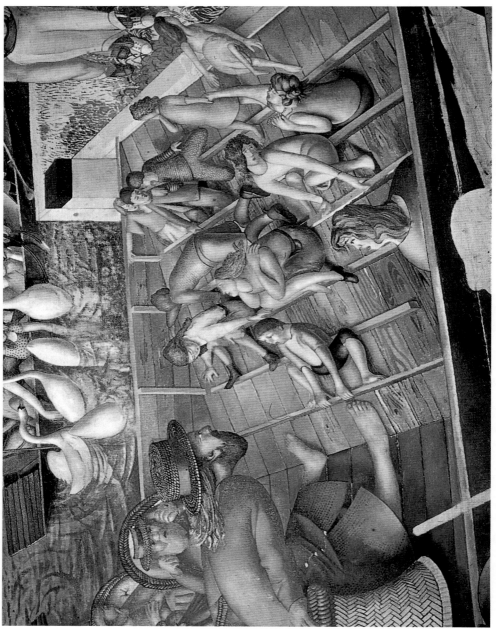

Christ Preaching at Cookham Regatta (1959). The unfinished seventh painting (of which this is a detail) in Spencer's series having to do with Christ in Cookham. It combines his deepest feelings of oneness with the village, the river, his childhood, and all that is holy. It would have been, had he lived to complete it, a summation and reassertation of his cherished belief that Cookham-on-Thames was an earthly paradise.
(Stanley Spencer Gallery/Estate of Stanley Spencer © DACS)

grasses', and a low wooded ridge that bounds 'the river-plain to the south and south-east, whence we had come . . . and through the hawthorn sprays and long shoots of the wild roses . . . the flat country spreading out far away under the sun of the calm evening, till something that might be called hills with a look of sheep-pastures about them bounded it with a soft blue line'.

As for the house and grounds: they are 'redolent of the June flowers, and . . . roses . . . rolling over one another with that delicious super-abundance of small well-tended gardens'. There are 'doves cooing on the roof-ridge . . . rooks in the high elm-trees . . . swifts wheel[ing] . . . about the gables'. Ellen 'laid her sun browned hand and arm on the lichened wall as if to embrace it, and cried out, "Oh me! Oh me! How I love the earth, and the seasons, and the weather, and all things that deal with it, and all that grows out of it, – as this has done!"' The beautiful girl has given voice to William Morris's *cri de coeur*.

Guest is describing Kelmscott and the surrounding landscape as it looked to Morris in 1890. This landscape needed no transforming, only preservation and respect. But there has been the 'great change' since Morris's day. The haymakers, 'gay-clad' and joyous, live in Nowhere, not Kelmscott. Now William Guest remembers how, in Kelmscott, in 1890, although the countryside was beautiful 'two or three spindle-legged back-bowed men and haggard, hollow-eyed women', whose labour was drudgery because it was involuntary and ill paid, cut the hay and 'wore down the soil . . . with their heavy hopeless feet, from day to day, and season to season, and year to year'. William Guest, sensing that his time in Nowhere is nearly spent, half expects them to appear.[18] In a sense they do, for soon enough Guest finds himself back in his own time and place where such figures are common. In *News from Nowhere* Morris thus acknowledges the worm in the bud, even alongside the river at Kelmscott. His earthly paradise is under threat and always will be until 'the great change' has come.

★

To another English visionary, the painter Stanley Spencer, born in 1891, a year after the publication of *News from Nowhere*, the Thames, or at least the stretch of river near the village of Cookham where he was brought up and lived a good part of his life, seemed an eternal heaven. Spencer, a much more inward-looking and self-involved figure than Morris, often drew upon the memories and associations of his childhood in Cookham for his art. These works involved the village (specific buildings and structures), and the village residents (specific people). But as with Morris at Kelmscott, the river runs through it, essential as air, an inextricable aspect of remembrance.

Cookham-on-Thames is thirty miles west of London, just past the stretch of river bordered by Cliveden woods. That short stretch, immediately before the village proper, where the stream makes a nearly right-angle bend, is straight as an arrow below the Cliveden bluffs, and outlined by stands of tall poplars on either shore. As I have seen, there is sufficient space between the trees for the glow of a late-afternoon sun to filter through, making the water sparkle and the white swans shimmer, illuminating four mallard ducks as, wings outspread and webbed feet forward, they come swooping in for a landing. Morris thought the Cliveden woods too tidy, 'game-keeperish' he called them, but today, as then, many people find them beautiful. Certainly Stanley Spencer did. He loved too the surrounding countryside, which is largely unchanged even now (despite some suburban sprawl), for there are still farms and fields dotted with grazing animals. But perhaps Spencer loved most of all the village of Cookham itself, with its tidy brick houses and shops, chapel (now the Stanley Spencer Gallery), church and churchyard and river spanned by a wrought-iron bridge, and the Horse Ferry Hotel and Turk's Boatyard on the southern bank. Stanley Spencer, in his childhood, thought this community 'perfect' and, borrowing the famous line from Morris, 'an earthly paradise'.

A hundred years ago Cookham-on-Thames was one of a series of increasingly fashionable small villages strung along the river made easily accessible to the metropolis by the coming of the railway. Wealthy Londoners built second homes in or near them; they organised annual regattas on the river, when there would be concerts, fireworks, boat races, and the like. Spencer did not come from a wealthy London family, his father taught piano and violin and served as a church organist, but he came from an inordinately happy, ambitious, cultured, accomplished and large one (he had eight siblings). Moreover they lived in one half of a big semi-detached house, built by his grandfather on Cookham's main street, while his father's brother's family lived in the other half. There were relatives scattered throughout the village as well. Parents, brothers, sisters, cousins, aunts and uncles constituted a community unto themselves. The children explored Cookham, and surrounding countryside. They swam and boated in the river. Every summer they waited anxiously for the annual regatta, which they adored.

This was not a family or a village in which socialism loomed large, or in which the contradictions of capitalism inspired rage and political engagement, although Spencer's later work does reveal a profound egalitarianism and democratic belief in the kinship of all humankind. His early days and environment, however, mainly seem to be bathed in the amber light of a long sunset, the late-Victorian and Edwardian garden parties, when England ruled an empire and peace and prosperity reigned. Young Spencer was an original, with an original mind, but unlike William Morris his originality did not lie in his understanding of politics and society.

His father was Anglican, his mother Methodist. Young Spencer attended both church and chapel. He preferred the latter, because it was less formal, but no formal religious association could contain his unconventional and boundless spirituality. As a boy he refused to be confirmed, objecting less to the doctrine than to the priest. An unorthodox Christianity suffused his world and world-view, from childhood on. 'It came into my vision quite naturally, like the sky and the rain.'[19] But it rarely rained in Stanley Spencer's memory. Recalling the golden mornings of his boyhood and early manhood he wrote:

> We swim and look at the bank over the rushes. I swim right in the pathway of sunlight. I go home to breakfast thinking as I go of the beautiful wholeness of the day. During the morning I am visited, and walk about being in that visitation. Now everything seems more definite and to put on a new meaning and freshness.[20]

He wandered the rural lanes, the fields and low hills of the Thames valley, in an almost ethereal daze. 'I could see the richness that under-lies the bible in Cookham in the hedges, in the yew trees.'[21] He found holiness and meaning everywhere: in places, people, things, including things cast away by others as useless. Such revelations filled him with joy. As he began to draw, and then to paint, he found the process of work itself to be spiritual; and his paintings expressed the ecstatic divin-ity he saw all around him.

Stanley Spencer was so content and felt so secure during his child-hood in this happy extended family and model village, and he believed so profoundly that he had been vouchsafed visions of holiness there, that he wished never to leave, and in fact did not really leave until dragged away by the First World War when he was twenty-six. He had attended the Slade School in London from 1908 to 1912 (and graduated with its highest prizes), but commuted daily, so that his fellow art stu-dents quickly dubbed him 'Cookham'. After the war he occasionally lived elsewhere, but a main theme of his adult life was the quest to return to and recreate the blissful years of his prolonged Cookham childhood by the river.

His love for the Thames valley is revealed in his very first pure land-scape painting in oils, *Cookham 1914*. In later life Spencer resented the time he spent working on landscapes, 'observed paintings', they have been called,[22] which, because they were more easily understood, were more

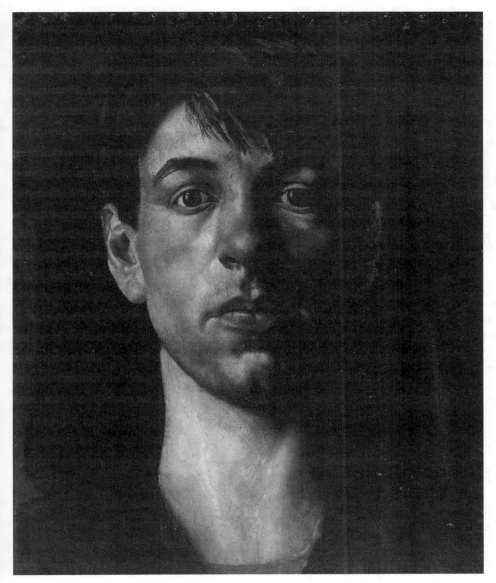

The young artist before the First World War dragged him away from Cookham. (*Self-Portrait*, Stanley Spencer (1891–1959)/Estate of Stanley Spencer/Tate, London 2004 © DACS)

popular and lucrative than his visionary, compositional paintings. The latter, by contrast, are obscurely personal, their themes are often mystical, the figures in them frequently swollen, or elongated, or otherwise weirdly proportioned. He thought his landscapes 'dead, dead', because they did not engage his mind or reflect his imagination as the compositional paintings did. His best landscapes, however, have been highly praised by experts for their depth of observation and sense of place,[23] and the pellucid *Cookham 1914* certainly is deeply observed, with its green foliage and dashes of yellow hinting at just the beginning of the season's turning, and its fence posts marking the tilled fields from the green ones, and its red-roofed Tudor farmhouse just visible in the distance. In fact the scene is so perfectly delineated, the sense of place so strong, that it has been possible to locate it precisely: Terry's Lane leading up to Winter Hill, a little beyond Rowborough House in Cookham.

But the scene is larger than that. It is an unmistakable English farm landscape, and as such it is deeply felt. When Spencer painted it he had been reading Hamilton Mabie's compilation of *English Ballads* (1896) 'and feeling a new and personal value of the Englishness of England'. His painting reflected this sentiment, he told its purchaser. We can still see that, nearly a century later. We can also sense the innocence of it; for it was an England that after 1914 would never be the same. When Spencer finished *Cookham 1914*, the First World War was only months away.

The war profoundly affected one of his next works, a composed painting in which the Thames itself figures largely. Because it was composed rather than observed, it is both more complex in conception and more important to the artist than *Cookham 1914*. Where the landscape painting evoked personal, local and national themes, *Swan Upping at Cookham* added historical and biblical ones. It is one of the best known, if not the best executed, of Spencer's early works, precisely because it resonates so much more deeply. But to understand it one must peer far down the line of years, to long before August 1914.

The painting *Swan Upping at Cookham*, is named for the ancient practice of actually physically carving a mark on to the beak of a cygnet in order to demonstrate possession. This practice, 'upping', dates at least to the twelfth century, some time during which the Crown, in an attempt to restrict ownership of swans, declared them to be a royal bird.[24] We can guess why it did this. The swan appeals to something deeply rooted in men and women. The Greek myth of Leda, ravished by Zeus in the form of a swan, inspires feelings of mastery or surrender. European legends of alluring 'swan maidens', women who were really swans, appeal to our sense of mystery and beauty. Certainly the Mute Swan of England (*Cygnus olor*) has a regal aspect. If it is white, it practically gleams; if it is black its long neck curves no less gracefully. When a fully grown male swan rears his head and begins to stretch his wings and to hiss his defiance at man or beast, he is magnificent. A single swan on lake or stream is lovely to watch. A flock of them gliding serenely along the river can cause the breath to catch. In 1496 the secretary of the Venetian ambassador, Capello, wrote with what must have been massive understatement to his master, 'It is a truly beautiful thing to behold one or two thousand tame swans upon the river Thames as I, and also your magnificence, have seen.'[25]

We know that by 1355 the king had appointed a Swan-master to care for his royal birds and more generally to supervise swan keeping throughout England.[26] This was when the formalities of swan upping began to take shape. The Swan-master, whose full title was Master of the King's (or Queen's) Game of Swans, oversaw the regulating of the birds: marking, checking marks, registering and the like; he and his deputies also enforced the myriad of laws pertaining to swans: their hunting, their sale, the stealing of their eggs, pinioning of their wings, and so on.[27] More important was the ceremony of swan upping itself. This would take place on different days, on different stretches of different waters over the course of the year. It was a major proposition, for every swan had to be identified, every mark checked, every one of them accounted for. The Swan-master and his deputies recorded each detail on a roll, or later in a book. Some of these have survived; the earliest vellum roll dates back to before 1500.

Over the centuries the Crown grew more jealous of its rights of ownership while individuals and corporations found reasons to become less so, in part because they did not relish challenging the Crown. But as the practice disappeared elsewhere, swan upping on the Thames continued, became in fact a more elaborate annual ritual than ever before. By 1793 ownership of swans on the Thames rested only with royalty and two of the livery companies of London, the Dyers and the Vintners. Every summer, usually in late July, six skiffs would row upriver from Sunbury, their crews dressed in red if they represented the Crown, in white if the Vintners, in blue if the Dyers. Each skiff was decorated with flags and carried two oarsmen, except for the queen's randan, which carried three. The Swan-master, most gorgeously arrayed of all, sat in the stern of this boat. Swan uppers sat in the others. By now the actual practice of carving symbols on to the birds' bills had devolved upon Thames watermen and lightermen only. No one else could perform the deed, and the marks of ownership had become complex works of art in their own right.

So the strikingly costumed Vintners, Dyers and Swan-master would arrive in Cookham, accompanied by the plebeian watermen and lightermen, with their leathers to protect them from a swan's thrashing wings and thrusting beak, and their baskets for transporting captured swans to the place where the ritual carving was performed, and their sharp blades for the actual incisions. Their appearance in the sleepy little community was redolent of England's history, a visible link between past and present. It made a deep impression upon the young Stanley Spencer, who named his painting for it.

Swan upping was a secular ritual. Spencer, in his work, made it into a holy one. He first began to conceive the painting on a Sunday while sitting in church. He sensed that the mood and feel of the place, the words of the minister, were not containable within a building. Spencer projected them outwards, through the walls and stained-glass windows, into the streets beyond. Then 'The village seemed as much a part of the atmosphere prevalent in the church as the most holy part of the church such as the altar.' And not only places and structures, but villagers as well. 'When I thought of people going on the river at that moment my mind's imagination of it seemed . . . to be an extension of the church atmosphere.' He had turned the village, river and all, into a vast church.

In *Swan Upping at Cookham*, the waterman, with swan constrained in a basket on his shoulder, is the central figure. Two swans, trussed up and deposited in a little scull, also demand the eye's attention, their straining long white necks a stark contrast to the brown of the boat and the grey-green of the river. But the painting is, in fact, a series of 'cameos', each a 'pocket of feeling'.[28] In the foreground two men shift a long punt. They are working men, with strong, long arms, reminiscent of the elongated necks of the swans. Two girls carry folded punt cushions behind the men. They are softer, less angular than the workers, so are their cushions softer and rounder than the hard narrow punt the men are awkwardly lifting. At the top of the painting an iron bridge spans the river. A man on the bridge seems almost to be studying something to his left. Is it the woman whose head and shoulders we can just make out near the end of the bridge or someone or something further distant?

For Spencer each of these cameos of feeling is suffused with a holy light. That is to say, each of them is sanctified by his all-encompassing vision of church and village as one. The labourers and the swan upper are engaged in the community's sacred rhythms of working life. So too are the girls with cushions engaged in holy village ritual, but in fact all the women in the painting are sacred to Spencer for the special position they occupied in his heart. He had painted them as the Bailey girls, daughters of a local builder who was an artist himself. The sister on the bridge was the most dear to Spencer, she had tutored him in art when he was a child: 'How much, Dorothy, you belong to the Marsh meadows and the old village. I love your curiosity and simplicity, domestic Dorothy.' But Spencer loved the Bailey girls not only for themselves. They, as much as or more than the unidentified workers, were members of the blessed Cookham community. 'The Bailey girls . . . Mr. Worcester, Pa, Mrs. Croper, or Mr. Francis or Mr. Pym . . . It's just heaven reciting those names.'[29]

There is still to consider the enigmatic male figure on the bridge, however. At what or whom, if not Dorothy Bailey, is he gazing so intently? Here, perhaps, history intrudes. Conceivably he represents the artist's increasing awareness of the threat posed from outside. The year was 1915, after all.

Spencer, when he finished at the Slade and began painting seriously at Cookham in 1912, was at the height of his powers. 'Everything seemed fresh and to belong to the morning.'[30] He did not then realise that, in fact, it was late afternoon and night drawing in, and the long English garden party finally about to end. But it did end, in August 1914, and the nightfall interrupted Stanley Spencer as it interrupted practically everyone else. Reluctantly he laid aside his paints and brushes and his unfinished painting, mute, idiosyncratic, testimony to a way of life now to disappear. He volunteered for service, first as a hospital orderly in Bristol. In the summer of 1916 he volunteered to be sent abroad. He thought he was going to India, but wound up in Macedonia, to take part in operations against the Germans and Bulgarians. Once again he volunteered: this time for the infantry. He spent several months in the front lines, experiencing danger and hardship, if not actual combat. It was not until December 1918 that he returned to Cookham.

He had gone into the army and then abroad and then into the infantry of his own free will. Nevertheless while in Macedonia he began to fear that he would never return to Cookham, never have a chance to finish painting *Swan Upping*. His art and his life were inseparable, or perhaps his art was more important to him than life itself. He longed to tell his officers 'I have a picture at home and I just want to finish it before going into this attack.' Of course he did no such thing. But 'it was just the fact that there was a remote possibility that I might still be living in a time of peace and no war and painting this picture up in my bedroom at home that was so agonizing'. By spring 1918 he thought peace was near. 'This made the sudden appearance of fresh supplies of ammunition arriving and orders for the beginning of a new offensive insupportable to the spirit.'[31]

Swan Upping had assumed immense significance to Spencer. Originally it had stood for home and the heavenly bliss of Cookham and a historic, sacred ritual in which the river figured; now it also stood for life itself and for all his future paintings.

> It can be imagined what I felt when I did at last in fact walk into my bedroom at home and see this picture leaning with its face to the wall on the far side of the big bed. I walked round the bed to it and laid my hands on it once more. Well there we were looking at each other; it seemed unbelievable that it was a fact. Then I wondered if what I had just come from was fact and caught sight of the yellow of the liddite or whatever the Bulgars used in their shells on my fingers and fingernails.

The war had been real all right. He could no more return to pre-war Cookham than other surviving soldiers could simply go home and pick up where they had left off. Everything was changed. But Spencer was a great artist. During 1927–32, at the Burghclere Chapel, he would produce 'the most powerful art to emerge from the carnage of the Great War'.[32] Of course it took him time to find his feet again. 'Oh no,' Spencer exclaimed. 'It is not proper or sensible to expect to paint after such experiences.'

Look carefully at *Swan Upping in Cookham* and you can see where he took it up again after nearly a four-year interval. In the upper part of the painting the Thames water sparkles in early morning sunlight. It shines like a whitened mirror where the light is most direct. Then look at the water close to the scull in which the swans are kept. It is muddy grey and crudely daubed in comparison. Or consider the girls with the cushions: originally Spencer had intended to paint the two young daughters of the proprietors of the Ferry Hotel, girls who really worked there.[33] But after his return: 'I could not seem to get on with drawing [them] . . .' Only by substituting the Bailey girls, who were sanctified in his memory as part-and-parcel of sacred pre-war Cookham, could Spencer rekindle the flame of his holy vision. But for a moment it had deserted him.

'The years of his Cookham earthly paradise were over,' writes Fiona MacCarthy, who knows Spencer's work well. The rest of his life, with all its contradictions, had now begun.[34] *Swan Upping* literally reveals the great caesura. It can stand too for the chasm dividing pre- and post-war England.

Stanley Spencer would spend the rest of his days lovingly burnishing the earlier years in his memory, recalling and exploring the village of his childhood over and over again. But not everything was retrospective. He continued to grow, and to develop his notions of interconnectedness, his belief that what he had witnessed as a child in Cookham and the surrounding countryside presaged what he would read in the Bible when he was only a little older, that the Thames valley remained what it had been before 1914, as much a holy land as any other place. Now came the series of paintings, perhaps little loved by the public at large, but much loved by the artist himself, in which biblical events are transposed to Cookham: *Christ Carrying the Cross* (1920), *Christ's Entry into Jerusalem* (1921), *The Betrayal* (1922–3). The Cookham he portrays in such works is less joyous than the village of the pre-war years, but still it is hallowed. Moreover these works are all leading to another great expression of joy, *The Resurrection, Cookham* (1924–7).

This is usually considered one of Spencer's most important composed paintings. It is an intensely personal work in which the artist himself appears reborn more than once, also many of his friends and relations, and perhaps most importantly the woman he loved, Hilda Carline, whom he married while the painting was still unfinished. All are in some stage of opening or leaving their coffins or the church cemetery. It is a complex and subtle composition whose deciphering demands minute knowledge of Spencer's life and circumstances. Here we will only note that the Thames, which can be seen in the upper left-hand corner of the canvas, far from being a black river Styx across which the dead are ferried to the underworld, is rather a 'river of life', carrying a steam launch of the resurrected towards a glowing dawn. Spencer told his sister that for the passengers aboard the boat 'the climax in heaven lay in the sunlit continuation of the marsh meadows beyond the bend in the river'.[35] It is here that Spencer reveals his kinship with William Morris. Heaven is to be found in this world not in any other, and in a meadow by the Thames.

During the early 1930s Spencer met Patricia Preece. He had to have her. He broke the marriage with Hilda Carline, but not his relationship with her: in fact he wished for a permanent *ménage à trois*, but this Hilda would not accept. So he married Patricia, lavished expensive gifts upon her, including his own house. She did not treat him well, but he was besotted. His money needs grew. To this we owe his return to painting the much-loved landscapes, the Cookham street scenes and studies of particular Cookham trees, flowers and bushes. These works – including *Gypsophila* (1933), *The May Tree* (1933), *The Cedar Tree Cookham* (1935), *Bellrope Meadow* (1936), *Gardens in the Pound, Cookham* (1936), *Cookham, Flowers in a Window* (1938) – are glimmeringly, gorgeously clear, closely, lovingly and yet unblinkingly observed. They, as much as the composed paintings, are testimony to the earthly paradise Stanley Spencer kept alive in his head at any rate. But because of these paintings the general public misunderstood him. It thought him, during the inter-war years, a nostalgic

Spencer thought such 'observed' paintings 'dead, dead, dead'. They did not interest him as much as his interpretative works. But the public loved them. [**Pic 1**] (*Bellrope Meadow*, Estate of Stanley Spencer/Stanley Spencer Gallery © DACS) [**Pic 2**] (*Bridle Path at Cookham*/Estate of Stanley Spencer/Stanley Spencer Gallery© DACS)

defender of traditional England, a *georgic* England if it is not anachronistic to use the term for a twentieth-century painter, the England of cosy cottages and villages, and harmonious social relations, as though he was a William Morris without teeth, a defender of the Thames valley in the way that, say, Kenneth Graham, author of *Wind in the Willows*, was a defender – which is to say a celebrator of something that had never been, but which many Britons liked to imagine had been.

In fact there is a profoundly democratic element in Spencer's approach to village life and indeed to all life. Royal Swan-master or common waterman, Cookham tradesman or day labourer, one was as holy as the other in his view. Even tin cans and cabbage leaves, the detritus of Cookham's most humble residents, the dustmen, were 'worthy of being adored'.[36] Spencer could never accept the social hierarchy that undergirded the traditional countryside, nor the little-England, chauvinist sentimentality with which it was imbued.

And from the democratic view to the internationalist: during a decade when fascist or fascist-like movements were sweeping Europe, and when even Britain faced the challenge of Oswald Mosley's blackshirts, Stanley Spencer set his face defiantly against, albeit in his own way. In a famous compositional work, *Love among the Nations*, he pictured men and women of every race and nationality embracing one another. In this sense, as well as in his love of the river and surrounding landscape, Spencer was again a true heir of the great leveller and anti-xenophobe, William Morris.

During the last phase of his life, from 1945 to 1959, Spencer lived once more in Cookham. He returned more determinedly than ever to the theme that had always sustained him, the exaltation of the quotidian in his village. His paintings were not unreservedly cheerful, for neither was Stanley Spencer, but he painted Christ being baptised in the sacred waters of the Thames, *The Baptism* (1952), and Christ sitting in an armchair, before a playground where children jump and skip at hopscotch, and adults in diamond-patterned sweaters sit looking for all the world 'like a football team being photographed', *Christ in Cookham* (1952).[37] At his death he was still working on an enormous composition, the seventh in this series having to do with Christ in Cookham. It combines his deepest feelings of oneness with the village, the river, his childhood, and all that is holy. It would have been, had he lived to complete it, a summation and reassertion of his cherished belief that Cookham-on-Thames was an earthly paradise. The painting is called *Christ Preaching at Cookham Regatta.*

Much has been written about this unfinished work, which depicts Christ, wearing a straw hat, leaning forward from a wicker chair on the old Cookham horse-ferry barge, exhorting (it would seem) villagers and holidaymakers on the shore in front of the Ferry Hotel, and even possibly a dozen children scattered about his feet, 'like little frogs which have jumped accidentally into punts from the riverbank', as Spencer told a friend.[38] But some of those little frogs are listening and looking very carefully at the man in the chair. In the front of the picture stands old Mr Turk, owner of Turk's boathouse during Spencer's youth. He is leaning against a long mop, paddles, oars, and punt poles, which he has gathered at the end of the day and wedged before him so that they rest at an angle on the ground and against his shoulders, and he can put his arms around them. Mr Turk has paused it would seem to listen to the man preaching from the old horse ferry. By contrast the rather calculating-looking hotel-keeper stands on the lawn, slightly behind his wife, who seems to be signalling him surreptitiously, her fingers curled behind her back. And all around are more people and children, both on the land and in punts on the river, and, once again, there are white swans.

It could not be clearer. We know already how the Spencer children eagerly anticipated the annual regatta. This English ritual was as holy to Stanley Spencer as swan upping. The river would be crowded with punts, so thick on the water that it might have been possible to walk across upon them without getting wet. The old horse-ferry barge, which was moored permanently before the Ferry Hotel, would again be put into use: as a stage for musicians, including Spencer's musical brothers. They would play Handel. It is hard not to think that they played the *Water Music*, as redolent of English history in its way as any river tradition or ceremony. The music had an even deeper meaning to Stanley Spencer. 'It isn't a far cry between people listening to Handel and people listening to Christ preaching,' he wrote.[39]

He had been thinking about the scene in the Bible where Christ preaches from a boat on a lake, and about the Cookham Regatta as a symbol for all that was holy to him, for decades. Finally he had combined them to reassert his most fundamental convictions: that the holy land was located on the river Thames; that all who came there, regardless of background, were surrounded by a divine light. All could be saved.

William Morris, Stanley Spencer: these two unlike figures, united in their love of the Thames, wound the river ever more deeply into the national consciousness. In Morris's work it is an essential part of the heaven England could yet become in spite of all; in Spencer's it is a crucial aspect of the heaven England already is, if we could but see it.

9

River of Fire

*N*ever was the Thames's role as a twisty guideline into London from the sea more important than during 1940–5; never was the opposite more true: that the river led out of England as well. So important was the Thames to the nation during those crucial years of peril and opportunity that it is difficult to separate the history of the first from that of the second. They merge; they become one.

Since London had never ceased to expand, her population to increase, her trade to develop, so, therefore and inevitably, great docks had grown up alongside the river that bisected her. Five giant systems of quays, jetties and pools, the first dating from early in the nineteenth century, eventually extended from Tower Bridge all the way to Tilbury, 26 miles downstream. Then there were also hundreds of individual wharves, many of them much older than the docks, competing for the shallower-hulled vessels that engaged in coastal trading;[1] also, behind docks and wharves there stood massive warehouses, many stories high, lining the broad waterway in both directions.

Into the warehouses tens of thousands of dock labourers (whose strike in 1889 William Morris had underestimated) daily trucked goods unloaded from ships: every raw material, every commodity, every luxury, every foodstuff and drink imaginable. London was the nation's capital; the Thames was the nation's river; 'dockland', as this section of east London was called, had become the nation's giant larder and collecting area. Early in the twentieth century the Millwall Docks could accommodate 24,000 tons of grain; the Royal Albert Dock had one cold store alone capable of housing 250,000 carcasses of mutton; the Surrey Commercial Docks could take more than a million tons of timber; the Royal Docks, with a water area of 230 acres, comprised the largest enclosed impounded dock water in the world.[2]

By 1900 dockland probably contained more wealth and more stuff that was crucial to the operation of the national economy than any other place in Britain, although the people who laboured on the docks and lived in the neighbouring warren of mean streets and alleyways remained, as they had been before the great strike of 1889, desperately poor. Nevertheless, dockland was a nodal point into which, and from which, flowed all that made Britain what it was. This was true later in the century too, even during the depression years of the 1930s, when the volume of trade through the port was declining. In 1939 some 60 million tons of cargo still passed through the London docks. From berth 33 at the Royal Albert Dock, every day dockers loaded 14,500 quarters of frozen beef, 2000 carcasses of mutton and 2000 packages of offal into 280 refrigerated trucks and ninety insulated railway wagons per eight-hour shift.[3] The London St Katharine's Dock where labourers regularly handled tea, wool, wine, spirits, coffee, rubber, ivory, gums, wax, canned goods, seasonal dried fruits, veneers and plywood was considered to contain 'the world's greatest concentration of portable wealth', economic depression notwithstanding.[4]

The route to this locus of prosperity and power, as every invader or potential invader, and as even Admiral Richard Parker of the floating republic, might have testified, was the river Thames. Even in the age of the aeroplane, hostile pilots and navigators knew, looking down from above, to follow the looping curving river. It would lead them into the heart of the empire, which is to say not merely into London but into dockland itself, which we might term the heart of the heart of the empire.

Accordingly dockland was England's most tempting target, the paramount goal of any modern enemy. British politicians and generals understood this. After the Great War they believed that the cost of defending dockland would be unacceptably high. Britain had been hard pressed to protect it against even the primitive Zeppelin and Gotha raids of 1915–18. Stanley Baldwin, looking back in 1931 – warned the House of Commons almost despairingly 'the bomber will always get through'. And once having passed England's defenders, what havoc could not a modern air force wreak with modern bombs? In 1939 the British Air Staff thought the Germans had 1600 long-range bombers, capable of dropping about 700 tons of bombs per day. They thought fifty people would be killed or wounded per ton of bombs dropped on a built-up area. The arithmetic was horrifying: Ministry of Health officials estimated that during the first six months of a second war with Germany 600,000 people would be killed and 1,200,000 wounded by bombs dropped from German aeroplanes.[5] Such sobering statistics, even though they proved to be exceptionally pessimistic, make the ill-judged policy of appeasement more comprehensible to later generations.

Perhaps, for east London, the solution was to divert trade and goods from the Thames to western ports, further from Germany and therefore less accessible to the Luftwaffe and, moreover, surrounded by lesser concentrations of population. There would be fewer bombs dropped over dockland if dockland was empty. Possibly this is what Winston Churchill had in mind when, on the very eve of war, he remarked consideringly, 'I think we shall have to abandon the Thames.'[6] No such abandonment occurred, however, although in the event much inbound traffic was directed to other harbours. Nevertheless the port of London continued to function throughout the war, in fact played a vital role as we shall see, and as a result the Thames near dockland became 'the most consistently and heavily bombed civilian target in the country'.[7] The fate of the nation and the fate of the river, particularly the stretch where it winds in a great arc round the Isle of Dogs where the greatest docks are located, were more inextricably intertwined during this period than ever before, so that, especially during September 1940 at the height of the Blitz, many, when they thought of England, thought simultaneously of the Thames.

Despite Churchill's musings, then, the government planned to protect the river and port, not to abandon them. For every major port in the kingdom it established Port Emergency Committees responsible to the Ministry of Transport. In London the chairman of the Committee was Mr (later Sir Douglas) J.D. Ritchie, who was already chairman of the Port of London Authority. Meanwhile the navy took control of Southend Pier, at the mouth of the Thames, a crucial strategic position, where entire convoys had room to shelter, and past which every in- or outbound ship must sail. Rear Admiral E.C. Boyle, Flag Officer in Charge, London, established his headquarters in the Port of London Authority's building on Tower Hill. Here then, taking shape during the year before the outbreak of hostilities, was the coalition that would regulate the port and the river from London to estuary during wartime: Admiralty, Ministry of Transport, Port Emergency Committee, and Port of London Authority.

Then came the crisis for which the coalition had been formed, ushered in by one calamity after another: first Germany's invasion and defeat of Poland in late 1939, then Germany's breathtaking and devastating advance west in the spring of 1940, leading to the conquest of the Low Countries and of much of Scandinavia, and of France in mid-June; finally, Germany's long-awaited assault upon England. Germany hoped for mastery of British skies, a precondition (though not the only one) for invasion. Throughout that summer the Luftwaffe bombed coastal

radar stations, airfields and sector-stations, the control centres of the
British Fighter Command. It engaged Spitfires and Hurricanes in running dogfights, so that the Royal Air Force was stretched near to
breaking. At the climax of the Battle of Britain, Churchill himself jour-
neyed from Chequers to the underground operations room at
Uxbridge. He watched aides, members of the Women's Auxiliary Air
Force, pushing counters on a vast map of England, the counters representing squadrons of RAF fighters rushing to meet wave upon wave of
incoming German aeroplanes. It was an enormous battle in the skies
over his country and more Luftwaffe kept coming. Soon all the RAF
squadrons were committed to the mêlée. The prime minister had
remained silent throughout. Now he turned to Air Vice-Marshal Park.
'What other reserves have we?' 'There are no reserves,' came the reply.[8]

The opening phase of the great struggle saw relatively few civilian
casualties. The Luftwaffe sought to destroy the RAF in the air and its
infrastructure on the ground, but not yet British industry, commerce
and cities, possibly because Hitler hoped for a compromise peace with
England. Nevertheless, on 8 and 24 August, German aeroplanes did
drop bombs on London. Churchill ordered the RAF to retaliate with
bombs on Berlin. Hitler was enraged. 'When the British air force drops
two or three or four thousand kilograms of bombs, we in one night will
drop one hundred and fifty, two hundred and thirty, three hundred or
four hundred thousand kilograms. When they declare they will increase
their attacks on our cities, we will raze their cities to the ground.' For
once he was as good as his word.

The chief of the German air force, Hermann Goering, told reporters
that he had taken 'personal command of the Luftwaffe in its war against
England'.[9] On 7 September he sent over a vast flying armada: more
than 350 bombers, escorted by more than 600 fighters. They formed a
phalanx twenty miles wide as they advanced across the Channel and
then westward up from the estuary of the Thames. They flew in waves,
in tight formations at 14,000 and 20,000 feet. English interceptors

Smoke rising from the docks after a German daylight raid. (Tower Bridge/CORBIS)

Nighttime raid on the docks, 1940. Flames leapt so high they blistered fireboats on the far shore. 'It was something,' said A. P. Herbert, who was on the river that night, 'to be the only boat in Hell.' (German Blitz/TRH Images)

scrambled to meet them. They assumed the attack would again be directed at airfields and radar towers, and positioned accordingly. But the Germans followed the ribbon of river where it led this time, and dropped their bombs on the initially undefended warehouses and docks and wharves and factories and, inevitably, homes of the East End. 'I saw the planes coming over and had mistaken them for flocks of pigeons,' one Eastender reported rather endearingly.[10] But these pigeons dropped tens of thousands of 1-kilogram electron incendiary bombs. The bomb cases were made of aluminium alloy mixed with 90 per cent magnesium, which melted at 650 degrees 'and burned like the fires of hell'. They dropped high-explosive splinter bombs. They dropped 500-kilogram and 1000-kilogram bombs packed with TNT.[11]

Dockland, England's storehouse, exploded in a hurricane of fire. The first blaze ignited at Millwall Docks, where two hundred acres of dry timber, 1.5 million tons of softwood, went up like so much kindling. 'Send all the bloody pumps you've got; the whole bloody world's on fire,' signalled the fire officer frantically.[12] Bombs continued to rain down. Firemen fought to contain blaze after blaze: at Woolwich Arsenal they worked amid boxes of live ammunition and nitroglycerine; in the warehouses that contained alcohol they saw barrels ignite, and rum and whisky arc flaming into the air; in the spice warehouses they inhaled and choked upon stinging black pepper. Tea burned 'sweet, sickly and very intense'; rubber fires produced asphyxiating black clouds of smoke; grain fires released millions of black flies and thousands of rats to plague the men who carried the hoses; sugar melted and continued to burn as it floated; so did wax. It looked as though portions of the river itself had caught fire.[13]

Finally the German bombers broke off the attack and turned back for the Continent. It grew dark. East London drew breath, though many fires continued to burn. And then the sirens wailed once more and the bombers returned, drawn like angry moths to the flames. Into the vast conflagration they poured more bombs and explosives. Blazes spread completely out of control now. Flames leapt so high and long that they blistered the paint of fireboats three hundred yards away on the far shore of the river. They created hurricanes of wind that tossed burning embers across roads, over rooftops and trees, to set new fires wherever they landed. The dean of St Paul's Cathedral stood inside his church, miraculously unscathed by bombs. 'The light was such,' he wrote after-wards, 'that I have never seen the stained-glass windows glow as they did then.'[14]

And this was only the overture. The planes would return night after night, every night except one, 2 November when the weather was too stormy, for sixty-seven consecutive nights. Not only dockland and the East End but the entire city reeled from the Luftwaffe's devastating attacks.

Here is not the place to retell the story of the London Blitz. Suffice to say that the Germans initially thought they could break the RAF as it tried to defend the capital but that the RAF showed them this was an illusion; and that day raids proved too dangerous for the Luftwaffe, which therefore turned to raids under cover of darkness. The human toll was terrible, though not so bad as British officials had feared it would be. To take the country as a whole: from the beginning of August 1940 until the end of May 1941 when at least the sustained bombing campaign had finished, the Germans killed more than 43,000 civilians; they seriously injured about 51,000, and slightly injured perhaps 88,000 more.[15] Still Londoners may be forgiven for having thought that the German Führer was concentrating his malevolent gaze upon them alone. In fact already he was contemplating the invasion of Russia, and 'the sooner the better'. With Russia out of the picture, Hitler believed, Great Britain would have to give up. It is hard to imagine a more griev-ous miscalculation from the Nazi point of view.

Meanwhile a great, if often tragic, chapter in the history of the Thames was being written every day and night by the men of the Luftwaffe who were attacking it, and the men of the RAF who were defending it, and by the civilians who worked and lived near it.

Among the latter consider Alan Patrick Herbert, a tall, lean man who lived in Hammersmith in a house with a garden that reached down to the river. He was a graduate of Winchester and Oxford who had served as a petty officer in the Royal Navy during the First World War. Qualified to practise law, he chose instead to earn a living by his pen. He wrote for *Punch*. He wrote plays and libretti, some of them extremely funny and clever, for the West End theatres. He wrote books, including the classic *Misleading Cases*, which contained mock law reports and bits of real if very odd law, which he punctured by extending to their most absurd limits. From 1935 to 1950, when his seat was abolished, Herbert also acted as one of Oxford University's two independent Members in the House of Commons. There he successfully brought forward legislation to liberalise divorce laws. All the while he wrote poetry as if addicted, slight but witty verses usually, sometimes political, of which the following, dedicated to the people of Germany and their Führer shortly after the Munich settlement of 1938, is a typical example:

> *The Roarer*
>
> Our Roarer is a simple soul, his heart is always bleeding:
> He's kind to his old mother, he is fond of flowers and reading:
> But he has cowed the Continent from Russia to the Riff
> By roaring into microphones and boring people stiff.
>   Oh rally round the Roarer!
>   Our Roarer beats the band;
>   We have a ruder Roarer
>   Than any other land!
>   He'll roar and rant and rage
>   Like something in a cage;
>   He rages, roars and rants

And no one kicks his pants.

The world may sigh and stop its ear,

But everybody has to hear,

And it's so very boring

That all the frantic nations say

'Oh, let the Roarer have his way,

And stop the Roarer roaring.'[16]

For all his other interests, however, it is fair to say that the river was A.P. Herbert's passion. As a young man he taught himself to sail upon its lower reaches, refining his technique by picking up driftwood with one hand while guiding his boat with the other. Soon he was president of the London Corinthian Sailing Club. Eventually he came to own a 38-foot motor launch called the *Water Gypsy*, which he kept tied up at a little pier at the bottom of his garden except when he was on it, exploring the river with his family. He served for thirty years as a member of the Thames Conservancy; he was president of the Inland Waterways Association. He was well known for advocating that London re-establish water buses upon the Thames, a great and underutilised highway he thought; also for advocating construction of a barrage to protect London from tidal surges. This campaign eventually bore fruit in construction of the Thames Barrier, although Herbert would not live to see it.[17]

In 1938 Herbert enrolled in the civilian River Emergency Service, a fleet of private motorboats whose owners drilled in preparation for the coming war. 'But what exactly will you do if a bomb does fall in the river?' friends would press him. 'I shall catch it,' he would reply with characteristic insouciance. During the period of 'phony war', after the fall of France and before the Battle of Britain, Herbert patrolled the lower reaches of the Thames in the *Water Gypsy* for the River Emergency Service, adding to his knowledge of the stream until he knew it fold, from London to the estuary. He helped keep track of incoming traffic.

He could give a 'pluck' or a tow to sailing barges, helping them into docks. But no bombs fell.

Then came the crisis of Dunkirk. Apparently the Port of London Authority sent employees wearing bowler hats and carrying umbrellas to help pull the stranded soldiers from French beaches.[18] More significantly, at this climactic moment in the nation's history the Thames sent over nearly all the boats it had: tugs, sail and motor barges, 'butterfly boats', shrimping bawleys, pleasure launches and yachts, fireboats, eight hundred Thames lifeboats, even one of Joseph Bazalgette's famous sludge hoppers. Herbert longed to go too, with his *Water Gypsy*, but he was kept to his Tideway Patrol. Afterwards the Admiralty merged this unit of the civil defence with the Royal Naval Thames (Auxiliary) Patrol. Most of Herbert's colleagues had to step down, 'but I said "Aye, aye sir"'.[19] He was once again a petty officer in the Navy. His boat received a coat of paint, battleship grey, and armament, and crew. For the duration of the war Herbert would be out on the river night and day. Few saw more of it, or observed it more closely during this crucial period, than he.

On 7 September 1940 he was at home in Hammersmith celebrating his wife's birthday with friends when they became aware of the great blaze downriver. Herbert reported to headquarters by telephone and received a summons to Tower Pier. With one of the party, a member of his crew called Seaman Longstaff, he went straight down to the *Water Gypsy* at the bottom of his garden, cast off and headed downstream. By now it was dark. There were no lights on the bridges but luckily there was no traffic either. Anyway, by the time they had reached Lambeth the great glow emanating from dockland made everything visible. They passed the Houses of Parliament, shining as if illuminated by floodlights. They were closer now to the action. Bombs whistled overhead. 'One felt a little naked and presumptuous alone with a tin hat in the middle of the lighted river,' Herbert admitted. But he did not think of turning back.

At the headquarters barge below London Bridge he received further instructions: get some wire from a lighter in the Pool of London and take it to Woolwich ten miles downstream for towing burning barges. The Pool itself, Herbert noted, was bright as 'Piccadilly Circus in the good old days', lit by fires the Germans had set raging throughout east London. At least that made it easy enough to find the lighter and pick up the wire. But the crew gave him dismaying news. He would never reach Woolwich. It was impossible to get past the Surrey Docks where, as we know, the Germans had set more than a million and a half tons of timber blazing. Herbert and Longstaff set off anyway.

Their journey brought them right into the centre of the maelstrom created by the Nazi bombers. Towers of flames raged along half a mile of the Surrey shore. Sparks and smoke, swept by a westerly wind, formed an incandescent cloud all the way across the river. 'We put wet towels round our faces,' Herbert recorded, and steamed directly into it. Inside the cloud, across from the Surrey Docks, burning barges drifted everywhere, yellow flames on black water. Fires roared on either bank, but the dense smoke and steam rendered them invisible, though not inaudible. In fact the air was full of crackling and hissing. Sparks whirled overhead. 'It was something to be the only boat in Hell.' Herbert's knowledge of the river came in handy now. He could not see, for the smoke, but steering by compass he brought the *Water Gypsy* through. A bomb dropped only thirty yards ahead of them. But Herbert delivered the wire.

It was not so dramatic and dangerous every night along the London reaches of the Thames, but whatever the drama and danger Herbert was in or near it. He was now carrying mail from London down to the estuary every other day and back to London the next. He loved the river's every twist and turn; its injuries pained him; he wrote almost as if he thought it a living thing. 'Day by day we saw the wounds of the river increasing.' He meant the tugs wrecked, piers demolished, colliers and merchantmen sunk, riverside houses, pubs and inns destroyed. The

Germans dropped mines into the stream from the Nore all the way up to London. All too often these lay undetected until a ship passed over, and set them off.

Every other night, having delivered his mail downstream, Herbert moored his boat in Sea Reach perhaps thirty-five miles east of the metropolis. It would be silent and dark, until the sirens went off. Then the German planes bound for London would roar over the little *Water Gypsy*, and the guns at Hole Haven and Southend would open up with terrific noise, and shrapnel would clatter on to the deck or fall hissing into the water. Herbert could trace the progress of the bombers as searchlights flashed in a westward progress along the river all the way up to London, and then far in the distance, too far to hear, he would see the ghostly flicker of shells as anti-aircraft guns in the capital fired at the enemy; and then the same sequence would repeat but in reverse as the Luftwaffe, twisting and dodging among the searchlights, retraced its journey down the river over his boat and out to sea, until it was dark and silent again.

During the first year of war more than four and a half million tons of shipping were lost, most of which had been destined for London. London's seaborne commerce declined to a quarter of pre-war levels. Still, the coastal trade remained strong and the port continued to function in spite of all. Convoys continued to sail, 3367 of them, 84,297 ships outward bound from London over the course of the war.[20] If the Thames was Germany's guideline into London it was also one of England's most crucial lifelines. Had the Germans really been able to block it up and to destroy the storage and distribution facilities, the consequences would have been enormous, possibly fatal. In this sense the destiny of the river, of London and of the country were inextricably enmeshed. Everyone knew it.

Even on the first day of the London Blitz it seemed as if Hermann Goering was reaching towards such an understanding of the battle, viewing the fate of England through the prism of city and river. 'This afternoon the Luftwaffe attacked the port and city of London for the first time with strong forces' reads the German air force communiqué of 7 September 1940. 'One single huge smoke cloud is spreading out from the centre of London towards the Thames estuary.'[21]

German officers must have conflated the fates of Thames, London and Britain in the briefings they delivered to Luftwaffe pilots prior to bombing runs, for certainly individual crewmen did so. For example, a pilot of Luftflotte 2, flying a Heinkel 111 nicknamed 'Monika', remembered the approach to London 'along the river Thames above silver-lined cloud mountains'. He remembered what London looked like burning beneath his aeroplane, 'a dazzling grim sight – tens, no hundreds of fires, too many to count'. He remembered imagining the devastation below: 'explosions in the factories, the bursting of the gasworks, the wailing of the sirens, the clattering of broken glass, the roaring of the flames and the hollow sound of buildings tumbling down'. None of this troubled him. Rather: 'we were thinking about the riches that had been amassed since time immemorial along the many kilometres of the river Thames in huge warehouses, wheat silos, oil reserves – everything that England now needed in large quantities for war. And then there were the formidable docks, which the island kingdom needed for its indispensable merchant navy.' Destroy the cluster of targets lining London's river and you would destroy England too. The bombardier dropped his lethal load, suddenly the aeroplane was lighter and easier to steer. 'Monika' had done her bit in this most crucial theatre of the war.[22]

The Reich Minister of Propaganda, Joseph Goebbels, sought to make the entire German nation understand these links: England–London–Thames–dockland. His office released a photograph of another Heinkel 111 flying over the great bend in the river round the Isle of Dogs, 'Zielraum [target area] G'. It shows a daytime raid, in fact ostensibly the raid of 7 September. The London Docks lie immediately beneath the aeroplane, the Surrey Docks below and a little to the right, the India and Millwall Docks a little further still to the right, where the Isle of Dogs juts into the river. It is an arresting image and a famous one that has been reproduced many times since the war: England prostrate beneath the German eagle's wings, but an England compressed into river and docks which symbolise the whole. The London Thames stood for everything Goebbels wished to destroy. (But in fact he had doctored the image to make the point. The Heinkel is superimposed upon an earlier photograph, taken before 1939, when there had been no cover over the north terrace of 'The Den', the ground of Millwall Football Club.)[23]

In September 1940 the river stood for Britain in the minds of the Germans. It did so for English too. A.P. Herbert said it in his own inimitable fashion. Traditionally invaders of Britain had gathered at the estuary and followed the Thames up to London. So, in 1940, had the Germans, but in aeroplanes, high above the stream. They understood less of the water than their predecessors. England would survive such ignorant would-be invaders. Herbert wrote to Hitler:

> *Invasion*
> Napoleon tried. The Dutch were on the way,
> A Norman did it – and a Dane or two.
> Some sailor King may follow one fine day:
> But not, I think, a low land-rat like you.

The RAF would not allow the German Luftwaffe to gain mastery of English skies. High above the winding Thames it mounted a stubborn, bitter, slashing resistance. The German onslaught on dockland faltered. It did not come to a complete end until the war itself had ended, and in the war's later stages 'doodlebugs' and V2 rockets provided fresh horrors, but after September 1940 with every passing day the possibility of invasion diminished. An extraordinary chapter in the history of the river was over, but another chapter, equally important, was beginning.

Goebbel's famous image suggesting England, symbolized by the Thames and London docks, prostrate beneath the wings of the German Eagle. But he had doctored the image. The Heinkel 111 is superimposed upon an earlier photograph, taken before 1939, when there had been no cover over the north terrace of Millwall Football Club's ground. (German Bomber/CORBIS)

With the invasion of Russia in June 1941, Hitler opened the Pandora's box of a two-front war for Germany. A quick victory would have shut it again, but after initial confusion and setbacks the Soviets proved at least as formidable on the ground as the English in the air. The German armies spread terror and atrocity in their wake as they raced east, but they could not take Leningrad or Moscow, and finally they confronted nemesis at Stalingrad. There they fought and froze and suffered beyond human endurance, until at last those who remained alive surrendered. The Russian army thirsted for revenge. Soon it would begin its pitiless inexorable march on Berlin. And meanwhile, far to the west, Hitler's other enemies were preparing to launch the second front. For the moment England's river was not at the centre of the action, but in the preparations for D-Day the men who worked along the Thames continued to play a crucial role. During the early phases of the war the river had proven that England could 'take it'; now it would prove that England could 'dish it out'.

We are all familiar with what happened on D-Day itself, 6 June 1944, when Allied troops finally landed on the beaches of Normandy and began to fight their way towards the Russians who were advancing from the east. Many, however, fail to appreciate the planning, organisation, invention and labour upon which the success of the D-Day soldiers depended. The logistics were complex enough: preparing and coordinating vast convoys of ships with men and matériel. Moreover such puzzles, once solved, would require millions of man-hours of labour to implement. And there were other problems too: for example, how to land the men and all their equipment on beaches where there were no docks? How to transport tanks, jeeps and other vehicles from ship to shore? How to provide fuel for their engines once they were ashore? The answers to these questions emerged from the very Thames-side docks the Germans had sought to destroy.

There were no harbours where the Americans and British intended to land in Normandy. Very well: English engineers designed giant prefabricated temporary ones, each referred to as a 'Mulberry', since that was the next available name on the Admiralty's List of Ship's Names from which codenames were chosen. Along the Thames, between Barking and Erith, where the land lay below river level and had to be protected by a great river wall, gangs of men dug out the turf in great squares and rectangles, and then cast immense concrete floorings where the turf had been. They knocked holes in the river wall, pried the floorings up, and pushed them through the holes. Tugboats pulled them down the river into the East India and Surrey and Tilbury Docks, where only a few short years before the German bombs had rained down. In these docks the men built watertight compartments, concrete caissons, over the floorings. They built five miles of them, weighing 668,000 tons in all. Then the tugboats towed and pushed the caissons from the docks into the river and down to the sea, where sailors pulled plugs letting in water so that they sank. The Germans never saw them, never knew precisely what was coming. Shortly before D-Day, however, the Allies pumped the water out of the caissons so that they rose to the surface again, and the Navy pulled them across the Channel to Arromanches and elsewhere. The caissons became the building blocks of 135 Mulberry harbours in all.

The famous 'Pluto' project, equally vital to the success of the D-Day landings, also took shape in the London docks. This was the famous Pipeline Under The Ocean, which, on the appointed day, would stretch from England's south coast all the way across the Channel to Cherbourg, supplying fuel to the Allied armies once they were on the beaches. The pipes were coiled on enormous floating reels called 'conundrums'. Just prior to the great day, tugs towed the 'conundrums' downriver and along the coast to where they needed to be.[24] A.P. Herbert saw them floating by. He could not imagine what they were.

And the Thames supplied many of the ships for D-Day as well. The great shipbuilding firms had long since departed London's river, but craft building and ship repair yards remained. As early as spring 1942, the craft-building shops were busy churning out wooden motor launches and sweepers (immune to magnetic mines). The repair shops were preparing landing craft. They cut the ends off lighters and 'dumb barges' never meant to go to sea, and fitted them with collapsible ramps, bridges, wheels, engines and propellers. A.P. Herbert watched these developments with satisfaction. He wrote:

> But they took them old lighters, a thousand or more;
> They cut out the ends and they put in a door;
> They gave 'em a wheel, and a motor so fine,
> And painted 'em camyflarge like a ship of the line.

The repair yards adapted other boats to different purposes. 'The vessels produced were diverse in size and type, but one feature was common to all,' writes a historian of the port, 'they were . . . designed for use in an offensive.'[25]

All along the Thames 'from Teddington to Southend one began to smell the spirit of attack', Herbert remembered. The river and its people were finally preparing to strike back. In early 1944 Thames lightermen were signing up to bring those strange vessels across the Channel. Herbert wrote of these volunteers:

> They came up from Tilbury, they came down from Kew,
> From the 'Prospect of Whitby', and the 'Dog and Duck' too,
> From Gallions, from Bugsby's from Bow Creek and all,
> For to help the Royal Navy crack up the West Wall.[26]

And now he began to see American stars and stripes fluttering from new ships, 'LSTs', capable of carrying and disgorging on the beaches of France as many as thirty tanks at a time. He noticed dockers loading even little Thames coasters with boxes of ammunition and oil drums. He saw big transport steamers, packed with military vehicles and men in khaki.

Every day and night a vast concourse of ships sailed up to London to take on men and cargo, and then back down the river to anchor off Southend Pier or below, in preparation for the great day. The port was busy as never before and the Thames was becoming again what it had been before the war, a great flowing highway, only now bearing primarily ships of war not commerce.

It required a massive effort from the men who worked on and alongside the Thames, loading and unloading literally tens of thousands of vessels during the months leading up to D-Day. Their labour was as much a prerequisite of success on 6 June as the invention of the Mulberry harbours and Pluto; and the hectic period leading up to that date, more even than autumn 1940, was to constitute their finest hour. But dock labour always had been, and was still, dangerous, difficult and exhausting; and since 1889 Thames dockers and stevedores had grown famous for the strength of their organisation, the depth of their militancy, the intensity of their class-consciousness. Did they, then, during the months and weeks surrounding 6 June, lay aside the old social antagonisms? Were they inspired by 'the spirit of Dunkirk'?

A number of historians have argued that 'the spirit of Dunkirk' was hardly as widespread as popular post-war myth would have it.[27] And it is true that class-consciousness did not disappear among dock workers during the Second World War. The union continued to defend its members with zeal. It negotiated a national wage rise of a shilling per day at the start of the war. Even at the height of the Blitz it engaged in ongoing negotiations with employers to 'raise the minimum wage of tippers, teemers [unloaders], weighers, hoistmen and boxmen' who moved goods from dockside warehouses to railway freight cars.[28]

It might well be thought that three years of war would do little to improve mood or morale among dockers or their union negotiators or anyone else. But among London's riverside workers, at least, morale did improve, in part because Winston Churchill had appointed their union's leader, Ernest Bevin, to be Minister of Labour. One of Bevin's first moves was a long-cherished scheme to establish dock labour on a permanent rather than a casual basis. Men would be paid a regular wage whether or not ships appeared for loading and unloading on a given day. For the first time in history the needs and hopes of Thames dockers were well represented within the corridors of power.

And then, as Britain's soldiers and sailors prepared for the last great push, the government discovered an evangelist of hard work as the precondition to victory who, for the moment, eclipsed even Ernest Bevin in popularity among London dockworkers. This was none other than the hero of the North African campaign and current chief among all British military personnel, General (later Field Marshal) Bernard Montgomery himself, an old friend of A.P. Herbert as it happened. With the details of the Normandy invasion settled he had undertaken a lightning tour of the troops, aboard a special train called the 'Rapier'. He intended to address every soldier who would be taking part in D-Day. But soon he was addressing as well the workers upon whom the soldiers relied. On 3 March he spoke to 16,000 Thames dockers, his words relayed round the port through loudspeakers. There is no record of his speech among his papers or in the contemporary press, but two weeks later he spoke at the Mansion House along what must have been similar lines.

'Can you imagine this conversation in after years?' Montgomery asked his audience:

'What did you do in the World War?'
   'I pulled hard to start with; but after a time I began to lose interest and let go the rope. I thought I wanted a rest; and I wanted more pay.'
   'And did you win?'
   'No. We lost. I let go the rope and we lost the match. God forgive me; we lost the match.'

Montgomery posed a second question to his audience: 'Is it possible that such a conversation could apply to us British?' He answered himself: 'No. It is impossible. Thank God it is impossible.'[29] It is likely he asked the same questions of the dockers, and provided them with the same answers. We know that he told them their labour was indispensable to victory. Here is the summary of his speech as it appeared in newspapers the next day: 'Together . . . the workers . . . and he and the soldiers would see the war through right to the very end.'[30]

When he finished speaking the dockers escorted him back to his car singing 'For He's a Jolly Good Fellow'.[31] Then they returned to work. It was appropriate that the men who had borne the brunt of Hitler's wrath at the beginning of the war should now provide the material for victory over him; that the river, which Germany's Führer had conceived as a guideline leading to Britain's soft underbelly, finally should demonstrate its muscle. Between January and March, 6626 ships came up and down the Thames; between April and June, 10,609; between July and September 11,024. The dockers loaded every one of them. Sometimes they worked for forty hours at a stretch. Montgomery had appealed to 'the spirit of Dunkirk' among them and it had worked. 'Not a single vessel has been held up or delayed through the action of the port workers,' the union journal reported proudly.[32]

Far from having to be abandoned during the war, ultimately the river had proven itself an asset. Its docks had been a tempting target, but they could not be destroyed; eventually they played their part in the great counter-attack. The men and women who lived near its banks had bowed but never broken; they too assumed a crucial role in the preparations for opening up a second front. If at first German pilots had followed its giant looping course to the primary target area, dockland, then later British and American ships followed the Thames back east towards France – and Germany. At the height of the Blitz its winding form, beneath the German bomber, had assumed the lineaments of a national symbol. We may almost imagine that the river coiled and flexed on 5 June 1944, the day before D-Day, like some vast water serpent, and then shot off the ten thousand allied vessels all the way to Normandy. The river had its revenge when it provided the sinews of victory.

10

Blue River

The Second World War marked Britain for ever and led to profound changes. The socialist Labour Party governed for six years after 1945, for five of them with an unassailable majority in the House of Commons. It embarked upon a massive programme of reform: nationalisation of major industries, erection of a generous welfare state. 'We are the masters now,' one Labourite warned honourable Members opposite, and when Conservatives broke into 'For He's a Jolly Good Fellow' upon catching sight of Winston Churchill entering the debating chamber, Labour drowned them out with a rendition of the 'Internationale'. Eventually Conservatives made their peace with the new ethos, even embraced aspects of it; when they regained political power in 1951, they largely accepted the 'Revolution of 1945'.

It was harder to accept Britain's reduced role in the world, and for a time some politicians of both major parties made their careers by pretending that in this regard nothing much had happened. Even during the war, however, Britain had been the obvious junior partner among the Big Three: British diplomats had consoled themselves by imagining that their country would play Greece to America's Rome. After the

war the Labour Foreign Secretary, Ernest Bevin, pushed hard and successfully for America to take up Britain's leading role in world affairs.
Meanwhile the retreat from empire had commenced: first from India
and Ceylon and Burma, ultimately from just about everywhere.
Eventually a Conservative prime minister acknowledged the 'winds of
change' blowing from Africa. To many Britons it seemed an ill breeze.

But some things do not change. The river continued to flow past
Westminster as always; certain customs, ceremonies, habits, including
habits of mind, lingered, in fact demonstrated great tenacity. Perhaps
after so many years of turmoil Britons took comfort in reviving or
returning to them. We may view the re-establishment of one tradition
immediately after the war in this context at any rate.

On Saturday morning, 30 March 1946, a perfect spring day, with the
sun shining through a thin mist and a light breeze blowing from the
south-east, two rowing eights bobbed upon the Thames at Putney. One
crew wore light blue and represented Cambridge University; the other
wore dark blue and represented Oxford. They were about to race each
other upstream to Mortlake, a distance of 4¼ miles, with the incoming
tide to speed them. This was the first Oxford–Cambridge Boat Race
since 1939, but the two universities had competed on an irregular basis
beginning in 1829 and annually since 1856; now thousands of spectators
eager to see the rivalry renewed had gathered at the starting and end
points of the course, and lined the towpath between, just as they had
done every year for eighty years before the war. Perhaps that morning
they had read *The Times*, which anticipating large crowds had reminded
readers 'to start early and if possible to choose a route avoiding
Hammersmith Broadway . . . Diversions of road traffic will be sign-
posted.' Not only Britons were anxious to witness the contest. So many
European journalists and commentators arrived in Putney that the
BBC had to find them an extra motor launch to follow the race for
broadcasting commentary.

At precisely 11 a.m. the umpire intoned the famous words: 'I shall ask

Hammersmith Bridge on Boat-race Day: an annual tradition that world wars might disrupt but could not destroy. (*Hammersmith Bridge on Boat-race Day 1862*/ Walter Greaves (1849–1930)/Tate, London 2004

you once if you're ready. If I get no reply I shall say "Go." If you are not ready please shout and raise your hand.' Nobody spoke or moved. The oarsmen, their backs angled forward, their knees bent, and their blades poised behind them, waited for the signal. The crowd was silent. The tension grew. Then the umpire gave his command and the men with the blades exploded into action, like so many tightened springs releasing simultaneously. Oxford, well trained but not favoured to win, in fact generally expected to lose because it was the lighter and smaller crew, took an early lead, held off a Cambridge charge later in the race, and flashed first past the finish line to claim victory.

So resumed an annual tradition with attendant rituals at a moment when one might have thought popular currents would be running all the other way. But then the Oxford–Cambridge Boat Race is a tradition whose meaning transcends the sporting contest it appears to be; in fact it is better understood not simply as a competition but as a bundle of meanings, most of them having to do with class and with Englishness. Twice since the Second World War these larger meanings have come to the fore, the first time to provide just a glimpse of some of what lay beneath the surface whenever the light and dark blues raced on the river, the second time to make more clearly visible things we might rather not have seen. In 1959 and then again in 1987 the Oxford crews 'mutinied' against their captains and coaches. These outbreaks hardly compare in importance with the real sailors' mutiny of 1797 when lives and perhaps England's future were at stake. Of course they pale in comparison with the subject of our preceding chapter, the London Blitz. Nevertheless both little 'mutinies', were revealing episodes in the social and cultural history of post-1945 Britain. And once again the river runs right through them.

The great figure in the post-war Boat Race world at Oxford was Hugh Robert Arthur 'Jumbo' Edwards. An accomplished oarsman who won a record three medals in a day at the Henley Regatta of 1931 and two medals on a single day at the 1932 Olympics, a racer of aeroplanes who placed second in the King's Cup air race of 1933, he made a career with the RAF rising to become squadron commander during the war. Afterwards he combined his interests in flying and rowing. In 1948 he helped to coach the RAF crew, in 1949 he helped to coach Oxford for the first time. During the early 1950s he coached Oxford more frequently. Still a member of the RAF and stationed in the headquarters of the 2nd Tactical Air Force at Bad Eilsen, he would regularly pilot his own plane to England for the afternoon to consult with other coaches, to help select the crew and to deal with any problems. He would then fly back to Germany in time for dinner. He would make the round trip seven times per academic year starting in October. 'I was never late.'[1]

Group Captain Edwards was one who regretted Britain's changed status in the world. He thought his country's recent losing record at the

Olympics and recent loss of international power and prestige were linked.

> When Great Britain won [the Olympics, rowing] in 1908 and 1912, our empire was intact, the vaults of the Bank of England were bulging with gold bullion, and for home defence alone our fleets consisted of eight battle squadrons of eight battleships each, together with their attendant cruiser squadrons, flotillas and auxiliaries . . . In those days we had not suffered the humiliation of having oil refineries and canals stolen by Moussadeq and Nasser and seeing the empire frittered away.[2]

He thought that England's post-1945 racing crews must recapture at least their former self-assurance if they hoped to win international competitions. He was confident they would recapture it. 'The British spirit will never die. It appears to flourish best when we have our backs to the wall and are outnumbered or at a disadvantage.'[3]

On the other hand, when it came to rowing Edwards was more than willing to experiment. 'Tradition is a wonderful thing but it must never be allowed to block progress,' he once wrote.[4] Richard Burnell, author of Edwards's entry in the *Dictionary of National Biography* and himself a former Oxford oarsman, judged that 'many of the technical innovations of modern rowing stemmed from [him] . . . the development of long oars and "spade" blades . . . "interval training" . . . the use of ergometers . . . strain gauges, accelerometers, and trace records . . .'

A traditionalist but also an innovator: possibly the contradiction worked against the success of the man who would coach the Oxford crew nineteen times during 1949–72. Some Old Blues (as former oarsmen for Oxford in the race against Cambridge were called) disliked his willingness to experiment, or thought he favoured the wrong rowing techniques. Others believed him to be a poor judge of men. In 1958 the treasurer of the university boat club described him as 'a crank'.[5] Some considered Group Captain Edwards a bit of a martinet. He would have been more popular if he had been more successful. But during the nineteen years he served as coach, Oxford won the Boat Race only five times.

In 1958 Edwards coached both the first Blue boat and the back-up Oxford crew, whose boat was called Isis. With the latter he was successful for a change. Indeed many thought Isis faster and better coached than the first Blue boat, which had been built around a graduate of Yale University, Reed Rubin, a 'massive American' (he was 6 feet 4 inches tall).[6] Yet in 1958, Rubin notwithstanding, the dark blues lost to Cambridge once again. In the twelve years since the war Oxford had won only in 1946, 1952 and 1954. This dismal record now provided the backdrop to an ill-tempered six-month-long fracas among Oxford boating circles, one that cracked open a door on certain sentiments and attitudes that otherwise might have remained hidden. If we listen carefully through the crack to the contending voices of 1959 we may hear the ugly sounds of class prejudice and anti-Semitism; of course we also hear their opposites.

How to reverse the losing streak? Reed Rubin believed that Oxford placed too much emphasis on physical fitness and not enough on rowing techniques.[7] He believed the university should import American coaches, more specifically the coaches who had so successfully trained the Yale crew (which had gone on to win the Olympics); also that the head Oxford coach should be sent to America before the Yale–Harvard race, to see American coaching methods for himself. As it happened, all the returning crew members of the first Oxford boat agreed with him. With their unanimous support Rubin stood for president of the Oxford University Boat Club (OUBC) on this platform. Had he won he would have been responsible for picking coach and crew.

Standing against him was a Worcester College oarsman, Ronnie Howard, who had rowed in 1958 for Isis under Jumbo Edwards, 'the only

Oxford coach I considered to be really first class'.[8] Howard agreed with
Rubin that Oxford should emphasise 'how to row properly' over mere
endurance training.[9] His plan was to put Edwards, who had left the RAF
and could focus exclusively upon coaching, in charge of the Blue boat
from beginning to end. This was an innovation in British practice, where
coaches, who volunteered their time, rarely did more than two- or three-
week stints; it was, in fact, the way the Americans organised things. But
there was no need actually to import American coaches, according to
Howard, nor for Edwards to visit the US and take tuition there, although
he could certainly consult with Americans if he wished.

It seemed a straightforward election. The electorate consisted exclusively of the thirty-five or so Oxford college boat club captains
(unfortunately for Rubin his support among resident Old Blues did
not translate directly into ballots); and when the ballots were tallied
Howard emerged as winner, although by the slimmest of margins, only
a single vote. So it was Howard not Rubin who now bore responsibility
for picking the crew of the 1959 Blue boat, and for choosing the coach.

Things might have rested thus. Howard did what he had promised to
do and appointed Jumbo Edwards to be head coach. He assumed Rubin
would form part of the crew. But the American and his supporters felt
too deeply to leave the matter alone. They tried to persuade Edwards to
adopt Yale methods. He refused. They tried to persuade Howard to drop
Edwards and to replace him with a Yale coach after all, or even with
Rubin himself. Howard turned a deaf ear. Stymied, Rubin and his allies
consulted once more, and agreed the fatal 'mutinous' step. They would
prepare a crew of their own, trained the Yale way. It would consist of all
the returning Old Blues including Jonathan Hall, secretary of the
OUBC, and David Edwards, Jumbo's own son, and as many new recruits
as necessary. One of these would be Charlie Grimes, another American
and former Yale crewmate of Rubin's, who had rowed with the victorious US Olympic team in 1956 and who arrived in Oxford to study law at
the beginning of the 1958–9 academic year.

On behalf of his 'pirate crew', as the newspapers already were calling it, Rubin challenged Howard to race. If his crew won, it would represent Oxford in the annual contest with Cambridge; if it lost, then Rubin would retire from the scene, while his followers could choose to row for Howard and Edwards, if the coach and OUBC president would have them. This, then, was the Oxford 'mutiny' of 1959, small beer no doubt in the great scheme of things, but more complex when examined and more revealing of certain unappealing post-war British attitudes than is at first apparent.

The Boat Race is 'a national event,' the Chancellors of Oxford and Cambridge universities had written in 1954.[10] It is 'as much a piece of England as the Downs in Sussex . . . church bells chiming in a country church on Sunday morning, or the sound of carols on the eve of Christmas', agreed Gordon Ross, whose history of the first hundred Boat Races appeared that same year.[11] It seems obvious that Britons might have resented an American claiming to know better than an Oxford coach how best to prepare for this quintessentially English occasion, and we may guess that anti-American sentiment played some role in the Oxford rowing establishment's reaction to a 'mutiny' led, after all, by the US-born Reed Rubin. On the other hand, there is no supporting evidence for this either in the newspapers or in the private papers of the OUBC. Perhaps British resentment was less powerful than British gratitude, which would still have been fresh, for America's role during the war.

At any rate, more than simple national pride lay behind Ronnie Howard's insistence on Jumbo Edwards's freedom of action. Deep-seated attitudes towards class were involved as well. For all that Britain had turned a corner in 1945 it remained a country in which social rank played an important, if decreasingly obvious, role. But it was more obvious at Oxford than in some other places, and more obvious still among the Boat Race community.

Ever since the first organised boat races on rivers in England an

unbridgeable gulf had separated amateur rowers from so-called profes-
sionals. The former were 'gentlemen' (and if from Oxbridge 'the very
pick of the manhood of Young England' according to one fan[12]), the
latter were 'menials', men who actually needed the money they might
win in a race. For example, Thames watermen and lightermen, who
worked the river for a living and who therefore knew better than most
'gentlemen' how to row upon it, were 'menials'. They never mixed in a
single crew with their social superiors; they did not race against them;
they belonged to separate rowing associations. As late as 1936 Henley
Regatta had barred an Australian crew because it included several
policemen; and though the ensuing furore caused even Henley stewards
to change their policy, twenty years later the old attitudes still prevailed, not least in Oxbridge.

The Oxford ideal was 'effortless superiority', a notion stemming from
British aristocratic traditions. For the Oxford crew 'effortless superiority' did not mean no practising, far from it, but it did mean no coaching
from men who accepted money for their tuition. To one not schooled
in this particular British tradition it must have seemed absurd. Reed
Rubin thought that professional coaches (from Yale) must know better
how to train a crew than, say, career air force officers who learned and
taught the sport in their spare time. But to Howard and Edwards and
much of the Oxford racing world a professional coach was unthinkable.
Thus the American found himself challenging a habit of mind that had
survived both the war and the following period of socialist government. If anything the resumption of the Boat Race had strengthened it.

In 1959 the world of the Boat Race seemed frozen in the era of Max
Beerbohm's famous creation, the beautiful Zuleika Dobson, who cut
such a swath through Edwardian Oxford that smitten young men
dropped as if poleaxed (into the Thames) when they saw her. Jumbo
Edwards was its avatar. He extolled as a model the superb racing eights
of St John's College, Cambridge, in 1949–50 which might as well have
dated from half a century before. The crew would appear for dinner

every night, Edwards wrote approvingly, 'immaculately dressed in gleaming white flannels, the original scarlet blazers and bow ties. They were obviously proud of themselves and they had a right to be. Not only could no other crew match them on the river, but they saw to it that no other crew could turn out so smartly ashore.' Later these wonderful oarsmen performed another ceremony taken straight from the halcyon age: 'Every evening after dinner they would gather round a table on the Leander lawn . . . to have their glass of port.'[13]

To those not steeped in British upper-class traditions Edwards's notion of proper conduct must have seemed egregiously anachronistic, possibly comic, or even offensive. Such sceptics would have adopted a different stance. Rubin, for instance, was hardly a 'menial', although perhaps his wealth was derived from trade; nevertheless he took what Edwards might have termed a 'professional's' attitude to the regular tipple. Rubin thought 'The energy and time wasted at the daily boat club sherry party . . . detract[s] from the final effort.'[14] He showed what he thought about the emphasis on sartorial display by turning up for practice in an old grey sweater instead of the uniform dark blue. Or perhaps he was ignorant of the custom; but it was all one to Edwards: 'A crew in which such a lapse can occur is not a good crew, and needless to say they were beaten.' When Charlie Grimes appeared wearing an engineer's cap Edwards insisted that he remove it.

Snobs do not only discriminate on the basis of class, and the Boat Race provided an outlet for ancient atavisms as well as for outdated social prejudices. Reed Rubin's American birth may or may not have stood against him, but he also happened to be Jewish and, as became clear during the run-up to the election for president of the OUBC, there were college boat club captains who would never vote for 'Mr Rubinstein', as Jumbo Edwards apparently had dubbed him. An ugly undercurrent of anti-Semitic innuendo is said to have permeated the campaign for election of the 1959 OUBC president.[15]

There were journalists, too, prepared to suggest, if only obliquely, that the American was a double outsider. Rubin wisely tried to avoid all journalists. 'I could crucify you on the front page of the *Daily Mail* tomorrow,' one of them is supposed to have threatened him. Television crews camped outside Merton College and would not leave until he appeared. Finally 'at about 10:30 p.m. he was angrily accused of "purposely evading the BBC", and was almost ordered to stand in front of the camera for an interview.'[18] He refused. Eventually, however, they wore him down and he agreed to a group session. The results were dismaying. 'Hawk-featured [Reed] Rubin . . . lounged back in his lodgings,' according to the *Daily Express*, 'suede shoes crossed and hands deep in his whipcord slacks.' This was not the attire Jumbo Edwards would have favoured. It was not what one expected an Oxford oarsman to wear. The American was not a gentleman. But then his 'features' betrayed him.[17]

And finally the icing on the cake, a last injustice: for having acceded in this one instance to the demands of the media we learn from the editor of the *British Rowing Almanack* that Rubin had supported his position 'by all the modern techniques of public relations including press-conferences'.[18] So he was pushy too.

In the end Rubin and the Old Blues backed down. They did not train as a 'pirate crew' after all. Rubin withdrew rather deftly, announcing merely that traditionally Americans did not race during their last year at Oxford. So the foreigner understood at least one tradition after all. Grimes withdrew as well, ostensibly because he could not bear to part with his engineer's cap, really because he did not wish to row for Edwards. Ronnie Howard brought all the other Old Blues back into the fold. In the end the traditional rivalry meant too much to them; they could not forgo the annual contest with Cambridge. On Boat Race day, Oxford won. If it was Edwards's greatest coaching triumph it was a victory for certain traditional attitudes as well.

The atavistic, class-ridden rhetoric that had sounded in comparatively muffled tones in 1959 blared like a klaxon at Oxford in 1987, when university oarsmen launched a second, bigger rebellion. Again Americans were ringleaders and this time their nationality did become an issue. But again let us be clear: this 'mutiny' ranks as a significant historic event no more than the first. Amidst the hubbub it produced, however, one may hear a rumbling, grumbling assertion of English identity late in the twentieth century.

During the second 'Crisis on the Isis', as the newspapers called this one, the Oxford coach was Daniel Topolski, son of a well-known East European artist, himself a photojournalist who travelled in artistic and bohemian circles — and a Jew. This seems as far from Group Captain Jumbo Edwards as may be; it is evidence of progressive evolution in Oxford, indeed in England, since 1959. And yet . . .

The bare outlines of the 'mutiny' may be recounted quickly. Under coach Topolski Oxford had experienced a great revival on the river, winning the Boat Race ten times in a row. They lost, however, in 1986. Chris Clark, an American on the losing team who had rowed for his country in the Pan Am Games, went home over the summer holiday to scout for talent. He returned in the fall with four oarsmen from the American national crew whom Oxford colleges obligingly agreed to admit: Daniel Lyons (Oriel), Chris Huntington and the coxswain Jonathan Fish (Mansfield), and Chris Penny (St John's). Here is a sign not of progressive but of regressive evolution at Oxford since 1959: Rubin and Grimes had been legitimate students; in 1987 the Americans came to Oxford to row. With the exception of Penny, a Princeton graduate who hoped to earn an M.Phil. in medieval history (he never did), they enrolled in one-year postgraduate courses that if successfully completed would lead to receipt of a diploma, not a degree.[19]

The Americans arrived with rowing accomplishments under their belts and egos worn on their sleeves. They were America's top rowers, trained by America's best coaches: they knew it and they said so. Perhaps Chris Clark displayed his sense of superiority most blatantly for he was to become a magnet for criticism later. At any rate the five recruits quickly concluded that Dan Topolski was a dinosaur so far as his coaching methods were concerned. Like most Oxford coaches he mainly emphasised fitness training. When Jonathan Fish saw Topolski's training schedule he immediately complained to OUBC president Donald McDonald. When Daniel Lyons saw it he exclaimed: 'That is more training than we did for the World Championships.'[20] Their coach ignored them.

The Americans thought that Topolski did not understand how fitness training should proceed anyway. Perhaps they were right. Eventually one of the Oxford coaches acknowledged that 'they knew a lot [more than we did] about the physiology of training and the benefits the various types of training had'.[21] But here too, Topolski turned a deaf ear. Then, the Americans, like Rubin and Grimes before them, wanted much more emphasis placed on rowing technique; and again perhaps they were right. 'When we rowed they searched for perfection in their blade-work,' a British crew member, Gavin Stewart, remembered. 'It was a new experience for a lot of us because for the most we'd been taught rowing by Topolski and the emphasis had been on hard work . . .'[22] But the coach made no concessions on this score either.

Resentment simmered; during one particularly heavy practice the Americans simply beached their boat and walked away. But there was another source of friction. Topolski placed OUBC president and Blue boat captain Donald McDonald in a key bow-side position, although that meant moving Chris Clark to stroke side and dropping from the Blue boat altogether a second oarsman, Tony Ward. The American vociferously objected; the entire crew thought the head coach was playing favourites, sacrificing boat speed in the process. Lyons and an English oarsman, Richard Hull, put it to McDonald: he must give up his place among the crew for the greater good. For three days, 19–21 January, the Oxford crew trained on the river with Clark at bow side, Ward at stroke side, and their captain on the bank. 'We are rocket fuel,' Chris Penny famously observed of this combination. But McDonald, who knew that the OUBC president alone had legal power to pick his crew, called a meeting of Oxford coaches and a sprinkling of influential Old Blues (including Ronnie Howard, who had experience of mutinous Americans). After taking their advice he emerged a few hours later to announce that it was not himself, nor even Tony Ward, who would be dropped from the boat, but the irritating Mr Clark.

Now the real 'mutiny' commenced. The four Americans remaining on the Blue boat informed McDonald that they would not row with him under any circumstances. Clark, of course, was out as well. Of the British-born crew only medical student Tom Cadoux-Hudson supported the president unambiguously. All the rest agitated hard for McDonald's removal. At an Oxford Union debate they gained a respectful hearing: 'This house believes that the Oxford University Boat Club has mishandled the organization of the Boat Race crew.' The resolution passed by 153 to 10. Emboldened, the rebels pushed for a meeting of the college captains. They hoped for a similar vote of 'no confidence' in McDonald's leadership which might lead to a reshuffling of the crew. The meeting took place, but the captains voted in favour of McDonald by a margin of 28–11.

The Oxford rowing world was in ferment and yet, as in 1959, with the coaches and college captains backing the president the outcome of the dispute could not be doubted. McDonald might nourish hopes that the Americans, *sans* Clark, would return to the crew. (They never did.) He was confident that the Britons would. It was harder for them to relinquish all hope of participating in the great Oxford–Cambridge Boat Race than it was for foreigners who had already won international and Olympic medals. One by one the British oarsmen trickled back, although Gavin Stewart first resigned the vice-presidency of the OUBC to demonstrate his frustration. Of course hardly anyone thought that Oxford without the Americans could beat Cambridge.

By 1987 the popularity of the Boat Race had declined since its heyday; on the other hand, those who still did care about the race cared intensely.

When the rebel American oarsmen failed to follow the precedent of Reed Rubin and Charles Grimes and swallow their discontent, they provoked a genuine storm in certain circles; and these were circles with access to the media, or even representing the media, so that radio and television commentators, journalists, even leader writers, not to mention innumerable letter writers, soon were debating definitions of sportsmanship and good manners, and more. From this tempest the 1987 Oxford Boat Race 'mutiny' crystallised a sense of the national virtues and world-view, that is to say of the national identity. Like the Thames during the frost fairs two hundred years earlier, so during the great Boat Race imbroglio of 1987: the river provided more than backdrop to the event; it was like a great mirror reflecting the nation, or at least one important view of it.

Part of Britain's problem with the US rebels was their style: understatement was not their forte. Numerous examples of American boastfulness could be cited but one will suffice here, Jonathan Fish in *The Times*, speaking of his countrymen: they could provide the nucleus of 'the fastest Boat Race crew ever'.[23] Britons winced at this sort of thing. I have not found similar statements by any British rower, but 'a former Oxford college oarsman' wrote a letter to *The Times* denigrating American 'self-opinionated arrogance'.[24] And Topolski, writing of his American tormentors but perhaps thinking also of two Americans at Wimbledon, Jimmy Connors and John McEnroe, referred almost despairingly to 'the new brattishness which has been abroad in sport'.[25]

Then the American rowers seemed to be culturally tone-deaf. For long Oxford rowers had thought Topolski's training regimen too harsh, but British-born oarsmen did not publicly question, let alone defy, their coaches.[26] Crew members had been unhappy with the archaic constitution, and particularly with the voting rules, of the OUBC for years, but had done nothing about them. The Americans, confident, brash, oblivious, simply charged straight ahead. They publicly defied their coach. After their defeat at the meeting of the college captains they called for 'changing the constitution of Oxford University Boat Club before next year's race', so that the meeting could be reconvened and the no-confidence vote could be called again, but this time with Old Blues and crew members voting.[27]

Perhaps needless to say, traditionalists were aghast not merely at their behaviour but at their presumption. The leader-writer of the *Daily Telegraph* noted that five Americans in the Blue boat would constitute a bloc vote. 'As the more articulate trade unionists say after they have rigged a ballot: "This was a decision reached democratically by our democratically elected members."' As if college captains might not constitute blocs also. As if there would always be five Americans in the Blue boat. As if it was a positive good that oarsmen should remain permanently voiceless. The leader-writer made no apologies. He preferred the OUBC's traditional 'autocracy'.[28]

The old class biases resurfaced too. It now was recalled that whatever their technical status the Americans were not legitimate students pursuing legitimate degrees, but rather hired guns brought to Oxford for a single purpose. They were practically professional oarsmen. If they had kept quiet and rowed there would have been no trouble, but they were brash and contentious. Suddenly the rowing world discovered it was time, as OUBC president Donald McDonald said, 'to get strategic oarsmen limitation talks going'.[29]

Here it is necessary to draw distinctions. Among the minority who cared deeply about the Boat Race no doubt some genuinely pined for the lost purity of university sports. Beneath other lamentations, however, lay a different sentiment. 'Why do not the appropriate authorities make a ruling that no one may take part in an Oxford v Cambridge match or race who is not an undergraduate in residence?' asked a reader of the *Daily Telegraph*, reasonably enough. But then he added: 'And while we are at it let's get rid of the coaches too.'[30] Running through the public discussion of the Oxford boat crew 'mutiny' was that same red thread of snobbery displayed by upper-class Englishmen for the past century and more. A vocal contingent still believed in the ideal of 'effortless superiority', as if there was something demeaning about working at a sport. The Americans, with their professional attitude towards rowing, were not gentlemen. The *Times* rowing correspondent thought they were employing 'business-school methods' out of place at Oxford University.[31] A student at the Oxford Union debate said it clearly: 'A professional ethos has been forced on them [Dark Blues] . . . The Boat Race has lost the English sense of sporting innocence.'[32]

It is hardly surprising that American oarsmen who did not under-stand British self-deprecation, or unique British Boat Race traditions, also failed to appreciate the distinctions so beloved by certain snobs. Here the clash between modern American professionalism and old-fashioned British ideals was most stark. When the Americans said that the coaching they were receiving at Oxford was outmoded a columnist riposted disdainfully that they found 'it hard to work with any coach other than the sort of $50,000-a-year professional to be found in the US colleges'.[33] When they said it was ludicrous to substitute Donald McDonald for Chris Clark, a man who had successfully rowed in the Pan Am Games, the English response was: 'The race is about big hearts, not big reputations.'[34] And when they said they were only making a fuss because they wanted to put together the fastest possible crew, David Miller, rowing correspondent for *The Times*, answered, 'the Boat Race is not, mercifully, just about being fast'. R.B. Bruce Lockhart encapsu-lated the attitudes of upper-class Britons towards the Boat Race and the men he considered to be American *arrivistes* in a letter to *Miller's* news-paper. 'To many of us a sporting contest conducted in a pleasant and gentlemanly manner can matter more than imported win-at-all-costs principles.' He wanted Cambridge to lose the race on purpose. That would teach the 'ageing Yank permanent students a thing or two about the institution which is *our* Boat Race'.[35]

The storm of anti-Americanism that burst upon the unsuspecting heads of the five oarsmen suggests that grateful memories of the wartime alliance had faded since 1959. Some anti-US expressions were merely snide and condescending. 'Chris Penny towers above the tow-path mud, a testimony to homogenized milk, red meat and two hot showers a day . . . Clark is a man whose every gesture conjures up images from *Gunfight at the OK Corral*.'[36] Others were personally wounding. 'Clark . . . sounds like the kind of American that Oxford and even America can do without.'[37] They could be vicious, if muddle-headed and obscure: one student at the Oxford Union opposed admitting Americans to Oxford because it led to 'the racial degeneration of the Boat Race'.[38]

Of course the Americans received support from the vast majority during the Oxford Union debate; and, of course, many Britons eschewed chauvinism in general and anti-Americanism in particular. Still, from the deluge of comment a portrait of late-twentieth-century Britain, as one section of the population conceived it, begins to emerge. It was the anti-America: understated and self-deprecating, respectful of tradition, interested more in playing the game than in winning it, and in doing good rather than in doing well.

One of the ironies of the '1987 Boat Race Mutiny' was that the Americans, in completely misunderstanding and underestimating Dan Topolski, thought he typified the old Oxford rowing establishment. In fact he did anything but. In his social attitudes and background he was hardly representative of Oxford's rowing traditions, and probably he had butted his head against a few of them. Significantly, he had learned the lore of the river and, in part, how to use an oar from professional racers, spiritual heirs of the 'menial' Thames-side watermen, with whom the old guard would never have deigned to speak.

Indeed Topolski's hard-won knowledge of the river turned out to be crucial to Oxford's chances on the day of the race. The weather forecasts were for stormy weather. The coach thought about the effect of wind on the different stretches of the river; he thought about the effect of choppy water on his boat and crew. The night before the competition he went down to the boathouse and re-rigged the boat to change the length and angle of the oars in the water. For the lightweight oars with which the crew had been practising he substituted willow oars, with a strip of carbon down the middle to give them stiffness.

Next day at Putney the sky was nearly black. There was thunder and lightning and hail and a fierce headwind that made the water in the middle of the river extremely rough. Urgently Topolski pulled aside the new cox, Andy Lobbenburg, who had replaced the American Jonathan Fish. The Blue boat must aim for the lee shore as soon as the starter told the boats to 'Go!' It must seek out the smooth, undemanding water and shelter from the wind on the Middlesex side of the river. Let gentlemanly Cambridge plough straight ahead into wind and chop. Oxford would row the longer, but easier and therefore faster race. Once in the lead Lobbenburg should steer back towards the centre, taking away the advantage Cambridge would have had otherwise as the inside boat at the Surrey bend in the river.

Photographs taken at the start of the race show the Light Blues stoically heading straight down the centre of the course, right into the heavy water. They show the Dark Blues rowing at a tangent towards the Fulham Wall. 'It was so rough . . . it felt like there were 70 mph winds and six foot waves.'[39] But then they were through it and into smooth water, and there was no looking back. A mile into the race they were clearly in the lead, and still following Topolski's instructions to the letter. At Hammersmith Bridge, Lobbenburg steered back to the centre, ahead of the Light Blues, as close to the Surrey side as their opponents. Already they had rowed a longer distance than Cambridge, but a less demanding one. They were fresher than their rivals. They began to pull away.

Against all odds Oxford won the Boat Race after all, by twelve seconds, by three lengths. It was a great triumph for Topolski and McDonald, although not so unalloyed as that of Jumbo Edwards and

Oxford University (right) and Cambridge University prepare to start the 1987 race in terrible conditions, with the Oxford boat already pointing around 10 degrees to the north of the direction of the Boathouse Reach. Coach Daniel Topolski had told the cox to steer for the Middlesex side of the river in search of smoother water and shelter from the wind. Oxford would row the longer, but easier and therefore faster race. (Empics/Alpha)

Ronnie Howard twenty-eight years earlier. For, in the final analysis, the Americans, even though they did not row the boat, can hardly be said to have been defeated in their 'rebellion'. Immediately after the race, chests still heaving, the victorious Oxford crew huddled round the giant oarsman Gavin Stewart on the bank of the Thames. He had a cell telephone in hand and was dialling the United States. His first thought, seconded by all the crew but one, Donald McDonald, who stood to one side, an isolated and lonely figure, was to share news of the great triumph with Dan Lyons.

The Americans, for all their shortcomings, for all that they had been the targets of abuse, were more popular among Oxford oarsmen than the president of the OUBC. They were the unlikeable spearhead of a movement long overdue, and they finally had broken the mould of Oxford rowing tradition, for in the end they proved more popular among the boat club captains too. Only a few days after the race, at the annual gathering of college captains and resident Blues, the American Chris Penny triumphed over Tom Cadoux-Hudson (McDonald's choice) in the ballot for a new OUBC president. And Penny then carried out the American rebel programme in its entirety: constitutional changes that would permit crew members to vote, and to have some control over the president's actions during the year-long run-up to the Boat Race.[40] Moreover, Penny made it clear that 'the amateur era has gone'. Topolski stepped down as head coach, although he would continue to advise the Oxford crew. In the 1988 season Steve Royle served as Oxford's first professional Director of Rowing.[41] That year, training according to the regimen favoured by the American, Penny led the Oxford crew to victory over Cambridge yet again.

Perhaps for once history provided the happiest possible of outcomes: for the only losers of the 1987 Oxford boat crew mutiny were those who favoured anachronistic class distinctions, and tribal identities. Every protagonist in the struggle could claim some form of triumph, while moreover the changes ushered in by the Americans did not lead to the predominance of big-business attitudes in the Oxford rowing world, but merely to less old-fashioned ones. It is a pity that the Americans mistook Topolski for a representative of the *ancien régime*. He was in the old school, but not of it. More tact on his part, or on theirs, might have averted the rebellion. But then history also suggests that without rebellion there is rarely quick change.

Finally, to place the event in its largest cultural context: despite the changes brought by war and the post-war Labour government, despite the 'winds of change' that made decolonisation inevitable, Britons had continued debating the role and merit of certain traditional values and practices in their society. Some bemoaned the growth of soulless suburbs and waxed nostalgic for the tight-knit working-class communities of their childhoods.[42] Others argued that, despite certain signs of progress, the country mainly languished in the grip of tradition's dead hand. They believed that the ancient universities, the clubs along Pall Mall, the famous public schools, were some of the fingers of that hand.[43] In the end this latter critique proved more influential. When the American scholar Martin Weiner published *English Culture and the Decline of the Industrial Spirit, 1850–1980* (1981), arguing that the thrusting, entrepreneurial spirit of the Victorian manufacturers had led to national economic supremacy, but that the spirit had died during the later nineteenth century and that Britain had lost her economic lead as a result, a prime minister signalled her approval.

Weiner believed, and Margaret Thatcher agreed, that for three-quarters of a century or more the British middle class had by and large disdained innovation, technology and ambition in favour of good manners, conservation, and pursuit of classical education. To these values it continued stubbornly to adhere, against its own best interests. What another cultural critic, Tom Nairn, had written of the House of Lords could be applied to Britain as a whole. Its 'true impulse is not really to "catch up" with the greater, evolving world outside, but to hold one's own somehow, anyhow, and defend the tribe's customs and weathered monuments'.[44] Thus, at this one point, anyway, the Conservative and the Marxist critiques of contemporary Britain bisected.

But could not Nairn's lament have been written with equal accuracy of the defenders of the Boat Race status quo? And did not Thatcher declare war, in fact, upon much that not merely the English establishment as a whole but the Oxford boating establishment in particular seemed to stand for: social exclusivity including the operation of an old boy network (although in this case they called themselves 'Old Blues'); archaic-seeming practices and methodologies coupled with disdain for modern ones; and contempt for the American 'win-at-all-costs' attitude? And therefore at some level did not opposition to American conduct during the lead-up to the Boat Race, and opposition to Thatcherism, go hand in hand, stemming from similar world-views? Politics makes strange bedfellows. And here perhaps it is not entirely irrelevant that the chief American troublemaker, Chris Clark, said he would vote for Thatcher if he could.[45] There is a sense in which the Americans were bringing to bear a Thatcherite approach to the Boat Race. Perhaps then they should have expected the reaction they received from the university that voted to deny Mrs Thatcher an honorary degree.

And running through it all is the silver thread of the river itself. It is peculiarly appropriate that the Thames, wound inextricably over centuries into English understandings of self, should provide the venue for these two twentieth-century struggles over values and identity. In 1987 the tide that carried Oxford to victory because Daniel Topolski had taught a coxswain to understand its erratic moods bore a good deal more than nine men in a boat.

11

Taming the Thames

Before the advent of Christianity in England, and for many centuries afterwards, men and women living near the Thames considered it a crucial but ultimately mysterious, indeed unfathomable, force in their lives. Source of drink and of water for crops, magnet for game animals, barrier against invasion, highway for trade, the river was essential; but also it was fickle, for when it flooded the consequences could be terrible. The inhabitants of the Thames valley worshipped river gods and goddesses. They sought to propitiate them with offerings and charms that archaeologists continue to find in or near the river.

But also Thames-side dwellers sought to bypass their deities or to make their interventions unnecessary. Incrementally, over many centuries, they learned to channel and to harness the power of the waterway. Fishermen set stakes along its margins with nets between them to catch the spawn and fry of fish as they drifted with the current. They stretched these 'kiddles', as they were called, from the shoreline more than halfway across the stream so that fish in the river were caught in fixed nets too. Millers learned to harness the river to turn great waterwheels for grinding wheat. This required the erection of dams, or weirs, across the Thames so that the pent-up water might power the wheel.

The effort to exploit and to control the flow of the river, and even to shape its contours, never ceased. Early on men learned to deepen and widen it with dredging operations, so that, as an Act of 1274, put it, 'ships and great barges might ascend from London to Oxford' unimpeded.[1] In fact barges were plying to and fro beyond Oxford, and even beyond Cricklade, at that date.[2] But they were hardly unimpeded. Weirs got in the way. Grudgingly (we may imagine) mill owners fashioned openings in the weirs, called flash locks. They kept them closed with paddles known as 'rymers', because opening them interrupted the flow of water powering the wheel. When a barge appeared, however, the miller would reluctantly lift the rymers, opening the lock, creating a flush or flash of water sufficient to equalise river levels before and behind the weir, so that the barge could pass by. Of course he milled less wheat that day.

Opening a flash lock was inconvenient to the miller. It was also inconvenient to the riparian landowner, for it might cause the Thames to flood, deluging fields and crops, jeopardising cattle grazing by the river bank. For centuries the Crown sought to force the destruction of weirs that obstructed trade and caused inundations. The solution, however, was not to destroy the weirs, which millers would never accept anyway, but rather to improve the flash locks. Alongside the weir, after all, one could enclose, or impound, a stretch of water no longer than the length of a boat itself, and then by letting the stream in or out through gates made of timber or stone, raise or lower the craft as necessary. Such a 'pound lock' would not interfere with weir or waterwheel, and would not cause floods. Yet pound locks were slow in coming to Britain. They may have been used in ancient Egypt. They certainly were used in Continental Europe by the mid-fifteenth century. Strangely, men did not install them along the Thames for two hundred years after that.

There is something almost magical about a pound lock in operation. The water rushes foaming into the compartment, inexorably raising a boat that two dozen straining men could not lift. A pound lock testifies to man's imagination and creativity. It reveals not merely ingenuity but the seeming mastery over nature. With a pound lock man appears to have channelled and contained the mighty river, to have made it do his bidding. That is the fascination of the device, which will almost always attract a crowd to watch it in process.

The first English pound locks were built on the Thames by the Oxford–Burcot Commission between 1630 and 1635 at Iffley, Sandford and in the head of the Swift Ditch. Over the next three hundred years a series of commissions and the Thames Conservancy constructed forty-five more, and generally improved the river's navigability.[3] Long before the last pound lock had been installed in 1928, however, barges were sailing up- and downstream relatively freely.[4] In the meantime men had widened and deepened the Thames; they had embanked it in stretches and, below London, cribbed it with flood walls more than five metres higher than mean sea level. Their victory over Father Thames seemed complete.

But human control of the river was always illusory. The river runs into the sea. More importantly, the sea runs into the river, salt water streaming all the way to Teddington. Vaster forces are at work on the tideway than upriver, and while man can attempt to defend against them he will never subdue them.

Two thousand miles west of the westernmost portions of the British Isles, in the region of the Newfoundland Banks off the coast of Canada, the warm waters of the Gulf Stream meet the icy cold Labrador Current. This produces low atmospheric pressure, a depression, as weather forecasters call it. The depression generates cyclonic winds that move eastward across the Atlantic Ocean. As the depression likewise shifts to the east, it sucks at the water below, raising it by about a foot.

This foot-high hump of water can reach as much as a thousand miles in diameter. It represents many millions of tons of water, racing at fifty miles an hour beneath cyclonic winds towards the European landmass. Its own motion raises the hump further. When it moves from the deep waters of the Atlantic into the shallower waters of the continental shelf, the hump gains in height yet again.

If the winds veer north-east at this stage, as they commonly do, then the hump of water dissipates harmlessly in the North Atlantic between Iceland and Scandinavia. Occasionally, however, the winds continue mainly easterly, towards northern Germany, pulling the hump of water into the upper reaches of the North Sea. Then, if the depression is followed by a system of high pressure, northerly gales will ensue. These will drive the depression and the hump of water beneath south into the funnel formed by the converging coastlines of England and the European Continent. Again the hump will gain in height, and the rotation of the earth will throw it against the east coast of England.

Even so, English coastal residents have little to fear — unless the northerly gales maintain their force so that they coincide with a normal high tide, and the normal high tide is a high 'spring' tide produced by the combined gravitational forces of sun and moon in a straight alignment with the earth.[5] Then the situation can become very serious indeed. The vast hump of water will reach the bottleneck of the Straits of Dover and pour into the Thames estuary, surging up the ever-narrowing river, spilling over sea and flood walls, inundating the land on either side, roaring in some cases all the way up to London.

A North Sea surge, as described above, is a rare but inevitable occurrence. We may guess that surges were responsible for the great Thames floods recorded over the centuries, for example that of 1236 of which Stow writes in his *Chronicles of England*: 'the River Thames, overflowing its banks, caused the marshes all about Woolwich to be all a sea, wherein boats and other vessels were carried by the stream so that besides cattle a great number of inhabitants there were drowned and in the great

Palace of Westminster men did row with wherries in the midst of the
Hall'. Stow wrote too of a flood six years later, in 1242, when 'the
Thames overflowing the banks about Lamberhithe drowned houses
and fields by the space of six miles, so that in the Great Hall at
Westminster men took their horses, because the water ran overall.'
Perhaps it was a surge tide on 7 December 1663 that moved Samuel
Pepys to record in his diary, 'There was last night the greatest tide that
ever was remembered in England to have been in this river, all
Whitehall having been drowned.'[6] David Beasley writes that the worst
Thames flood occurred in 1809 when the central arches of Wallingford
Bridge collapsed.[7] There were floods too in 1894 and 1928, when four-
teen died, and in 1947, and many other years.

At midday on Thursday 29 January 1953, a merchant ship south-west
of Iceland reported a developing depression in the area. Weather forecasters christened it 'LZ'. All that afternoon 'LZ' deepened, propelled
eastwards by cyclonic winds at a rate of between 17 and 23 miles per
hour. Beneath it ran the famous hump of water. That night 'LZ' merged
with another depression and strengthened, while continuing to move
towards Scotland. Atmospheric pressure at the centre of this enlarged
disturbance continued to drop. By early morning on Saturday 31
January the depression had reached its lowest level, 968 millibars. This is
considered to be a very low barometric pressure since average pressure
in the north of the British Isles is 1009 millibars.[8] Meanwhile winds
north of Scotland were driving water from the open ocean towards the
North Sea.

Behind 'LZ' a ridge of abnormally high pressure had built up over the
Atlantic, creating gale-force winds that soon enough were gusting
across the British Isles at record speeds. In Orkney a blast of air was
recorded at the unprecedented rate of 125 mph. As far south as
Southampton, the wind was so strong that the captain of the Cunard
liner *Queen Mary* refused to take his 81,000-ton ship from the dock,
although she was scheduled to sail. Between Orkney and Southampton

the wind wreaked havoc. In the end ten ships sank that Saturday, including the *Princess Victoria*, a British Railways car ferry, struggling up Loch Ryan to the Irish Sea on her regular crossing to Larne. One hundred and thirty-two men, women and children went under with her and died.

South-eastern England might have been spared the worst of it. Between noon and 6 p.m. on Saturday the storm centre stayed north. It seemed to be headed towards Denmark. Then, unaccountably, it turned south, with the trailing great winds now directly over the North Sea, whipping at the surge, icy waters which in turn were gathering in a rising spring tide, for sun, moon and earth happened to be in the fatal conjunction. This meant that the tide, when it came smashing in on England's east coast, would have been preceded and amplified by the surge after all, and would have the gale behind it.

In Yorkshire when the tide came pounding in it surged up the Humber overflowing embankments, spreading inland all the way to the village square at Easington, a mile from the sea. In Lincolnshire it flooded coastal villages and towns, higher than predicted, higher than ever before. Every automatic tide gauge between the Wash and Southend-on-Sea was either destroyed or rendered temporarily inoperable. At King's Lynn, the river Ouse overflowed so swiftly and heavily that fifteen people drowned, trapped in their houses. At Sea Palling, near Great Yarmouth, 'vast waves hurling themselves over the sand dunes . . . burst a 100-yard gap through them, engulfed the café, public house and dwellings at the seaward end of the village, ripped away the walls as if they had been blasted open by a bomb, and swept thousands of tons of sand up the village street beyond, to lie there afterwards in drifts five feet deep'.[9] Further south, water encircled the town of Harwich, flooded homes, destroyed shops. A member of the Harwich town council scrambled upstairs with her family as the water lapped under her door. 'We could hear our furniture and crockery hitting the walls downstairs and several small things – kitchen chairs, cushions,

small tables, floated through the windows . . . I looked down the stair-
case and saw the water was still rising, step by step . . .'[10] At Colchester
a desperate farmer watched the water pour into his barn while seven-
teen prize Friesian cows stood docile in their open stalls as it rose above
their shoulders. All but the farmer and one bull drowned.

But, of course, fatefully, the water attained its greatest force and
greatest height when it reached the funnel-shaped Thames estuary,
squeezing between the narrowing shoreline, rushing ever inland up
the great river. And it was here in the most heavily populated areas, and
also where industrial development was most complete, that the surge
and the tide proved deadliest and did the greatest damage.

Canvey Island lies on the north side of the estuary beneath the bulge
of Essex, Suffolk and Norfolk which juts east and north, largely shel-
tering it from the open sea. And yet the sea hammers it with every
incoming tide. In 1607, before residents erected walls for protection,
William Camden said the island was 'so low-lying that often it is all
overflown'.[11] By 1953 men had long since walled it in entirely: part of
Canvey was still farmland; part of it was earmarked for industry; most
of it was residential, though many residents lived there on a seasonal
basis, treating it as a holiday resort convenient to London. All of it lay
below sea level during spring tides with only the sea walls for protection.
Starting late on that fatal Saturday night and continuing into the next
morning, first the surge, many million tons of water, and then the
spring tide, many million tons more and backed by howling gales,
crashed against those walls with breathtaking ferocity, overtopped
them, pounded them to bits, eventually breached them and poured
through.

In low-lying areas men, women and children awoke in darkness as
water and debris — including uprooted trees, caravans, sheds, cars —
smashed against the walls and doors and windows of their homes,
forcing entrance for the icy deluge. Some people rushed from their
homes, only to confront gale-force winds and successive waves of

freezing waist-high water crashing through the breached sea walls. Some rushed upstairs into attics to wait out the storm. They 'shivered and chattered all night. I have never been so cold in my life,'[12] but they were the fortunate ones. Many had no upstairs to rush to, or could not reach the stairs. They stood on chairs, tables, stools to keep dry. But the water kept rising: above the furniture, above their knees and waists and shoulders. Mothers tried to keep their babies and toddlers clear of it. Even if they were strong and determined enough to hold them all night long above their heads the air was freezing cold: 'After a while he did not speak any more and appeared to go to sleep,' one mother reported of the baby son who died in her arms.[13] Some, made desperate by the rising water, used what came to hand or even bare fists to smash holes in their ceilings. Then they climbed through, pulling their children after them on to the rooftops.

But Canvey Island was not the end destination of the many million tons of water raging through the estuary and up the river. The surging tide inundated the island and kept going, past the marshlands of Fobbing, Corringham, Mucking, Tilbury and West Thurrock. A century earlier, the tide would have swirled across open uninhabited marshland and spent itself. Now contained by flood walls, it swept upstream through the tidal basin at Tilbury Dock, flooding the town, cutting off the Tilbury and Riverside General Hospital with water four feet deep. At Thurrock a wave three feet high burst through the main drainage works, bowling 3-inch-thick concrete water pipes along the ground as if they were tin cans. Further upstream at Purfleet it did burst the river wall, submerging sheds and outbuildings at the Purfleet Deep Wharf and Storage Company. It coursed along the railway track behind, reaching and wreaking havoc at Esso and Shell-BP yards. It destroyed the Van den Bergh and Jurgens margarine factory. It also backed up and overflowed the contributory streams of the Thames along these stretches of the river, the Ingrebourne, the Roding, the Lea. Rushing up Rainham Creek it caused much destruction at the Phoenix

Canvey Island in the aftermath of the disastrous spring surge tide of 31 January–1 February 1953. (Canvey Island/Topfoto)

Timber Company. Farther up still it flooded the Dagenham sewage disposal works.

The tide reached all the way to the Royal Docks at West Ham, 6 feet higher than predicted, half a foot higher than ever previously recorded, higher than defence provided for. Now Canning Town, upon which German bombers had rained destruction only thirteen years before, 'took it' once again, this time in the form of 141,750,000 gallons of Thames river water. It was less deadly but hardly less uncomfortable than the Blitz. Two hundred and fifty acres of east London containing 9 miles of roads, plus factories, shops, railways, schools, churches and, of course, houses, lay 3½ feet under water.

At London Bridge the surge crested at a higher level than ever previously recorded. It even briefly threatened central London, reaching just to the top of the parapet running along the Victoria and Chelsea embankments. But the wind had turned and the surge backed off and then reversed. Holland would take its full brunt only hours later.

In Essex alone, the surge tide of 1953 drowned more than three hundred people, fifty-eight of them on Canvey Island. It damaged more than 24,000 houses, flooded more than 200 industrial premises, twelve gasworks, two power stations, eleven major roads, 200 miles of railway track, 160,000 acres of agricultural land. It killed 9000 sheep, 1100 cattle, 2600 pigs, 34,000 poultry and 70 horses.

So much for man having mastered the river.

The catastrophe of 1953 provided impetus to a long-standing demand for increased flood protection from the Thames. Some people thought it would be sufficient to strengthen and further raise flood walls. Most believed something more fundamental was needed.

For three-quarters of a century plans had been circulating for construction of a barrage across the river, downstream of the major London docks, to stop the tide entirely. Historically the primary motivation had been not so much to protect Thames-side residents from flooding as to protect them from the stench of the muddy, scummy, river banks when the tide ebbed. In 1907 advocates chose Gravesend as the site for the barrage. The scheme gained support from the Radical Liberal politician John Burns, a member of the Liberal government.

A barrage would have had incalculable environmental and ecological effects both up- and downstream, though this was little appreciated at the time. More to the point, ships wishing to pass the barrage would have had to be raised or lowered in locks. Backlogs would have stretched for miles, the impact upon trade would have been devastating. For this reason, no doubt, the scheme went nowhere. Nevertheless, during the 1930s indefatigable A.P. Herbert took it up, arguing that a tideless river, a great lake really, in the centre of London, would prove to be a major and popular urban amenity. Even his championing of a Thames barrage proved fruitless, however.

Not a barrage, then, but some form of barrier, whose gates could be left open in normal times for ships and water to flow through, but slammed shut against an advancing surge tide. After the 1953 flood, the government appointed an investigative committee, chaired by Lord Waverley, the former Sir John Anderson, nemesis of trade unionism during the lead-up to the general strike of 1926, better known for air-raid shelters named after him during the Second World War. Waverley's committee reported in favour of a barrier, not a barrage, to be erected between Purfleet and Tilbury, in Long Reach, about twenty miles downriver from London Bridge.

But how to engineer the barrier? One proposal called for a lifting bridge with barrier gates that could be lowered on to the river bed when the bridge was in the down position. For the bridge to work when two ocean liners travelling in opposite directions were passing through, it would have had to have two openings each 500 feet wide and 130 feet tall. The top of the structure would have towered 200 feet above the riverbed. As one historian puts it, 'there were planning and environmental objections.'[14] Another proposal called for erection of a swing bridge barrier;

but this required too much river space. A third proposal suggested a retractable bridge barrier; this required too much empty space on land. Then in 1961 the Port of London Authority authorised construction of massive jetties in Long Reach. No barrier of any sort could be built on that stretch of river any more.

Planners suggested a new site at Crayfordness. Difficulties peculiar to this site meant that neither a lift nor a swing bridge barrier would work, and the proposals eventually advanced for a retractable bridge barrier contained cost estimates far beyond what the government was willing to pay. By now it was 1966, and Prime Minister Harold Wilson wanted a new commission to consider the matter all over again. At the suggestion of his science adviser Sir Solly (later Lord) Zuckerman, he appointed Hermann Bondi, Professor of Mathematics at King's College, London, to lead it. Professor Bondi's committee confirmed Anderson's initial recommendation: action was necessary, and building a barrier not a barrage was the proper action to take. Earlier Wilson had passed the London Government Act, creating the Greater London Council (GLC), which replaced the smaller and outdated London County Council (which, it will be recalled, had replaced the Metropolitan Board of Works). In May 1970 the GLC finally took responsibility for the entire flood prevention scheme. It accepted Professor Bondi's report, obtained approval for the expenditure of necessary funds, chose a site at Woolwich for the barrier (after further study) and appointed Rendel, Palmer & Tritton Consulting Engineers to design and build it.

Things were moving at last, but still not very fast. They would have moved even slower, however, if not for Charles Draper, a member of the Rendel, Palmer & Tritton design team, who on Christmas Day 1970 knelt to turn on his gas fire at home and suddenly realised that the principle for turning on a gas tap could be applied to opening and closing the gate of a barrier. He called it a 'Rising Sector Gate', and it obviated the weight and span problems of lift, swing and retractable bridges, and the deep underwater excavations necessary for any kind of falling gate.[15]

Essentially, as Draper designed it, the gate rests flat on a concrete sill on the river bed. It is attached at a right angle to a metal disc fitted to a pier. Hydraulic cylinders rotate the disc, which when turned pulls the gate up to face the river rising a little more than 200 feet above the river bed, 50 feet above the surface of the Thames itself. The Thames Barrier when completed had six Rising Sector Gates attached to piers in the middle of the waterway, and four more traditional 'Falling Radial Gates' closer to the banks where the water is shallower, making ten gates in all. When they are in the upright position they block the Thames at Woolwich entirely.

The Rising Sector Gate represented a conceptual breakthrough that occurred in a moment. Implementation of the concept, however, required a long hard slog. The piers rest on concrete foundations. The concrete could not be laid until interlocking corrugated strips of steel driven more than 52 feet below the river bed formed watertight compartments for labourers to work in. The sills, concrete slabs, were built in dry dock, and, like the caissons for the Mulberry harbours of the Second World War, floated into place between the piers. Then workmen pulled the plugs to let in water, which made them heavy enough to sink. The large gates, weighing 1500 tonnes each, were manufactured in Darlington, assembled at Port Clarence on the river Tees, and shipped 300 miles in barges to the Thames. Given the size and weight of the objects under construction, the precision required was remarkable. Every individual part of the barrier must fit perfectly with the others. For example the largest sills weighed 10,000 tonnes. They were 196.8 feet long and 91.6 feet wide. When labourers placed them between the piers, using floating cranes, they had only four inches clearance to work with. And, to make matters even more difficult, they were working during a winter storm in near-blizzard conditions.

Given the scope and complexity of the operation it is not surprising that once construction finally began it took eight years to complete, and that the cost – originally estimated at £171 million, not merely for the

The Thames Barrier. According to Ted Hollamby, former chief architect and planner of the London Docklands Development Committee, when 'the steel helmets come down and the great visors rise to hold back the tide, they can be imagined as five Don Quixotes preparing to throw back the North Sea'. (Thames Barrier/Julian Calder/CORBIS)

Barrier but for raising flood walls all along the estuarial portion of the river as well, and additional barriers for some of the Thames's tributaries – finally totalled £525 million. But the glimmering stainless-steel shells surmounting the finished piers at Woolwich are not merely effective, they are beautiful. They remind one of so many Sydney Opera Houses stretching in a row across the river. To quote Ted Hollamby, former chief architect and planner of the London Docklands Development Committee, when the 'steel helmets come down and the great visors rise to hold back the tide, [the Thames Barrier] can be imagined as five Don Quixotes preparing to throw back the North Sea'.[16] In conception, utility and grandeur the Thames Barrier is an engineering accomplishment of which Isambard Kingdom Brunel might have been proud.

And, as in Brunel's day, there was a political dimension. It was not so much that the Victorian engineer engaged actively in politics as that politicians engaged with him and his projects. A century later the men who worked on the Thames Barrier were not particularly political, but the politicians simply could not keep away.

In 1970 the GLC had taken responsibility for preventing another Thames flood, as we have seen. Conservatives controlled the Council in that year; Labour gained a majority in 1973; Conservatives won it back in 1977. Work on the Barrier proceeded apace. Then in 1981 Labour took control of the GLC again, this time under the leadership of a young, fire-breathing left-wing politician, Ken Livingstone. But if Labour was the majority party on the GLC, Conservatives now held a majority in Parliament. Their leader, the prime minister of the nation, was Margaret Thatcher.

Everybody knows that the Thatcher government believed it must cut taxes and public spending in order to roll back the 'nanny' (welfare) state and revitalise the national economy. But the Labour-controlled GLC, led by Livingstone, believed in the opposite: activist government funded by progressive taxation. GLC Labour candidates pledged during the election campaign of 1981 to maintain public services, most importantly housing and, especially, public transport, whose fares they promised to reduce. After the election, the Thatcher government slashed grants to 'high-spending' councils including the GLC so that they could not pursue such policies; but the GLC cut fares anyway and, like other Labour-dominated councils, raised local taxes to compensate. Conservatives had foreseen this move. They calculated it would be politically damaging to Labour, and perhaps it was. Unexpectedly, however, the spectacle of central government dictating to the localities proved damaging to Conservatives as well. Moreover, in Livingstone, Thatcher confronted an opponent who, though he often enraged many with hard-left pronouncements, including many members of his own party, never missed an opportunity to cock a snook at her. To give an example: with unemployment rising sharply during the early 1980s, Livingstone raised above GLC headquarters, diagonally across the Thames from Parliament where Conservative and government Members could not help but see, an enormous sign, tracking every month the rate of joblessness.

Livingstone was a practitioner of political judo, adept at turning the weight of his opponents to his own advantage. The courts declared that the policy to cut transport fares had been illegal and that the GLC must not only raise fares back up again, but also must find £125 million to make up the difference for the six months when they had been lowered. To most of the GLC Labour contingent this seemed a disaster and an enormous victory for the Conservative government. Livingstone was not so sure. He insisted that the £125 million be paid off immediately, in a single year, 1982, realising that the taxes imposed to make the payment possible would remain after the debt was gone, and that many Londoners would not hold the GLC responsible for the taxes anyway, but rather the government that had reduced the GLC grant in the first place. As a result, in following years, when every other local authority in the country was scrimping and saving and cutting because its central funding had been reduced, the GLC literally had more money than it could spend. Livingstone complained to colleagues: 'There is a general problem of under-spending on agreed programmes in 1983–4 as there was in 1982–3 . . . We must introduce procedures which will make such under-spending against budget less likely to occur.'[17] This despite having made increased disbursements for the usual social services, and to a host of less obvious organisations: disarmament groups (including one called 'Babies against the Bomb'), women's groups, gay groups, and many others. Moreover, after taking advice from lawyers, the GLC advanced a new and only slightly less ambitious low fares policy that the courts accepted.

The government was furious. During the general election of 1983 Conservatives pledged to pass a law that would make it illegal for local councils to raise taxes beyond a certain level. More pointedly they promised if re-elected to abolish the GLC altogether, as well as six other metropolitan councils scattered through Britain, all of which had Labour majorities, ostensibly because they represented a 'wasteful and unnecessary tier of government'. If Thatcher had her way the GLC would expire in May 1985 when the four-year terms of its members had finished. In response Livingstone launched the campaign of his life. The ensuing Donnybrook was slightly bizarre: Margaret Thatcher, champion of 'the little man', of localism, against the overweening power of central government, was using precisely the overweening power of central government to crush localism; Ken Livingstone, the avatar of state planning, was fighting just as visibly to preserve the pre-rogatives of a local council from national intervention.

This is not the place to recount that strange and divisive contest, except to note that the outcome could never be in serious doubt, since Thatcher commanded a huge majority in the House of Commons and could see off even a score of Tory rebels if necessary, and that, nevertheless, Livingstone led his troops with great verve, imagination and skill. At one point, the Conservatives in the House voted to cancel GLC elections that were due to take place before abolition. They would then let the Tory-dominated London boroughs run the metropolis until abolition was complete. The House of Lords rebelled at this – yet another irony: the socialists of the GLC temporarily saved by the unelected chamber – and Thatcher had to diverge slightly from her plan. She insisted that the elections be cancelled, but she also extended the terms of GLC councillors for as long as the GLC should continue to function. This meant at least an additional year of life and agitation. Livingstone put up another banner over County Hall: 'GLC thanks House of Lords', just where Mrs Thatcher and Conservative MPs could view it from the House Terrace across the river.

Possibly a majority of London's Conservative councillors thought the government campaign ill-advised. These Conservatives may have judged they had a good chance to beat Labour in the next election (since the socialists *would* keep putting up taxes), and that the powers of the abolished GLC would inevitably devolve to a new body anyway (although in this they were mistaken, Thatcher only maintained the Inner London Education Authority, all other GLC functions were given either to the boroughs or to temporary quangos). But certainly there were Conservative councillors in London who supported Mrs Thatcher's plan unreservedly. Of these the most strident and visible was Lady (later Dame) Shirley Porter, Conservative leader of Westminster City Council and heiress to the Tesco supermarket fortune. At her urging Westminster announced it might sue the GLC for lowering Tube and bus fares again. Lady Porter argued that well-off Westminster residents paid a disproportionate share of the taxes used to subsidise cheap public transport. She took pride in the low rates paid by Westminster residents and, intending to keep them low, campaigned enthusiastically for abolition of the GLC. She reached out to friends and contacts in the business community. For a gift of £1000 or more to the campaign for abolition, she would arrange a meeting with the prime minister. Unfortunately a Livingstone supporter received one of these solicitations. He gave it to the GLC leader, who gave it to the press.

Meanwhile, work on the Thames Barrier finished in October 1982; staff first closed its gates against the river in February 1983; the GLC set its official opening for 8 May 1984. Livingstone thought the occasion could be turned to advantage in his fight with Thatcher. The Barrier is a marvellous sight and a miraculous device, testimony to the effectiveness and drive of the body ultimately responsible for its construction. This was not the national government but the council Mrs Thatcher wanted to abolish. The Labour group on the GLC determined to broadcast this point as widely as possible.

At first Livingstone assumed that he and another Labour figure, or he and one of the workers who had actually helped to build the Barrier, would preside on the appointed day, and push the button to activate the gates. But, as the GLC leader later admitted in his autobiography, 'When the workforce heard of this, they made it quite clear that they expected the Queen to perform the opening . . . I went down to the site to meet them and they reiterated that if we tried to get anyone else they would strike and put a picket line across the ceremony.'[18] Gleefully Thames TV polled viewers on the question and reported the results: seven votes for the chair of the GLC to perform the ceremony, more than 14,000 for the queen.

Labour councillors with republican sympathies were aghast. Yet demos had spoken. Moreover it would have been a public relations disaster not to invite the queen now. The GLC entered into communication with Buckingham Palace. The queen agreed to preside. Livingstone, ever the master of political judo, believed that even this embarrassment could be turned to advantage. He told the *Paddington Mercury*, 'I think it is quite interesting that, given all this controversy surrounding the GLC, the Queen is happy to come and open the barrier. I think the Queen is trying to tell us something – that she doesn't agree with the abolition of the GLC.'[19] It may even have been true, although Buckingham Palace quickly issued a disclaimer: the queen was above politics. In any event, Livingstone's chutzpah rendered Lady Porter apoplectic: 'It is disgraceful for Ken Livingstone to attempt to drag the

Queen into this political campaign against the government. This is one of the most disgraceful acts I have seen. It is ludicrous for Mr. Livingstone to try to deceive the public.'[20]

On the great day itself the queen, 'dressed in lime green . . . with a matching hat decorated with bobbing baubles that appeared to act as some form of royal bird scarer',[21] accompanied by the Duke of Edinburgh, various retainers and other figures including the GLC leader's mother, Mrs Ethel Livingstone, took the royal barge downstream from Festival Pier. They sailed beneath bridges decorated with bunting. An armada of smaller craft, colourfully decked out and jammed with cheering pensioners, schoolchildren and the families of Barrier workers, accompanied the barge, kept at a careful distance by five police launches. Vessels along the shore sounded their klaxons and sent up water jets as the convoy passed by. It was the twentieth-century version of London's ancient water pageants, of royal Thames processions in the days of Henry VIII. Or perhaps of a slightly later period: for when the queen's barge docked at Barrier Gardens Pier, the Newham Borough Band struck up an extract from Handel's *Water Music*. Certainly the river spectacle, upon which the GLC had cheerfully spent £346,000 of the money so begrudged it by Mrs Thatcher, was meant to evoke patriotic and historic associations. And dignitaries and workers waving blue paper GLC flags, children holding balloons in the silver and blue GLC colours, the Barrier's ten piers each sporting enormous white letters, 'GLC', suggested not very subtly to viewers (the event was televised) which side in the struggle to abolish the Council identified most closely with national traditions.

Waiting for the queen at the Barrier stood Ken Livingstone and an additional 133 dignitaries. The head of the GLC shook the queen's hand. The queen made a speech: 'It is a great tribute to the wisdom of Parliament and of successive governments and to the unswerving purpose of the Greater London Council that London has now been made free from the threat of flooding.'[22] The queen was 'a very nice person', Livingstone allowed afterwards. He had received as close to a royal endorsement of the GLC, perhaps, as he could reasonably hope for.

The very next day Parliament took up debate on the Council's fate. Polls would show that a mere 16 per cent of Londoners favoured abolition. Livingstone had won the war for the hearts and minds of metropolitan residents, but Thatcher won the war to abolish the GLC. With her ironclad majorities in both Houses she could not lose. There would still be fireworks, but two years later she set the seal upon her victory. At midnight on 31 March 1986 the council ceased to exist. County Hall with its anti-Conservative banners across the river from Parliament ceased to exist as well. The Thatcher government sold it to a Japanese hotel chain, spurning a bid from the London School of Economics.

And yet the denouement was not, perhaps, what the prime minister had expected. Practising his political judo even from beyond the grave of the GLC, Ken Livingstone stood for Parliament during the general election of 1987, as a spokesman for those rendered mute by Thatcher's attack on local government. He won his seat. In 1992, shortly after the Tories turned upon Mrs Thatcher and drove her from the leadership, voters re-elected him. Five years later the country finally turned on the Tory majority itself, and a New Labour government decreed that London must elect a mayor. In the year 2000 Livingstone resigned his seat in Parliament to campaign for the post. He was not the sort of candidate New Labourites had in mind, in fact he stood against the formally endorsed New Labour candidate, despite having promised not to. For this he was expelled from the party for five years. Ever a Houdini, however, the representative of nearly everything Tony Blair wanted people to forget about old Labour beat the New Labour candidate and all others. He has proven a popular mayor: so popular that the Labour Party readmitted him in January 2004. He was re-elected, as the Labour candidate, to a second term on 10 June 2004.

As for Lady Porter, the Mrs Thatcher of local government: she had condemned 'Red Ken' for claiming the queen's support in his struggle to save the GLC. 'It is ludicrous for Mr. Livingstone to try to deceive the public,' she had charged. His conduct had been 'disgraceful'. But Lady Porter was to learn something more about disgrace.

In 1986 the voters of Westminster sharply reduced the Tory majority on the city council. Lady Porter took fright. During 1987–9 she and a coterie of supporters sold empty council houses (that could have been used to shelter homeless people) to likely Conservative voters in eight marginal Westminster wards. Someone smelled a rat. The local district auditor, John Magill, launched an investigation. In 1991 the Thatcher government made Lady Porter into Dame Shirley Porter, but this did not deter Mr Magill. Eventually he concluded that she, and five colleagues, had been guilty of 'wilful misconduct', of 'disgraceful and improper gerrymandering'. He held them liable for monies either wrongly spent or lost to Westminster due to local Conservative policies, £31.6 million in all. The case wound through the courts with the final result that the Law Lords of the House of Lords held only Dame Shirley Porter and her deputy, David Weeks, liable – for a slightly reduced amount, £27,023,376. By now Dame Shirley Porter was living in Israel and claiming to be worth a mere £300,000, though once she had been judged one of Europe's twenty wealthiest women. The hunt for her assets was on. On 5 November 2003 investigators froze about £30 million which they said belonged to her and her husband and son in numbered bank accounts in Guernsey, and in a family trust in the British Virgin Islands. They thought Dame Shirley Porter controlled additional funds in Swiss bank accounts.[23] Meanwhile interest on the original surcharge continued to mount. Perhaps Dame Shirley began to feel the pressure. At any rate she finally struck a bargain with her opponents, and on 1 July 2004 paid £12 million into Westminster Council's bank account. That settled what Labour MP Peter Bradley, an ex-councillor at Westminster, has called 'the most costly conspiracy of political corruption in this country in the modern age'.[24]

*

The magnificent Thames Barrier puts the machinations of Dame Shirley Porter and the political calculations of Ken Livingstone into perspective. We look upon the massive steel gates, rising high as a five-storey building above the river, we think of the giant, concrete kerbed sills on the river bed and, as Shelley's Ozymandias, 'king of kings', intended men to do when gazing upon his terrible colossus in the desert, we compare it with our own puny achievements and we are awed.

But as the sand eventually ravaged the desert colossus, so the river never ceases to work at the Thames Barrier. Queen Elizabeth might say at the opening ceremony of 9 May, without conscious hubris, 'the power of the great river, flowing through our capital has been tamed'. We may say that she lacked perspective. Ten thousand years ago a tremendous weight of glacial snow and ice depressed northern Britain. Now the glacier is gone and northern Britain springs upwards, albeit at a nearly imperceptible rate, with the result that southern Britain tilts downwards. As the land of England subsides in the south, the water about it rises, including the waters feeding the estuary of the river Thames. Every year the river laps a little higher against the Barrier walls. Meanwhile the earth grows warmer. The polar ice caps are melting. The sea and river rise at a slightly increased rate. We are warned by experts to expect increasingly violent weather: harder rains, stronger gales. The sun, moon and earth will align again. We must expect ever more powerful surge tides, more powerful, even, than the ferocious spring surge tide of 1953. Eventually one will overtop the Barrier. Humanity's struggle with the river never ends.

12

The Thames Transformed

*O*ver millennia the Thames in London provided a living to any number of men. During a good part of the nineteenth and twentieth centuries it helped make possible not merely a living but a way of life for dockers and ancillary workers, men whom we have already noticed loading and unloading ships as they entered and departed the great port before and during the Second World War.

For long it was a difficult way of life, in part because vessels arrived depending on wind and tide. Until the advent of steam most dockers could not know whether they would find work on a given morning. They would kick their heels inside the depot sheds waiting for a ship to turn up, unpaid perhaps for days or even weeks at a stretch. When a vessel did appear it might pass by, depending on what it was carrying, for dockers specialised in different cargoes: they would handle only coal or meat or wine or timber or tobacco, for instance, and the port was very much compartmentalised, with wharves, warehouses, sections of docks cut off from each other in a sense, because they accepted such different kinds of freight. But when the proper ship did finally come in to the proper section of the proper dock, then the men waiting there would always compete ferociously, debasingly, for the attention of the hiring foreman. Always there were more men available for the job than could be hired, so that many remained still wanting work even after the 'call' had taken place. But if a man was lucky enough to be taken on, then he often found himself working at a gruelling pace, for the boat might have to be turned around very quickly. Dockers routinely laboured for eighteen, twenty-four, even thirty-six hours at a stretch. It was a punishing, sometimes dangerous, even killing experience, but finally, when the job was finished and they had been paid off, the men could splurge on food and drink. The ethos in dockland was individualistic, rough and ready. Dock work appealed mainly to single men who preferred to take their chances, and to desperate men, down on their luck, who had been laid off elsewhere perhaps, and for whom the dock hiring shed was a sort of court of last resort. During the Victorian era such figures helped make east London a byword for poverty, drunkenness, and crime.[1]

But there were countervailing forces operating in the docks. Dock labour required teamwork. The men laboured in gangs whose members must learn to trust and depend upon one another. Moreover, as steam-powered vessels grew more common, it became possible to plan for their arrival, to follow schedules, and therefore to count on work, even to demand it. More regular labour could mean more regular wages, a prerequisite for stable family life. Over the decades most dockers came to believe that in union there is strength. They learned to overcome the differences that divided, say, coal heavers from stevedores, or, most basically, the divisions between men who worked on ship and men who worked on the quaysides or in the warehouses on land. Painfully they built their protective associations, contributed their pennies to union treasuries, established sickness and unemployment and burial and strike funds, elected representatives to negotiate for them with the owners, demanded the exclusion of non-union labour from the hiring sheds so that the number waiting for jobs might be reduced. In 1889 they successfully struck for sixpence an hour, perhaps 50,000 men all at once, taking their employers by surprise, gaining the support of the country (indeed of much of the world) when they publicised their terrible working conditions. The dockers' union, which was formally constituted after the great strike of 1889, would go on to help form the Labour Party, and to elect members from its own ranks to represent its interests in Parliament. It would, too, contribute the nucleus of Britain's largest trade union, the Transport and General Workers' Union, of which Ernest Bevin became the first and greatest leader.

Over the decades the ethos of individualism on the docks had given way to an ethos of cooperation. The ethos spilled over beyond the dock gates and into dockland as a whole, which is to say into the East End of London itself. There developed a vibrant local culture, ever shifting, always contested, defined in great part by poverty and the struggle to cope with and overcome it by cooperative means. The area was hardly homogeneous, it was a magnet for successive waves of immigrants, it was home to English, Irish, Russian and East European Jews, Italians, 'Lascars', Chinese, and many others, and they did not always get along, but for the most part everyone belonged to the working class. The men who laboured on the docks provided a crucial component of the identity of this larger working-class community. They had learned from their own experience to emphasise solidarity, mutuality, community, class distinctions. We do not want to exaggerate or to romanticise. During the 1930s the fascist Oswald Mosley developed a following in the East End too. But it never outnumbered those who believed in the values of brotherhood promoted by the labour movement. Undoubtedly this more generous outlook helped all East London cope with the terrible German bombing campaign during the Second World War.[2]

After the war the Port of London Authority rebuilt the infrastructure of dockland and east London more generally. Labour and Conservative governments rebuilt housing, much of it in the form of council estates. During the 1950s the national economy boomed, and it reached all the way to the East End. Trade along the river resumed, indeed increased. By 1959 the London docks were handling one-third of Britain's entire seaborne trade. In 1966 London dockers handled more than 91 million registered tons of cargo, an all-time high.[3] And, although Ernie Bevin was gone, trade union membership had continued to rise.

But it was too good to last. Nineteen sixty-six proved to be an apogee, not an indicator of things to come. Shippers discovered they could pack their cargoes into large containers that could be easily transferred from boat to lorry at dockside by a single worker operating a crane, with just a few labourers on ship and quay to help. Moreover the containers were thief-proof and inexpensive. Naturally the shipping companies built massive new freighters that could carry thousands of them. But the new ships were too deep-hulled to sail all the way up the river to London, and they were too large and difficult to manoeuvre inside the east London docks. Moreover the quayside lorries to which the containers were transferred were becoming too big for the East End's narrow, crooked alleyways. So the great freighters stopped at Tilbury, which had been built to modern specifications, 26 miles downstream (and where the union was less strong), or at Felixstowe, on England's eastern coast, which enabled them to avoid the Thames and London altogether. At Tilbury a mere 3000 dockers could handle 50 million tons of cargo per year. First ships and then jobs began to disappear from the Port of London; labour unrest began to grow, even as union rolls began to shrink. During the 1960s and early 1970s Jack Dash, a charismatic communist port worker, led a series of bitter dockers' strikes mainly against containerisation, opening his daily quayside address to strikers with the words: 'Good morning brothers!' But the union could no more stop the haemorrhaging of jobs at dockside than the PLA could outlaw containers and the giant freighters and lorries that carried them.

The ramifications were profound. As trade in the port declined, local industries shut down or moved. Then, in 1967, the East India Dock closed. Nearly unremarked at the time, in fact the closure was a harbinger. The London and St Katharine's Docks shut down during the following year; the Surrey Docks in 1970; the West India and Millwall Docks a decade later; the Royal Docks, last to hold out, in 1982. For every job lost in the docks three more were lost in related industries. During 1966–76 the five east London boroughs, Greenwich, Lewisham, Newham, Tower Hamlets and Southwark, lost 150,000 jobs, 20 per cent of all the jobs in the area. As unemployment rose, population declined. For example, during 1961–71, Tower Hamlets lost 18 per cent of its population, and Southwark lost 14 per cent.[4]

Neither Labour nor Conservative politicians could suggest a realistic plan for regenerating the area, let alone for bringing work back to the docks. Early in the 1970s the Conservatives favoured an arrangement that would have led to gentrification: private development of a golf course, erection of convention centres and of owner-occupied housing for between 50,000 and 100,000 new residents.[5] Not surprisingly, working-class east Londoners, that is to say the vast majority, were generally opposed. What was in it for them? But when Labour offered an alternative, the London Docklands Strategic Plan, it seemed stale and unimaginative. As the preface to the document put it: 'Existing industry must be encouraged to remain in the area but it is also essential to provide scope for new growth . . . The river Thames has been the main artery of the area throughout its history . . . The Plan reflects the Joint Committee's desire to see a flourishing and viable port.'[6] This hardly seemed to come to grips with the challenge posed by containerisation or the loss of manufacturing jobs. But even when Labour did acknowledge that the port as it once had been was gone for ever, the best it could suggest was that the docks be drained and filled with cement, so that public housing and old-style factories might be built over them. Moreover, during the critical years while Labour was in power, 1974–9, government deference to local susceptibilities, competition between local authorities, the democratic process itself, upon which Labour placed great emphasis, taken all together produced paralysis and ensured that nothing was accomplished.

Meanwhile the area as a whole continued to deteriorate. Really it was in a terrible condition, with many of the people who still lived there in desperate straits. In 1979 Margaret Thatcher's first Secretary of State for the Environment, Michael Heseltine, flew over in a small aeroplane. He saw below 'immense tracts of dereliction . . . rotting docks . . . crumbling infrastructure . . . vast expanses of polluted land left behind by modern technology and enhanced environmentalism. The place was a tip.'[7] The waste of it all made Heseltine indignant. A formidable figure, energetic, decisive and ambitious, he was determined to regenerate the area where his predecessors had failed, and to do it quickly. Taking advantage of the Local Government Planning and Land Act (1980) he established in 1981 the London Docklands Development Corporation with powers to override local government and other interests in an area stretching 8 miles down the river from Tower Bridge, 21 square kilometres of land in all (there was another Urban Development Corporation for Liverpool as well). The LDDC would be funded with public monies, but it would spend them in order to strengthen private enterprise, which, Heseltine believed, would lead to rejuvenation of the poverty-stricken areas, especially those east of Tower Bridge.

The Conservative Secretary of State knew how to get what he wanted. When Mrs Thatcher objected to the LDDC as an example of interventionist central government, (she claimed to want to roll back the powers of central government) he told her the Corporation would create prosperity in the East End, undercutting all the communists there.[8] Moreover, by definition, the LDDC would weaken high-spending, Labour-dominated local authorities, just what Mrs Thatcher was trying to do in her battle with Ken Livingstone and the GLC. On what may have been the crucial issue Heseltine and Mrs Thatcher were already as one: regeneration of the East End would increase London's prosperity, which would in turn attract international investment and capital. And this would ensure London's traditional role as a hub of European, indeed of world, finance.

So Thatcher told Heseltine to proceed with the LDDC for many reasons. It will be noted, however, that the needs of unemployed dockers and other East End workers were at best a peripheral concern and that maintenance of the dockland culture did not figure in either politician's calculations.

There was an additional dimension to the project, however, precisely because England's national river, rich in cultural and historical associations, ran twisting through it all. This made the East End more than merely a derelict no man's land at the ragged edge of an otherwise great city. Reg Ward, first chief executive of the LDDC, understood. In his initial week on the job, the former chief executive of London Borough of Hammersmith and of Hereford and Worcester County Council lunched in the National Westminster Bank tower overlooking his new domain. He saw 'eight miles of river opening up into the Thames Estuary, all the docks, and so on . . . It was the most magnificent waterscape you could ever have hoped to see . . . I was totally taken aback and I could not help saying, "But where's the bloody problem?"' Ward had a crucial insight: 'The problem in my view was one of perception, of actually seeing the area differently.'[9]

Ward called his domain 'Docklands' so that others would see the area in the same light he did. Although he merely added a single letter, 's', to the colloquial appellation, it was an inspired adaptation. A businessman said: 'Docklands . . . You think of ships arriving and there's a spirit of adventure.'[10] Another expressed the same idea in slightly different terms: 'I thought constantly . . . just standing in that dereliction and looking towards St. Paul's and Tower Bridge, this is London, it's the Thames.'[11] Perhaps the Conservative project of regeneration would have proceeded as it did whatever they called it. But Ward and the LDDC never ceased to stress the historical resonance of *Docklands*, in order to remind people that when they invested in east London they were investing in their nation's heritage.

Ward took concrete, hard-headed business steps to facilitate investment in Docklands as well. He successfully appealed to Thatcher's Chancellor of the Exchequer, Geoffrey Howe, to declare the Isle of Dogs, at the heart of the East End, an 'Enterprise Zone'. This enabled the Corporation to offer extremely generous tax allowances and other incentives to developers and entrepreneurs: freedom from planning restrictions, exemption from local property taxes, and so on. Suddenly businessmen, who were perhaps deaf to Ward's evocation of the nation's heritage, discovered the advantages of an East End location after all. 'If you spend £100,000,' one explained, 'when tax was 60 per cent you could . . . wipe out your tax bill in the first year if . . . your building had cost you £40,000. You could then let it, and in three or four years you can cover the whole cost.'[12]

With such inducements developers might consider investing much more than £100,000. In 1982 three American banks, discouraged by astronomical rents in the City, which lies only a mile or so upriver from Docklands, proposed constructing a 10-million-square foot office complex on the Isle of Dogs at the old Canary Wharf, where the West India Docks once had been. At the last moment the British adviser to the banks, G. Ware Travelstead, proved unable to secure sufficient funding, but then a Canadian firm with extensive interests and experience, Olympia & York, stepped in. The owner of this firm, the Torontonian Paul Reichmann, may not have shared Ward's romantic vision of the Isle of Dogs. He was visionary enough, however, to realise that 'the Square Mile' of the City did not contain sufficient office space for the giant trading floors increasingly required by the financial world. Reichmann proposed to the LDDC a tremendous scheme, bigger even than Travelstead's: a 12.2-million-square-foot development at Canary Wharf that would include what turned out to be the second-tallest building in Europe (designed by Cesar Pelli, and now called 1 Canada Square). But he would proceed only if the state agreed to help improve transportation to the site. He explained to Heseltine, who appealed to the prime minister. She was amenable. The Conservative government agreed to provide funds for the extension of the Docklands Light Railway system, and of the Jubilee Tube line past Canary Wharf and all the way to Stratford. So the Brobdingnagian-scale scheme went forward.

We can see now that Reichmann, Ward, Heseltine, perhaps even Thatcher herself already conceived of Docklands as a second nodal point of finance in London, an alternative to the City, a 'Wall Street on Water'. They intended to guarantee London's world financial role. To succeed, then, Docklands must be accessible not merely to the rest of the metropolis via light rail and Tube line, but to all the world via every means of modern transport. The Conservatives approved construction of new roads that cut through the Isle of Dogs, displacing hundreds of residents. They helped fund construction of London's third airport, the City Airport, which opened in 1987, on a strip of land wedged between two disused docks. At first it could accept only relatively small propeller-driven aircraft but once its runways had been extended, it began accepting jet aircraft too. Meanwhile Heseltine had heard that the Channel Tunnel Rail Link might run from the coast to Waterloo Station, south of the Thames, without ever coming near the Isle of Dogs. He rushed to a meeting of the Department of Transport where 'I argued . . . if we sent the rail link north of the Thames and included a stop at Stratford it could help to rejuvenate that rundown and poverty-stricken part of East London.' Essentially, it would prove convenient, and would represent a further inducement, to the businesses Heseltine hoped to lure there. British Rail, however, had other interests. It had already bought property along the southern route. By now Mrs Thatcher had been forced to step down, but Heseltine was on very good terms with her successor, John Major. 'I was delighted,' Heseltine reports, 'when the arguments that I had advanced . . . appealed to him.'[13]

Anticipating that lines of communication were assured, Reichmann thought the Canary Wharf project could go forward. Foundation work commenced in May 1988. Cesar Pelli's great tower 'topped out' in January 1990. The first tenants moved in during August 1991. By October 1993 the working population at the complex stood at 7000; at the end of 1994 it stood at 12,800; at the end of 1997 it had reached 21,000; by the end of the year 2000 it stood at 35,000; and in December 2002 it had climbed to 55,000.

It was not all smooth sailing, of course. The early 1990s saw a downturn in the international economy, culminating in the stock market crash of 1992. Olympia and York Canary Wharf Ltd London was placed in administration; Paul Reichmann filed for bankruptcy protection in Toronto. The government began backtracking on its commitment to extend the Jubilee Tube line. Companies that had been considering moving to the Isle of Dogs developed second thoughts. But the recession turned out to be only a hiccup, if a frightening one. One year later the banks refinanced the Canary Wharf project. Two years after that Reichmann repurchased it at the head of another consortium of property developers. Construction, development and refurbishment recommenced.

The tens of thousands employed in the Canary Wharf complex worked for the largest and most important banks, insurance companies and brokerage firms in the world. They acted as a magnet for additional business. By 1997 some 2300 companies, including most of Britain's national newspapers, had made the move to the Isle of Dogs.[14] The pace of development increased. Cheek by jowl with the council houses of unemployed dockers there now rose up glass- and granite-faced buildings, sleek, shining, some like the skyscrapers of New York City and Hong Kong, incongruous in London, perhaps, all of them overlooking London's river. Clustered among and behind were the restaurants, health clubs, hotels, shops of every description, and apartment complexes.[15]

In fact, and not surprisingly, Docklands experienced a housing boom unprecedented for east London, and perhaps unprecedented for Britain. Within the 21 square kilometres that comprised the territory administered by the LDDC, in the fifteen years after 1982 builders constructed 21,600 homes. The original population of 39,400 more than doubled. Speculators realised fortunes. During 1982–3, 99 per cent of all houses were sold in Docklands for less than £40,000. By the first half of 1985 only 43 per cent of houses sold for so little. In fact, house prices were going through the roof, trebling between 1984 and 1987, sometimes more than trebling. For instance, a two-bedroom flat on the Clipper's Quay development cost £39,495 in 1984 and £199,950 in 1987.[16]

That was at the Isle of Dogs on the northern side of the river. On the south bank too, where once derelict wharves, warehouses and factories had rotted, now the shops, restaurants, pubs, wine bars began to appear. Also new housing, including a few architecturally adventurous, mixed income low-rise blocks, but more commonly lofts in converted warehouses, and striking, expensive, low and high-rise condominiums. A series of new office buildings grew up on the south bank too. Their construction and refurbishment formed the accompaniment to a sequence of regenerative cultural projects funded by Lottery money, gaining pace as the twentieth century neared its end and climaxing with the opening of the new millennium: these included the 'London Eye', a giant Ferris wheel, that looks down upon Parliament; the planned refurbishment of the South Bank Centre containing theatres and concert halls; the new Shakespeare's Globe Theatre; and, in Southwark, across from St Paul's Cathedral, the old Bankside Power Station, a massive, not to say brutal but also visually arresting structure, largely unoccupied after 1981, converted in 2000 into the most startling and impressive museum, housing the Tate Gallery's modern collection. Immensely popular, the Tate Modern draws millions of visitors annually, many of them arriving from the north bank via a graceful new pedestrian bridge, a 'blade of light', as it has been termed by its architect, Lord Foster of

The old Bankside Power Station, now the Tate Modern, and Lord Forster of Thameside's 'blade of light', the bridge connecting the north and south banks of the river. (Rachel Royse/CORBIS)

Thameside. Other pedestrians arrive by boat, for various water services have begun to ply the river again; the great-great-grandchildren of at least a few old Thames watermen have reappeared.

Much of the development was due to the LDDC, which folded up in early 1998 after an eighteen-year run. But even today the construction boom has not run its course, and the spirit and original vision of Michael Heseltine continues to hover over an unmistakably revived east London. Moreover, Heseltine was never content to rest. Development on the Isle of Dogs and on the south bank, tremendous though it was, had transformed only a first part of the riverside wasteland. Downstream too the area was victim to the nationwide shift away from industrial manufacturing; it had undergone the same sort of decay as the original dockland itself. Cement factories along the Kent shore, which previously had accounted for more than 20 per cent of national production, now lay idle. Once flourishing paper-manufacturing companies near where the Medway flows into the Thames hardly functioned any more. Chemical and engineering industries located along the river banks also had sharply declined.[17] But, Heseltine asked himself, could not the same vision and methods that were revolutionising the Isle of Dogs and south bank be applied to this larger area? Could not the entire gravity of London, already responding to the weight of Docklands, begin to shift east, facing outwards towards the Channel and Europe? Heseltine, or one of his colleagues, found the term to encapsulate the deepest meaning of his expanded project as he was coming to understand it: *Thames Gateway*. He hoped that it would be every bit as evocative as *Docklands*.

On 12 December 1991 the Minister of State for the Environment went on television to outline a grandiose scheme of continuing and more extensive regeneration. As on the Isle of Dogs, new, clean, technologically advanced industries, vastly improved lines of transport and communication, public amenities and private housing would provide its basis. And, as with Canary Wharf, the presence of the river would be key. After all, historically, the Thames had been the highway that bore

Britain's commerce, and that made London great and prosperous. The river could take centre stage again, as it had upstream from Westminster to the Isle of Dogs, even if only as an amenity. It would provide a perfect backdrop to the regeneration not merely of a derelict stretch east of London, but of Britain itself. For Heseltine believed that, when once revived, the East Thames Corridor would link his country ever more closely with Europe, and that this was the crucial connection that would safeguard Britain's economic future.

As Canary Wharf had been the key to Docklands, so another enormous structure, the Millennium Dome, with an overall diameter of 365 metres and a circumference of an entire kilometre, was intended to jump-start the Thames Gateway project. The Dome was not another office building but a public space, designed by Richard Rogers (Lord Rogers of Riverside), architect of the Pompidou Centre in Paris among other structures. When complete it would contain hundreds of exhibitions, restaurants, and shops; it would employ thousands. Given that its construction was intended to celebrate the turning of the great wheel, the end of a thousand-year period and the beginning of a new one, it could not have been built anywhere except Greenwich, 'home of world time', although other sites were considered. That Greenwich had lost 500 businesses and 10,000 jobs in the last two years, and that the site for building would have to be reclaimed from the most awful pollution, was also important.

It is still too soon to say whether Thames Gateway will succeed in the manner of Docklands. Heseltine writes proudly of the night the Millennium Dome opened: '31 December 1999, [when] my family and I had the privilege of sailing down the Thames in the company of Her Majesty the Queen and the Duke of Edinburgh to attend the spectacular . . . ceremonies in Greenwich.'[18] In fact, only a little more than a year later the Dome stood empty, exhibitions, restaurants and shops all closed, the government no longer sure what to do with it. Since then, however, Sol Kerzner, the swashbuckling South African hotel and spa developer, and an American partner, Philip Auschutz, a dotcom billion-aire, have announced plans to turn it into a vast Las Vegas-style casino, complete with gaming tables and nine hundred slot machines. A six hundred-bed hotel will be attached. But first the Labour Government must amend Britain's gaming laws.

Further downstream housing estates, shopping malls and new clean industries are sprouting along the old East Thames Corridor. As on the Isle of Dogs they glitter and sparkle amid post-industrial squalor. It is a question whether Tony Blair's Labour Party, or Ken Livingstone, mayor of London, and his allies, will temper the Thatcherite model, but indubitably the river has been transformed.

What of the old East Enders, however, and especially what of the dockers, made redundant by containerisation? Did regeneration hold promise for them?

If it did, most could not see it. A local poet wrote:

Cranes standing still, no work for them
No movement, a monument to times past.
Silhouette outlined against a London sky.

Their reflection, mirrored in the waters of a silent dock
Casting their shadows across the decks of pleasure yachts.

Like a cancer spreading, with unchecked speed,
Wharves, warehouses closed overnight
Transformed, renovated
Not for people who have no place to live,
But for those who with obscene ease
Sail their yachts whenever they please,
Leaving them moored outside their second homes.
It's all part of our social disease.

Docks closed
Once where dock workers played their part,
Shifting cargo, keeping London alive.
Now silence reigns, it is supreme
Thrusting aside this industrial scene.

Gone now, this way of life,
Testimony to the power of those few
Whose decisions carry far and wide,
Eroding, encroaching, changing the
Character of our riverside.[19]

During the 1980s and early 1990s many residents of the Isle of Dogs interpreted regeneration as an attack upon their way of life and values. How could they not? Twenty years on we may liken them to Luddites who stood in the path of a juggernaut. They were doomed. But of course they could not know it at the time.

Some diehards, perhaps including the poet above, believed the PLA had closed the docks because it made more money selling property to developers than it did unloading ships. They thought that the old factory owners had deserted the Thames Corridor in search of cheaper labour. It followed that the next socialist government, if it stuck to its principles, could induce or force them to return, and could reopen the docks as well. The Port of London would flourish again.

Other east Londoners, more numerous undoubtedly and more realistic, were resigned to the closing of the docks and the departure of traditional heavy industry, but nevertheless resented the LDDC approach. They longed for one that was more humane and less obviously materialistic. East London, after all, had been a heartland of Labour socialism. How could men and women steeped in its traditions welcome the unbridled capitalism for which the LDDC stood?

The Isle of Dogs in particular remained a redoubt of old Labour.

Occupying a bottom corner, as it were, of the East End, it had always seemed slightly distanced from the rest of London. Residents were relatively socially homogeneous, which is to say white and working class. For generations sons had followed fathers into the docks, much as the sons of miners followed their fathers into the pits. To visit the Isle of Dogs was 'like going back in time', said one who moved there in the 1980s.[20] The literature abounds with nostalgic accounts of the area's neighbourly attractions and communal identity. This was no 'imagined community', but a real one, if poor and slightly isolated. Or rather, it had been a community. Now at breathtaking speed came the transformation, and old-time Islanders did not like it.

Housing was a main arena of contention. In 1981, 83 per cent of residents in the three Dockland boroughs lived in public housing estates. Margaret Thatcher wanted to cut back public housing, in part because she thought home ownership would inculcate values that were likely to benefit Conservatives. Her government encouraged council tenants to purchase their homes, often at cut-rate prices. Meanwhile, of course, private developers were descending upon Docklands in search of profits. They were less interested in building for the impecunious locals than for the much wealthier newcomers who, perhaps, now had jobs at Canary Wharf. In any event they had no intention of building houses for rent; they built for owner-occupiers only.

Some of the better-off among the old residents managed to ride the wave. They were able to purchase their council homes, to sell them for refurbishment, at a profit, to the interlopers, and then to move away. The majority, however, could not afford this route. Instead they found themselves surrounded by newcomers, aliens, who were much richer than they, and who were living for the most part in extremely glitzy quarters. The contrast with the shabby old council estates, the disparity between rented and newly purchased accommodation, between private wealth and public squalor as the apt phrase had it at the time, was vivid, and galling. In July 1986 local residents held a protest demonstration

Wall Street on water: Canary Wharf as it appears today. (Getty Images)

The docks three hundred years ago. (Engraving of St Katherine's Dock in the East End from *Old and New London: The City Ancient and Modern* (vol. 1) by Walter Thornbury, 1897. Photo by Time Life Pictures/Mansell/Getty Images)

outside the offices of Christopher Benson, chairman of the LDDC. His bland response can have done little to reassure them: 'The variety of life in Docklands is very much the key to its unique character and it is encouraging to watch it increasing by the day.'[21]

But the old-timers did not respond well to this kind of 'variety', which they saw rather as 'disparity'. 'They think they own the . . . waterfront,' complained one of them about the newcomers. A rumour now swept the Isle of Dogs: previously, in hot weather local children had swum in the empty docks; these had been turned into yacht basins and now the children could not enter.[22]

And the newcomers did not much care for the old. Attempts to interleave the two groups were disastrous. At Tobacco Wharf, angry owner-occupiers threatened to sue. They had not known the development would be socially mixed. As one middle-class newcomer told a journalist, he had not paid more than £200,000 'to live in a council estate'. His neighbours were noisy litterbugs who hung out the washing and put up television aerials. Moreover, some of them were Asian. His newly formed tenant association would seek compensation for the alleged drop in property values.

Class distinctions on the Isle of Dogs, always sharply drawn, teetered on a knife's edge. An extreme sect of anarchists emerged. They called themselves 'Class War'. 'The rich flaunt their wealth under our very noses,' they wrote in their newspaper. The rich would learn to rue the day, however, for eventually the poor would rise up against 'gentrification, trendification . . . Yuppiefication'. Class War advocated mugging middle-class newcomers and vandalising their fancy cars. Members of the group pushed letters through East End letter boxes: 'For some reason you have chosen to move [here],' one of them read. 'It should be pointed out to you that this may be a grave mistake.'

But nothing could stop the influx of newcomers on to the Isle of Dogs. Developers merely adapted to the resistance put up by the old-timers. They built gates and other protective devices to keep the anarchists out. For example the 'Free Trade Wharf', a complex of more than three hundred apartments, offered '24-hour porterage with a secure reception area, door telephones, alarms to detect attempts at forced entry, panic buttons in each flat, and video cameras around the development'.[23]

The struggle for housing grew increasingly ugly. Whether anyone paid much attention to Class War may be doubted, but the advocates of race war gained a hearing. In fact there was a recrudescence of Mosleyism. The local council had begun sending homeless Bangladeshi families into such council houses as the Isle of Dogs still possessed. And it was not just the middle-class newcomers who objected to living near them. After all, the Bangladeshis were competing directly with the old white working-class residents for scarce public accommodation. They had neither wealth nor powerful supporters, and their customs were stranger even than those of the yuppies. The Labour Party had been campaigning against the Conservatives on the slogan 'Housing for all', but in such desperate times this traditional appeal for equity seemed out of date to some. A fascist candidate for the British National Party, Derek Beackon, now appeared, demanding that the Bangladeshis be sent elsewhere. In local council elections held in September 1993 he won a seat. Labour changed its slogan to 'Homes for local people'. In elections held nine months later this opportunistic catchphrase (it could be turned against the wealthy newcomers, or against the Bangladeshis) proved just ambiguous enough. Labour regained the seat. But the BNP received 2041 votes, an increase of 561.[24]

Housing was the main issue, but it was not the only one; unemployment was another. The docks had closed. The local industries that so often had depended upon manual labour were going or gone, replaced by high-tech new ones, and by service industries. Eastenders' old skills were next to useless in this brave new world. Here, as in housing, one sees a growing disparity. On the one hand, employment overall increased in Docklands, doubling between 1981 and 1996. The number employed in banking, finance, insurance, leasing and business services increased from 1500 to over 20,000.[25] On the other hand, long-time East End residents who possessed outmoded skills, or semi-skills, or no skills, usually remained unemployed. Between 1981 and 1985 unemployment on the Isle of Dogs rose from 18.7 per cent to 24 per cent.[26] As late as January 1997 the unemployment rate for Millwall on the Isle of Dogs was 12 per cent, and for Blackwall 19 per cent. The absolute number of unemployed in the LDDC area was greater, fifteen years after regeneration had begun, than it had been at the outset.[27]

And impalpable but omnipresent was the sense of lost community, of the passing of a way of life. In the old days East End neighbours kept their doors open, they sat on front steps and chatted with each other, they met at the butcher's and baker's and greengrocer's shops, or at the pub. In the new housing complexes, however, residents kept themselves to themselves, they purchased delicacies at expensive shops or ate in restaurants. 'There is nothing here for people with no money,' said Mrs Shirley Sempare, a welfare recipient and resident of 'Tobacco Wharf', the socially mixed development of new flats. 'It's too quiet, there are no supermarkets . . . I have got to pay £8 for a taxi to Bethnal Green just to get food.'[28]

Nor did regeneration take into account the precepts of the welfare state, once an animating force in the East End. In Heseltine's view regeneration meant precisely the opposite of the welfare state: entrepreneurship, competition, individualism. To dockers and their families, steeped in the lore of their union, however, it meant a return to the days when men fought each other for a job in the hiring shed. It was this sense of an antithesis, as much as the tangible difficulties with jobs and housing, which animated local opposition to the regeneration of east London.

But what could the old residents do? There was no point complaining to local government, because local government, while it agreed with them, had no power over the LDDC. In fact, for a time, there seemed precious little point to local government at all, since when the LDDC invited representatives from each council to join, they all refused, preferring to boycott. Why turn to politicians who chose isolation and impotence?

Activists thought for a while that they might sue the developers who were forcing them to live with the noise and dust and general inconvenience of massive construction projects. They floated a figure they thought might compensate, £100 million. Another, smaller group who were to be relocated because they lived in the path of a new road, broached a smaller suit, £10 million. Neither suit ever went to court. Yet another group drew up a 'People's Charter for Docklands'. No single document could better have illustrated the profound gulf between Heseltine's vision for the area, and their own. The Charter demanded public housing and jobs for people with traditional local skills. It called for funds for retraining programmes, and for improved public trans-port in and to the area, and for essential public services like health and education. One sunny day in 1984 advocates of the Charter put together a 'People's Armada', which sailed from Woolwich to West-minster, the Charter aboard the lead boat. They delivered their petition to 10 Downing Street where, perhaps needless to say, they did not enjoy a warm reception. (Ken Livingstone had received them warmly enough first, in Jubilee Gardens, but he was powerless to help.) Like the original Chartists they delivered the petition twice more (in 1985 and 1986), three times in all.[29] And like the original Chartists they met with a blank refusal to seriously consider their demands.

The historical analogy may be taken a little bit further. The first Chartists, who were calling for democratic political reforms during the 1830s and 1840s, failed in part because they confronted an unyielding state with massive power, so much stronger than they, and in part because their own difficult working and living conditions began to improve, so that their demands seemed less pressing to many. In the

East End in the 1990s, the latter-day Chartists likewise faced an unyielding powerful government, and likewise a situation that, in some ways at any rate, began to improve. Under pressure, new leadership of the LDDC had finally begun sponsoring job-retraining programmes; it put money into local education projects, for example £3 million into Bacon's City Technology College; it purchased £1 million worth of computers for local elementary schools. The children of the latter-day Chartists understood that the path forward, or at least to a job, lay not through the dock gates, but through the schoolhouse door. Where in 1981, 75 per cent of Docklands students had quit school as soon as they were old enough, in 1997, 75 per cent were staying on for some form of higher education.[30]

Like the earlier movement for a People's Charter, the movement of protest against regeneration in east London died not so much with a bang as with a whimper. The ideals to which the old residents of the East End clung were not necessarily irrelevant, but the material world that had shaped them was dead. Their children would learn to live in a new world, the one envisioned for them by Michael Heseltine. Many of them would move to the new private housing estates springing up further east along the Thames Corridor, where they would learn to 'speak Estuary'. More importantly they would learn the new technologies, and they would go to work in the new service industries. Perhaps they would vote New Labour.

But the Thames that had meant life to generations of working-class East Enders had finally doomed our twentieth-century Chartists. It had brought to 'Docklands' wealthy men and women who elbowed them out of the way because they wanted, from their sleek, towering office blocks, and glossy new four-bedroom flats, a river view.

Conclusion

The Thames and the Nation

*T*he river rolls in from the sea and up to London with the tide; at the other end it rises in a field near Cirencester to dampen the green grass in a dark curving line that soon becomes a stream. The salt water from the sea and the clear sweet water from the low Cotswold hills meet at Teddington. Some things do not change.

Many of the meanings with which Britons have invested this 220-mile-long waterway are changeless too, or anyway they are extremely long-lived.[1] Always the Thames was crucial to those who drew their drinking water from it; always it meant life to the men and women who farmed along its banks; always it was a path followed by invaders (although military technology has changed so dramatically since 1940 that probably the river will no longer continue to signify in this regard). For two thousand years, until the 1960s, it was Britain's prime commercial artery. For half a millennium or more, from before the reign of Henry VIII right through to Ken Livingstone's leadership of the GLC, England's rulers, or London's, have used it as a flowing stage. On the river Thames they scripted pageants and spectacles intended to strengthen their political positions. Doubtless they will continue to do so.

For centuries the river has given pleasure to anglers and boaters and swimmers and many more: until old London Bridge came down in 1831 the people used to walk upon the Thames when it froze, flocking to the great frost fairs. West of London they used to sail and paddle and motor on it, as William Morris did during the summer of 1880, and they still do, in boats and barges that slide or chug upon the winding stream through fields and pastures and woodlands. For a hundred and fifty years they have crowded on to its bridges and, like so many thousand dancing beads on a long, long string, they have lined its banks, to watch and cheer the oarsmen during regatta week in a dozen Thames-side villages.

We know that the river has had more awful meanings too. Once it was the stopped bottleneck that trapped the mutinous seamen of 1797; once it provided a dismal backdrop to the hellish convict ships anchored in Thames-side mud; for years it was a streaming sewer, producing a 'Big Stink'; in 1878 it was the monstrous, dripping apparition with clutching tentacles that snatched at a thousand despairing passengers thrown from the doomed pleasure cruiser, the *Princess Alice*; in 1953 it was a freezing spring surge tide that drowned fifty-eight residents of Canvey Island.

The Thames, as we have seen, is really two rivers. The tidal river, with its swift currents running through the flat salt marshes that stretch from the estuary all the way to London, is the river that directly links Britain with the rest of the globe. It bore the world's traffic even in Roman times; eventually it made London the world's greatest port. This is the river that the Elizabethan sea dogs knew. They glided in their sailing ships down from London, past the royal palace at Greenwich, under the watchful eye of the Virgin Queen, on their way to 'singe the beard' of the Spanish king, as one of them put it; and then across the oceans and back again with prizes and booty, and wounded sailors. In the end, as we have learned, the last of the great sixteenth-century adventurers, Sir Walter Raleigh, did not know this river well enough. He

might as well have thrown himself from a bridge to drown in it, as plan
to row upon the Thames to freedom, and miss the ebb tide. But many
seamen have better understood the river's changeable moods. They
form a line that begins long before Sir Walter was born, and that extends
beyond A.P. Herbert who, during 1939–45, learned the currents and the
two shorelines and the great mouth of the river by heart, and who
loved it all with the undying love of unshakeable patriotism and who
was willing to defend it with his life.

Then there is the other river, the sweet Thames running softly west
of London. That is the river that William Morris loved best, and that
Stanley Spencer worshipped. It is the Thames beloved by many poets
and artists, but not only by them. Walk the Thames Path, just east of
Oxford, on any fine autumn morning and you will see the sculls and the
fours and the racing eights slipping swiftly, noiselessly past. Take the
path west from the town out along Port Meadow and you will see a
riverscape essentially unchanged for a thousand years, with geese and
ducks and graceful swans; and on either side grazing cows and horses.
This is a bucolic Thames that is far from the salt sea, and the powerful
tides, and the teeming port.

The Thames is England's river, it is a thread woven through the tapestry of national history. Before the Romans came, part of it served as a
boundary between rival tribes; after the Romans left, part of it was the
borderline separating Britons ruled by King Alfred's law from Britons
ruled by Danelaw. Because it held military significance and economic
significance, it is historically significant. We have seen that a field at
Runnymede, along the banks of the Thames, afforded neutral ground
for the barons and King John to meet upon. There they were safe to discuss and agree the Magna Carta. And because the winding river made
possible the great Port of London and was therefore crucial to the
national economy, and because it provided a plain, if twisty, route to the
world's metropolis, therefore, as we have seen also, invaders from time
immemorial all the way up to the German pilots of 1940 followed it

from the sea to the city, which they wished either to capture or destroy. Great events have taken place on, or near, or above the river. It has been central to English life and therefore to British history.

At certain moments the river has helped to crystallise a vision of the nation. Turner's *Rain, Steam, and Speed* with its fiery locomotive blasting over the river like a military conqueror captured in an instant a new understanding of a transformed Britain. The Thames symbolised what England had been; the steam engine and Brunel's bridge suggested what it had become. In 1940 Britain's German would-be conquerors, raining down bombs upon old dockland, made the river into a national symbol again. For them the Thames, where it wound through the docks, represented British power, British economic might, in a sense it represented British history. For Britons it stood for national defiance and for all the national virtues. The river practically *was* Great Britain for a time during the spring of 1940. Nearly half a century later, during the Oxford boat club mutiny of 1987, arguably some Britons associated the river with a socially exclusive vision of the nation too.

National identity is a complicated concept that we have addressed only in passing. In any event perhaps the Thames is more bound up with regional than national identities, although these too shift over time. For example, as we have seen, most residents of the Isle of Dogs understood themselves and their community very differently a hundred years ago from the way they do today. When the docks along the river provided a livelihood then they stamped east London: it was, in its heyday, close-knit, working-class and communitarian. That is gone now. When the docks and other industries closed, and the banks and insurance companies and stockbrokers and private developers moved in, the character of the area altered profoundly. Perhaps something similar may be said of the identity of south-east England more generally, for it is undergoing a similar evolution.

West of London, too, the Thames has contributed to senses of

regional identity, for example to the one many viewers thought they
saw in Stanley Spencer's landscapes with their cosy cottages, neat fields
and hedgerows, and particular English flowers. Here we would seem to
have a notion of identity hooked into a misunderstanding of the great
artist, since viewers thought, quite mistakenly, that Spencer meant to
suggest the absence of social tensions in this countryside.

More generally the Thames's accumulation of meanings over the
centuries, its interconnectedness with so much history, has linked it
with evolving understandings of the nation and its heritage. Britons
identify themselves as heirs to a record through which the river has
always run.

When Winston Churchill died he was honoured with a funeral procession upon the Thames. At Tower Pier on 30 January 1965, just as the
clock struck one, just when the tide was full, a bearer party of Grenadier
Guards placed his flag-draped coffin upon the afterdeck of *Havengore*, a
survey vessel belonging to the Port of London Authority. Royal Navy
pipers skirled a lament. Huge crowds pressed against the pier gates; they
lined the banks of the river ten deep; they crammed the bridges that
Havengore would pass beneath. A Royal Marine band struck up 'Rule
Britannia', a saluting battery fired a seventeen-gun salute from the
Tower of London, and *Havengore* cast off, accompanied by three other
large PLA motor launches and as many police boats. Royal Air Force
fighters screamed overhead in boxes of four.

As the procession moved slowly west, towards Festival Pier, all the
cranes on both sides of the river, erect until now, swung and dipped, like
men removing their hats in respect, or like flags at half mast. It was an
eerie, extraordinary gesture (one that could not have been performed
only a few years later; there would have been no cranes left to dip), and
it was enough to make the hair stand up on the necks of some observers.
On the BBC, to a worldwide audience estimated at 350 million, President
Dwight D. Eisenhower of the United States paid a final tribute: 'Upon

the mighty Thames, a great avenue of history, move at this moment to their final resting place the mortal remains of Winston Churchill.' At that moment, the sun broke through the clouds, turning the grey river silver and gold.[2]

Churchill had been the captain when, twenty-five years earlier, England's fate was fought out above that very river. In a previous world war, while he was First Lord of the Admiralty, he had been responsible for every fighting ship that nosed its way down from the London docks and out into the sea. The river ran through his personal history as it ran through his country's; now his water-borne funeral procession evoked events that had transpired long before he was born: most obviously the great Thames processions of the lord mayors and kings and queens, including the first Queen Elizabeth, whose body had been transported downriver to Whitehall in a procession of black-draped barges in 1603; also England's naval traditions and its past as a great trading nation that depended upon command of the seas. But England had fought, in 1940, for the right to decide its own future. The sombre ceremony marking Churchill's death pointed forward, as well as to the past.

Winston Churchill's funeral procession upon England's river concentrates understanding. Great Britain's history; a people's consciousness of that history, which is to say, national identity at last; a future beyond sight: the Thames informs them all. *Havengore* rides the flood tide upstream.

Notes

PREFACE

1 The Severn is longer than the Thames.
2 See, for example, W.V. Emanuel, *River Thames*, London, n.d.; L.S.R. Byrne and
   E.L. Churchill, *The Eton Book of the River*, Eton, 1935; A.P. Herbert, *The Thames*,
   London, 1966; Paul Atterbury, *The Thames: From the Source to the Sea*, London,
   1998, L.T.C. Rolt, *The Thames, From Mouth to Source*, London, 1951; W.H. Owens,
   Royal River, London, 1953.

1 THE REEDS OF RUNNYMEDE

1 There are more books about the Thames than a single scholar can read.
   Among those the present author found helpful are: Paul Atterbury, *The
   Thames: From the Source to the Sea*, London, 1998; Leslie Banks and Christopher
   Stanley, *The Thames: A History from the Air*, Oxford, 1990; Hilaire Belloc, *The
   Historic Thames*, London, 1887; Geoffrey Boumphrey, *Down River: A Canoe Tour on
   the Severn and Thames*, London, 1936; L.S.R. Byrne and E.L. Churchill, *The Eton Book
   of the River*, Eton, 1935; Basil Cracknell, *Portrait of London River*, London, 1968; W.V.
   Emanuel, *River Thames*, London, n.d.; Paul Gedge, *Thames Journey*, London, 1949;
   Roger Griffiths, *An Essay to prove that the Jurisdiction and Conservancy of the River of
   Thames, &c. is committed to the Lord Mayor and City of London . . .*, London, 1746; A.P.
   Herbert, *The Thames*, London, 1966; W.H. Owens, *Royal River*, London, 1953;
   L.T.C. Rolt, *The Thames, From Mouth to Source*, London, 1951; Fred S. Thacker, *The*

Stripling Thames, A book of the river above Oxford, London, 1909, and *The Thames Highway, A General History*, London, 1914; Alwyne Wheeler, *The Tidal Thames: the History of a River and its Fishes*, London, 1979; David Gordon Wilson, *The Victorian Thames*, Dover, NH, 1993; Patrick Wright, *The River: The Thames in Our Time*, London, 1999.

2   For 600 million years the earth was a lifeless planet. The first microscopic organisms appeared perhaps 4000 million years ago in warm nutrient-rich pools in rock crevices. The first membrane-bound cell nucleus in which genetic information could be stored and transmitted appeared perhaps 2000 to 1000 million years ago. The atmosphere reached its present oxygen levels, permitting complex forms of life, perhaps 600 million years ago. The first human-like bipeds appeared less than 5 million years ago.

3   Our current trend of global warming may only represent another swing of the pendulum; alternatively (and probably) it is the result of human interventions. In either case it is momentary when understood in context. The world endures. If humankind does not survive, if global warming leads to scarcity and famine and finally provokes a nuclear war, then the glaciers may yet return to scour clean whatever debris remains from our brief moment on earth.

4   All information on geology and geomorphology of Britain and the Thames is derived from the following secondary sources: J.R.L. Anderson, *The Upper Thames*, London, 1970; Ron Freethy, *The Natural History of Rivers*, Lavenham, 1986; Anna Grayson, *Rock Solid, Britain's Most Ancient Heritage*, London, 1992; Luna B. Leopold, *Water: A Primer*, San Francisco, 1974; Richard and Nina Muir, *Rivers of Britain*, London, 1986; Michael Reed, *The Landscape of Britain*, London, 1990; I.G. Simmons, M.J. Tooley (eds), *The Environment in British Prehistory*, London, 1981; N.A. Verona, *Past Worlds: The Times Atlas of Archaeology*, London, 1988; 'The River Thames – Its Geology, Geography and Vital Statistics from Source to Sea'.

5   All information on Swanscombe and our earliest ancestors is derived from the following secondary sources: Anderson, *Upper Thames*; D.R. Bridgeland, *Quaternary of the Thames*, London, 1994; V. Gordon Childe, *Prehistoric Communities of the British Isles*, London, 1940; Nick Ashton, Bernard Conway and John McNabb (eds), *Excavations at Barnfield Pit, Swanscombe, 1968–72*, London, 1996; Peter Drewett, David Rudling and Mark Gardiner, *The South-East to AD 1000*, London, 1988; John Evans, *The Environment of Early Man in the British Isles*, London, 1975; Grayson, *Rock Solid*; Reed, *Landscape*; Simmons and Tooley, *Environment*; Verona, *Past Worlds*; Robert J. Wenke, *Patterns in Prehistory: Humankind's First Three Million Years*, Oxford, 1999; David Gordon Wilson, *The Making of the Middle Thames*, Bourne End, 1977. See also *The Times*, 4 June 2002, 'Anglia Man' becomes earliest Ancient Briton.

6   For post-Swanscombe Woman neolithic Britain see: Tim Allen, Nicholas Barton and Andrew Brown, *Lithics and Landscape: Archaeological Discoveries on the*

Thames Water Pipeline at Gatehampton Farm, Goring, Oxfordshire, 1985–92, Oxford, 1995; T.G. Allen, T.C. Darvill, L.S. Green and M.U. Jones, *Excavations at Roughground Farm, Lechlade, Gloucestershire: a Prehistoric and Roman Landscape*, Oxford, 1993; T.G. Allen and M.A. Robinson, *The Prehistoric Landscape and Iron Age Enclosed Settlement at Mingies Ditch*, Oxford, 1993; Anderson, *Upper Thames*; Banks and Stanley, *Thames*; I. Barnes, W.A. Boismier, R.M.J. Cleal, A.P. Fitzpatrick and M.R. Roberts, *Early Settlement in Berkshire: Mesolithic-Roman Occupation Sites in the Thames and Kennet Valleys*, Salisbury, 1995; D.J. Briggs, G.R. Coope and D.D. Gilbertson (eds), *The Chronology and Environmental Framework of Early Man in the Upper Thames Valley, A New Model*, Oxford, 1985; Childe, *Prehistoric*; D.W. Harding, *The Iron Age in the Upper Thames Basin*, Oxford, 1972; John Hawkes and Vince Jenkins, *The Past in Progress: The Archaeology of the Thames Valley Business Park*, London, 1989; Hoskins, *The Making of the English Landscape*, London, 1988; George Lambrick and Mark Robinson, *Iron Age and Roman Riverside Settlements at Farmoor, Oxfordshire*, Oxford, 1979; F.H. Thompson, (ed.), *Archaeology and Coastal Change*, London, 1980; Reed, *Landscape*; Wilson, *The Victorian*.

7   See Stewart Needham, *The Passage of the Thames: Holocene Environment and Settlement at Runnymede*, London, 2000, p. 242.

8   All information on the Runnymede settlement is taken from Needham, *Passage*, and Drewett et al., *South East*.

9   According to linguists the name Londinium is probably pre-Roman, possibly derived from the pre-Celtic Old European *Plowonida*, from two roots, *plew* and *nejd*, meaning something like the flowing river or the wide flowing river. Londinium therefore meant the settlement on the wide river.

10 Material on Roman London taken from Keith Branigan, *Roman Britain, Life in an Imperial Province*, London, 1980; Peter Marsden, *Ships of the Port of London: First to Eleventh Centuries AD*, London, 1994; Gustave Milne, *The Port of Roman London*, London, 1985; Brian Hobley and Gustave Milne (eds), *Waterfront Archaeology in Britain and Northern Europe*, London, 1981. More generally see R.G. Collingwood and J.N.L. Myres, *Roman Britain and the English Settlements*, Oxford, 1975; H.C. Darby (ed.), *An Historical Geography of England before A.D. 1800*, Cambridge, 1951; Malcolm Todd, *Roman Britain, 55 BC–AD 400*, London, 1981. For Roman military tactics see Norman Longmate, *Defending the Island, Caesar to the Armada*, London, 1989.

11 Allen, Darvill et al., *Excavations*.

12 For Roman farms and villas see: Allen, Darvill et al., *Excavations*; Lambrick and Robinson, *Iron Age*; Allen, Barton et al., *Lithics*; Hawkes and Jenkins, *Past*; Drewett et al, *The Southeast*. For Beddington particularly see Drewett et al., *South East*.

2 THE RIVER AND LIBERTY

1 For an idiosyncratic version of this period see Major Philip Thomas Godsal, *The Storming of London and the Thames Valley Campaign*, London, 1908. For a more scholarly approach see Norman Longmate, *Defending the Island, Caesar to the Armada*, London, 1989.

2 C. Warren Hollister, *The Making of England, 55 B.C. to 1399*, Lexington, Mass., 1983, pp. 48, 51.

3 Although N.A.M. Rodger is not so sure. See his *The Safeguard of the Sea, A Naval History of Britain, Vol. 1, 660–1649*, London, 1997, pp. 14–17.

4 For Windsor Castle see Michael De-la-Noy, *Windsor Castle, Past and Present*, London, 1990; Olwen Hedley, *Windsor Castle*, London, 1994; Christopher Hibbert, *The Court at Windsor*, London, 1982; John Martin Robinson, *Windsor Castle, A Short History*, London, 1996.

5 J.C. Holt, *Magna Carta*, Cambridge, 1991, pp. 160–1.

6 For Magna Carta in addition to Holt see V.H. Galbraith, 'Runnymede Revisited', *Proceedings of the American Philosophical Society*, vol. 110, no. 5, 27 October 1966; Anne Pallister, *Magna Carta: The Heritage of Liberty*, Oxford, 1971. See too Jerome K. Jerome, *Three Men in a Boat*, London, 1989, p. 96.

7 Clayton and David Roberts, *A History of England, Prehistory to 1714*, Englewood Cliffs, 1985, p. 122.

8 And did not cease even then. The plague returned to England in 1390, 1407 and periodically throughout the fifteenth century.

9 Simon Schama, *A History of Britain*, Vol. 1, London, 2000, p. 246.

10 Rodney Hilton, *Bond Men Made Free*, London 1973, p. 183.

11 Quoted in Schama, *History of Britain*, p. 247.

12 Quoted in Schama, *History of Britain*, p. 248.

13 H. Fagan and Rodney Hilton, *The English Rising of 1381*, London, 1950, pp. 94–5.

3 THE TIDES OF HISTORY

1 Of course the Tower of London served not only as a prison but as a residence for the royal family. It contained a menagerie. For more on the Tower see G. Abbott, *Great Escapes from the Tower of London*, London, 1982; Christopher Hibbert, *Tower of London*, New York, 1971; W.J. Loftie, *Authorised Guide to the Tower of London*, London, 1888; Geoffrey Parnell, *The Tower of London, Past and Present*, London, 1998; A.L. Rowse, *The Tower of London in the History of the Nation*, London, 1972; Derek Wilson, *The Tower of London*, London, 1989.

2 For Arbella Stuart see G. Abbott, *Great Escapes*; David N. Durant, *Arbella Stuart, A Rival to the Queen*, London, 1978; Sara Jayne Steen (ed.), *The Letters of Lady Arbella Stuart*, Oxford, 1994. I regret that I could not consult Sarah Gristwood,

Arbella; England's Lost Queen, London, 2004, which was published after I had written this chapter.

3 For Walter Raleigh see Robert Lacey, *Sir Walter Raleigh*, London, 1973; Rowse, *The Tower*; Wilson, *The Tower*.

4 STAGING THE RIVER

1 For Anne Boleyn see E.W. Ives, *Anne Boleyn*, Oxford, 1986; Retha M. Warnicke, *The Rise and Fall of Anne Boleyn*, Cambridge, 1989.

2 Henry, who died in 1612, did not live long enough to influence his father's policies, a tragedy for Walter Raleigh, whom the young man thought to have been unfairly imprisoned. Who but his father, Henry had been heard to mutter, 'would cage such a bird'?

3 Quoted in Godfrey Davis, *The Early Stuarts, 1603–1660*, Oxford, 1959, pp. 148–9.

4 See Pepys's diary entry for 23 August 1662.

5 Handel had composed some bits and pieces of the *Water Music* for a concert on the river on 22 August 1715.

6 Although note here that one of Handel's biographers considers the *Water Music* to exude 'Gallic charm'. See Jonathan Keates, *Handel: The Man and His Music*, London, 1985, p. 77.

7 For Handel see Donald Burrows and Robert Hume, 'George I, the Haymarket Opera Company and Handel's "Water Music", *Early Music*, vol. XIX, no. 3, August 1991; Otto Erich Deutsch, *Handel, A Documentary Biography*, London, 1955; Keates, *Handel*; H.C. Robbins Landon, *Handel and His World*, London, 1984; Jacob Simon (ed.), *Handel: A Celebration of his Life and Times, 1685–1759*, London, 1986; Julia K. Wood, '"A flowing harmony": Music on the Thames in Restoration London', *Early Music*, vol. XXIII, no. 4, November 1995.

8 The provincial ports were very much secondary, although Southampton had mounted a brief challenge.

9 Roy Strong, *The Tudor and Stuart Monarchy: Pageantry, Painting, Iconography*, Vol II, Woodbridge, 1995, pp. 26–32.

10 For the procession of 1610 see Nathaniell Fosbrooke, *London's Love to the Royal Prince Henrie, Meeting him on the river of Thames at his return from Richmonde, with a worthie fleete of her citizens on Thursday the last of May 1610, with a briefe reporte of the water fight and fire workes*, London, 1610; David Bergeron (ed.), *Pageants and Entertainments of Anthony Munday: A Critical Edition*, New York, 1985. For the procession of 1662 see John Tatham, *Aqua Triumphalis; Being a True Relation of the Honourable the City of Londons Entertaining Their Sacred Majesties Upon the River of Thames, and Wellcoming Them From Hampton-Court to White-Hall. Expressed and set forth in Several Shews and Pageants the 23 day of August 1662*, London, 1662. For the Lord Mayor's processions see David M. Bergeron (ed.), *Thomas Heywood's Pageants: A Critical Edition*, New York, 1986;

Sheila Williams, 'A Lord Mayor's Show by John Taylor, the Water Poet', *Bulletin of the John Rylands Library*, vol. 41, no. 2, March 1959, pp. 502–29. See also W.V. Emanuel, *River Thames*, London, n.d.; Strong, *Tudor and Stuart*; Jean Wilson, *Entertainments for Elizabeth I*, Englewood, 1980.

11 Timothy Barringer, *The Cole Family: Painters of the English Landscape, 1838–1975*, Portsmouth, 1988, p. 98.

12 For frost fairs see Robert Beddard, 'The London Frost Fair of 1683–84', *Guildhall Miscellany*, vol. IV, no. 2, April 1972; D. Brown, *An Historical Account of the Late Great Frost in which are Discovered in several Comical Relations the various Humours, Loves, Cheats and Intreagues of the Town, as the same were managed upon the River of Thames during that Season*, London 1684; Charles Corbet, *Blanket-Fair, or the History of Temple Street. Being a Relation of the merry Pranks plaid on the River Thames during the great Frost*, London, 1684; Ian Currie, *Frosts, Freezes and Fairs*, Coulsdon, 1996; Icedore Frostiface of Freeseland, *An Account of all the principal Frosts for above an Hundred Years past*, London, 1740; G. Davis, *Frostland: Or a History of the River Thames in a Frozen State . . .*, 'Printed and published on the Ice of the River Thames, 5 February 1814'; Henry Humpherus, *History of the Origin and Progress of the Company of Watermen and Lightermen of the river Thames with Numerous Historical Notes*, London, 1859; James Moran, 'Printing on the Thames', *The Black Art*, vol. 2, no. 3, Autumn, 1963; Michael Srigley, 'The Great Frost Fair of 1683–4', *History Today*, vol. 10, part 12, 1960; Edward Walford, *Frost Fairs on the Thames*, London, 1886.

13 Walford, *Frost Fairs*, p. 13; Srigley, 'Great Frost Fair', pp. 848–87.

14 *Erra Pater's Prophesy, or Frost Faire in 1683*, quoted in Davis, *Frostiana*, p. xix.

15 Anon., *News from the Thames; or the Frozen Thames in Tears*, London, 1684.

16 Quoted in Davis, *Frostiana*, p. xxviii.

17 Corbet, *Blanket-Fair*.

18 *Great Britain's Wonder: Or London's Admiration*, quoted in Davis, *Frostiana*, p. xxix.

19 Corbet, *Blanket-Fair*.

20 Corbet, *Blanket-Fair*.

21 Corbet, *Blanket-Fair*.

22 *Blanket Fair, or The History of Temple Street*, quoted in Davis, *Frostiana*.

23 Mr Cartwright, quoted in Frostiface, *Account*, p. 5.

24 *A Frigid Essay upon Frost Fair*, 'Printed and Sold at the Golden King's Head Printing Booth, in Frost Fair, and by C. Corbet, publisher, over-against St. Dunstan's Church, Fleet Street', 1740, p. 15.

25 *Erra Pater's Prophesy, or Frost Faire in 1683*, quoted in Davis, *Frostiana*, p. xix.

26 Quoted in Beddard, 'London Frost Fair', p. 85.

5 THE RIVER AND THE AGE OF REASON

1 For a description of Sheerness in 1797 see David T. Hughes, *Sheerness and the Mutiny at the Nore*, Minster-in-Sheppey, 1997.

2   Oatmeal gruel called burgoo or skillagolee, rations of rock-hard salt beef and salt pork composed mainly of bone, gristle and fat, weevil-ridden biscuits, wormy cheese, rancid butter.

3   I thank Michael Belleisles for this information.

4   The best scholarly treatment of impressments is Nicholas Rogers, 'Vagrancy, Impressment and the Regulation of Labour in 18th Century Britain,' Paul Lovejoy and Nicholas Rogers (eds), in *Unfreee Labour in the Development of the Atlantic World*, London, 1994.

5   Rogers, 'Vagrancy', p. 107.

6   Letters written by the crews of the *Shannon* and the *Winchelsea* quoted in G.E. Manwaring and Bonamy Dobrée, *Mutiny: The Floating Republic*, London, 1987, p. 8.

7   Roger Wells, *Insurrection: The British Experience, 1795–1803*, London, 1983, p. 81.

8   For example, Colonel Edmund Despard and Thomas Spence. See Peter Linebaugh and Marcus Rediker, *The Many-Headed Hydra: Sailors, Slaves, Commoners and the Hidden History of the Revolutionary Atlantic*, London, 2000, pp. 277–80.

9   Quoted in Manwaring and Dobrée, *Mutiny*, p. 7.

10 Quoted in Manwaring and Dobrée, *Mutiny*, p. 43.

11 Quoted in James Dugan, *The Great Mutiny*, London, 1966, p. 181.

12 Moreau de Jonnès (trans. Cyril Hammond), *Adventures in the Revolution and under the Consulate*, London, 1929, p. 146.

13 C. Cunningham, *A Narrative of the Occurrences that took place during the Mutiny at the Nore . . .*, Chatham, 1829, p. 13.

14 A contemporary anonymous pamphleteer claimed falsely that he hailed from Perth, that 'his parents were poor and wretched to the extreme', that he was brought up to be a weaver, but inspired by the ideals of the French Revolution had become 'a flaming politician' in Edinburgh to which he had tramped 'bare legged and bare a——d'. From Edinburgh, the pamphleteer wrote, Parker fled eventually to England and joined the navy, landing finally aboard the *Sandwich*. See *The Life and Extraordinary Adventures of Parker the Delegate and Ringleader of the Mutiny at Sheerness*, London, 1797, pp. 2–5.

15 For these more deeply researched accounts of Parker's early life see Manwaring and Dobrée, *Mutiny*, pp. 121–2; Cunningham, *Narrative*, p. 86; Dugan, *Great Mutiny*, pp. 199–200; Conrad Gill, *The Naval Mutinies of 1797*, Manchester, 1913, p. 128. I rely on these sources for my narration of events unless otherwise noted.

16 Dugan, *Great Mutiny*, p. 215.

17 Cunningham, *Narrative*, p. 34.

18 Quoted in Manwaring and Dobrée, *Mutiny*, p. 177.

19 Quoted in Rogers, 'Vagrancy', p. 108.

20 De Jonnès, *Adventures*, p. 147. See, too, Sir William Laird Clowes, 'The French Share in the Mutiny at the Nore', *Cornhill Magazine*, July 1902, pp. 38–52.

21 Eventually they agreed that the fleeing ships would all rendezvous at Cromarty Firth.
22 Christopher Lloyd, 'New Light on the Mutiny at the Nore', *The Mariner's Mirror*, vol. 46, no. 4, 1960, p. 293.
23 For the trial see Job Sibley, *The Trial of Richard Parker Complete . . .*, London, 1797.
24 For the execution see Anon., *A True and Particular Account of the Execution of Richard Parker . . .*, London, 1797.
25 Wells, *Insurrection*, p. 89.
26 Manwaring and Dobrée, *Mutiny*, p. 257.

6 WATER, AIR, EARTH, FIRE

1 Ozias Humphrey quoted in James Hamilton, *Turner: A Life*, London, 1997, p. 84.
2 Hamilton, *Turner*, p. 89.
3 Quoted in David Hill, *Turner on the Thames*, New Haven, Conn., 1993, p. 24.
4 Hill, *Turner*, p. 36.
5 Quoted in Hill, *Turner*, p. 127.
6 For more on this connection between Turner and Brunel see James Hamilton, *Turner and the Scientists*, London, 1998, pp. 100–2.
7 See here Adrian Vaughan, *Isambard Kingdom Brunel, Engineering Knight-Errant*, London, 1991, p. 76.
8 Tim Bryan, *Brunel: The Great Engineer*, Shepperton, 1999, p. 55.
9 Elizabeth Barrett Browning quoted in Michael Freeman, *Railways and the Victorian Imagination*, New Haven, 1999, p. 41.
10 Charles Dickens quoted in Freeman, *Railways*, p. 45.
11 See Francis Klingender, *Art and the Industrial Revolution*, Chatham, 1968, pp. 134–65.
12 See Judy Egerton, *The British School*, London, 1998, p. 308.
13 Hill, *Turner*, p. 156.
14 Egerton, *British School*, pp. 306–11, is particularly illuminating on this debate.
15 Although, again, the critics differ. See Egerton, *British School*, p. 320.
16 Quoted in John Gage, *Turner: Rain, Steam, and Speed*, London, 1972, p. 19.

7 DARK WATERS

1 19th Geo. III, cap. 74, quoted in Henry Mayhew and John Binny, *The Criminal Prisons of London and Scenes of Prison Life*, London, 1862, p. 198.
2 James Hardy Vaux, *Memoirs of James Hardy Vaux, A Swindler and Thief*, London, 1827.
3 Vaux, *Memoirs*, pp. 241, 261; W. Branch-Johnson, *The English Prison Hulks*, London, 1957, p. 51.

4   Reg Rigden, *The Floating Prisons of Woolwich and Deptford*, London, 1976, p. 5.

5   Vaux, *Memoirs*, pp. 262–3; Branch-Johnson, *English*, p. 16.

6   Vaux, *Memoirs*, p. 262; *Scots Magazine*, July 1777, quoted in Branch-Johnson, *English*, p. 5.

7   Branch-Johnson, *English*, p. 180.

8   Branch-Johnson, *English*, p. 134.

9   L.S.R. Byrne and E.L. Churchill, *The Eton Book of the River*, Eton, 1935, p. 10. See also Alwyne Wheeler, *The Tidal Thames: the History of a River and its Fishes*, London, 1979, p. 19; Fred S. Thacker, *The Thames Highway. Locks and Weirs*, London, 1968, p. 39.

10 Quoted in Anthony Wohl, *Endangered Lives: Public Health in Victorian Britain*, London, 1983, p. 233.

11 Wheeler, *Tidal*, p. 23.

12 Bill Luckin, *Pollution and Control: A Social History of the Thames in the Nineteenth Century*, Bristol, 1986, p. 118.

13 Quoted in R.K. Webb, *Modern England*, New York, 1980, p. 295.

14 For Faraday's famous letter to *The Times*, see Stephen Halliday, *The Great Stink of London: Sir Joseph Bazalgette and the Cleansing of Victorian London*, Stroud, 1999, p. ix.

15 Quoted in Edwin Guest (ed.), *The Wreck of the Princess Alice*, London, 1878, pp. 85–6.

16 *Illustrated London News*, 14 September 1878.

17 Guest, *Wreck*, p. 10.

18 *The Times*, 5 September 1878.

19 *The Times*, 7 September 1878.

20 Guest, *Wreck*, p. 10.

21 *The Times*, 4 September 1878.

22 Guest, *Wreck*, pp. 38–9.

23 Guest, *Wreck*, pp. 20, 15.

24 Guest, *Wreck*, p. 16. It is interesting to note that for weeks afterwards correspondents bombarded *The Times* with letters suggesting how the passengers of the *Princess Alice* might have saved themselves. For incongruity, not to say sheer fatuity, some of them are hard to beat. 'Every man possesses in his hat an efficient means of support in the water,' wrote T.S.P. on 10 September. It 'should be held firmly in front of the individual (with the thumbs on either side on the upper surface of the brim) and brought backwards and downward till the chin is enabled to rest on the crown, when the body will float easily in an upright position with the whole of the head above the surface of the water'.

25 *The Times*, 6 September 1878.

26 *The Times*, 27 September 1878.

27 Gavin Thurston, *The Great Thames Disaster*, London, 1965, p. 123.

28 *Saturday Review*, 21 September 1878.

29 Thurston, *Great*, p. 20.

30 *The Times*, 14 September 1878.

31 Guest, *Wreck*, p. 47.

32 *Saturday Review*, 5 October 1878; *The Times*, 19 September 1878.

33 *The Times*, 28 September 1878.

34 *The Times*, 11 September 1878.

35 *The Times*, 6 September 1878.

36 It may be pointed out that in this way the Board was practically replicating what it had done during the year of the Great Stink, when Bazalgette had moved the problem downstream, east of London. Now the Board had moved the problem as far downstream as possible, while still deferring a permanent solution. It was not until 1998 that marine dumping came to an end. Moreover the Board did nothing about waste from factories, which still poured untreated into the river. Today sludge is compressed and incinerated; the heat is recovered to generate electricity. The liquid is so carefully filtered that it is purer than the river into which it is finally released. See Halliday, *Great Stink*, p. 107.

8 THE EARTHLY PARADISE

1 See their *London: a Pilgrimage*, London, 1872.

2 Henry James, *English Hours*, Oxford, 1981, 'Essay on London at Midsummer (1887)', p. 95.

3 For Morris see especially Fiona MacCarthy, *William Morris*, London, 1994; Peter Stansky, *Redesigning the World*, Princeton, 1985; Edward Thompson, *William Morris*, London, 1976. Morris was unhappily married to the faithless Jane Burden, model female figure for the Pre-Raphaelite movement.

4 William Morris, *News from Nowhere*, London, 1993, p. 101.

5 He has William Guest cry in *News from Nowhere* (p. 204), 'I know every yard of the Thames from Hammersmith to Cricklade.'

6 Quoted in MacCarthy, *Morris*, p. 424, upon whose description of the trip my own is largely based.

7 Norman Kelvin (ed.), *The Collected Letters of William Morris*, Vol I, Princeton, 1984, William Morris to Georgiana Burne-Jones, 19 August 1880, p. 582.

8 Morris so enjoyed this journey that he repeated it the next summer, 1881.

9 Quoted in Thompson, *Morris*, p. 174. Originally Rossetti and Morris's wife Jane shared the house while Morris worked in London. Rossetti and Jane were already in the midst of their affair.

10 *News from Nowhere*, p. 221.

11 Quoted in Thompson, *Morris*, p. 175.

12   Quoted in Alfred Noyes, *William Morris*, London, 1908, p. 127.

13   'The Message of the March Wind'.

14   *The Pilgrims of Hope*.

15   *Commonweal*, vol. 5, no. 182, 6 July 1889, quoted in Nicholas Salmon (ed.), *Political Writings of William Morris: Contributions to Justice and Commonweal, 1883–1890*, Bristol, 1994, pp. 426–30.

16   It is perhaps significant that Ellen is physically opposite to Morris's wife, Jane Burden, who was tall and dark, the first and best model of Pre-Raphaelite beauties.

17   *News from Nowhere*, p. 208.

18   *News from Nowhere*, pp. 217–20.

19   Quoted in Fiona MacCarthy, *Stanley Spencer: An English Vision*, London, 1998, p. 8.

20   Quoted in Kenneth Pople, *Stanley Spencer: A Biography*, London, 1991, p. 24.

21   Quoted in MacCarthy, *Spencer*, p. 7.

22   Pople, *Stanley*, p. 68.

23   MacCarthy, *Spencer*, p. 16.

24   Norman F. Ticehurst, *The Mute Swan in England*, London, 1957, p. 10. The precise date has not been established, but it was prior to 1186. See also Mike Birkhead, *The Mute Swan*, London, 1986, p. 19: 'Giraldus Cambrensis, in an undated manuscript of the late twelfth century, possibly as early as 1186, describes the swan as a Royal bird.' In 1553 there were more than 800 registered owners of swans in one small section of the Fens. During the reign of Elizabeth I there were some 600 distinct swan marks. See Birkhead, p. 20, and also David Reed, 'Swan Upping', *Thames Guardian: Journal of the River Thames Society*, summer 1997, p. 21

25   Ticehurst, *Mute*, p. 16.

26   In that year Edward the Black Prince appointed Simon de Biflet and Nicholas de Mideford to keep all his swans in the water of Thames between London and Oxford 'by the supervision and advice of Thomas Gerveys'. Ticehurst, *Mute*, p. 54.

27   To pinion a swan is to amputate the last section of one wing, so that the bird cannot fly.

28   Pople, *Spencer*, p. 73.

29   Quoted in Pople, *Spencer*, p. 77.

30   Quoted in Duncan Robinson, *Stanley Spencer*, Oxford, 1990, p. 23.

31   Quoted in Tate Gallery, *Stanley Spencer: A Sort of Heaven*, Liverpool, 1992: Introduction by Anthony Gormley, p. 13.

32   Simon Schama, 'The Church of Me', *New Yorker*, 17 February 1997, pp. 52–7.

33   The Crown Hotel is sometimes referred to as the Ferry Hotel.

34   MacCarthy, *Spencer*, p. 21.

35   Quoted in Pople, *Spencer*, p. 238.

36 Quoted in MacCarthy, *Spencer*, plate 19.

37 Quoted in Pople, *Spencer*, p. 473.

38 Quoted in Pople, *Spencer*, p. 506.

39 Quoted in MacCarthy, *Spencer*, plate 60.

9 RIVER OF FIRE

1   There were over 300 wharves along the east London Thames in 1909. W. Paul
    Clegg, *Docks and Ports*, Shepperton, 1987, p. 37. Beyond the warehouses a warren
    of roads and railway lines trailed into the hinterlands so that whatever came
    into the port could be distributed to the rest of the country.

2   James Bentley, *East of the City: The London Docklands Story*, London, 1997, p. 44.
    Moreover, of course, London exported internationally as well. So the process
    worked in reverse. From the great larder labourers conveyed goods of all
    descriptions down to the quays, and other labourers loaded them into vessels,
    and then England's merchant marine carried them down the Thames past
    Sheerness and the Nore, to anywhere that ships could sail.

3   R. Douglas Brown, *The Port of London*, Lavenham, 1978, p. 109.

4   Brown, *Port*, p. 111.

5   Alfred Price, *Blitz on Britain 1939–45*, London, 2000, p. 2.

6   A.P. Herbert, *The Thames*, London, 1966, p. 147.

7   Brown, *Port*, p. 111.

8   Quoted in Cajus Bekker, *The Luftwaffe War Diaries: The German Air Force in World
    War II*, Edinburgh, 2001, p. 174.

9   Quoted in Bekker, *Luftwaffe*, p. 172.

10 Rotherhithe representative of Dockland Settlements, a project of the
    Malvern College Mission in east London, quoted in Ben Tinton, *War Comes to
    the Docks*, London, 1942, p. 61.

11 George Goldsmith-Carter, *The Battle of Britain*, New York, 1974, p. 82.

12 Quoted in Philip Ziegler, *London at War, 1939–45*, London, 2002, p. 25.

13 Constantine Fitz Gibbon, *The Blitz*, London, 1957, p. 48.

14 Quoted in Fitz Gibbon, *Blitz*, p. 48.

15 Price, *Blitz*, p. 138.

16 Quoted in Sir Alan Herbert, *A.P.H., His Life and Times*, London, 1979, pp. 57–8.

17 For which see chapter 11 below.

18 Arthur Bryant, *Liquid History*, London, 1960, p. 51.

19 Herbert, *A.P.H*, p. 172. For Herbert's adventures during the war see A.P.
    Herbert, *The Thames*, London, 1966, pp. 147–200, and A.P. Herbert, *Independent
    Member*, London, 1970, pp. 108–31, on both of which my account is based.

20 Herbert, *Independent*, p. 221. Oil imports actually increased by 300 per cent
    from 1940–45, though they fell drastically in 1942.

21 Quoted in Armand van Ishoven, *The Luftwaffe in the Battle of Britain*, New York, 1980, p. 90.

22 Quoted in van Ishoven, *Luftwaffe*, pp. 94–6.

23 See www.millwall-history.co.uk/Origins-4.htm.

24 J. Grosvenor, *The Port of London*, London, 1957, p. 72.

25 L.M. Bates, *The Thames on Fire: The Battle of London River, 1939–45*, Lavenham, 1985, p. 24.

26 From 'The Ballad of the "Bluebell"', A.P. Herbert, *Light the Lights*, London, 1945, p. 28.

27 See Steven Fielding, Peter Thompson and Nick Tiratsoo, *'England Arise!' The Labour Party and Popular Politics in 1940s Britain*, Manchester, 1995.

28 *T&GW Record*, October 1940.

29 Quoted in Alan Moorehead, *Montgomery: A Biography*, London, 1946, p. 190.

30 *Evening Standard*, 3 March 1944.

31 *Daily Herald*, 4 March 1944.

32 *T&GW Record*, July 1944.

10 BLUE RIVER

I am grateful to Boris Rankov, Michael Suarez and Michael Barry for talking with me about the 1987 Oxford Boat Race Mutiny, and other rowing subjects; and to Reed Rubin for corresponding with me about the mutiny of 1959.

1 H.R.A. Edwards, *The Way of a Man with a Blade*, London, 1963, p. 11.

2 Edwards, *Way*, p. 141.

3 Edwards, *Way*, p. 143.

4 Edwards, *Way*, p. 23.

5 As in, for instance, Oxford University Boat Club President's Notebook, private collection, in which Roderick Carnegie, president, 1957: 'I felt that his emphasis on technical points often affected the crew's confidence and that this had been partly responsible for [defeats of] 1953 & 1955.' I rely primarily on this book for my account of the 1959 'mutiny'.

6 *Oxford Daily Mail*, 10 October 1958.

7 *Oxford Daily Mail*, 10 October 1958.

8 OUBC President's Notebook, '1959 – Notes by R.L. Howard.'

9 *Oxford Daily Mail*, 21 October 1958.

10 Earl Halifax, Lord Tedder, jointly written foreword to Gordon Ross, *The Boat Race: The Story of the First Hundred Races Between Oxford and Cambridge*, London, 1954, p. 7.

11 Ross, *The Boat Race*, p. 193.

12 Frederick Gale, *Modern English Sports: Their Use and Their Abuse*, London, 1885, p. 37.

13 Edwards, *Way*, pp. 125–7.

14 *Oxford Magazine*, vol. LXXVII, no. 2, 23 October 1958, p. 34.

15   I am grateful to Lara Heimert for this information.

16   *Oxford Magazine*, vol. LXXVII, no. 3, 30 October 1958, p. 49.

17   *Daily Express*, 21 October 1958.

18   *British Rowing Almanack*, 'Review of the Year 1959', p. 6.

19   But in Penny's case, too, I am told, rowing came first, study came second.

20   Alison Gill, *The Yanks at Oxford: The 1987 Boat Race Controversy*, Lewes, 1991, p. 40.

21   Gill, *Yanks*, p. 41.

22   Gill, *Yanks*, p. 28–9.

23   *The Times*, 7 February 1987.

24   Christopher Pearson in *The Times*, 17 February 1987.

25   Daniel Topolski with Patrick Robinson, *True Blue: The Oxford Boat Race Mutiny*, London, 1989, p. 106.

26   In 1982 and 1983 successive OUBC presidents Richard Yonge and Boris Rankov had complained to Topolski, but when he made no changes they let the matter drop. Gill, *Yanks*, p. 59.

27   *Guardian*, 5 February 1987.

28   *Daily Telegraph*, 30 January 1987.

29   *The Times*, 30 January 1987.

30   *Daily Telegraph*, 3 February 1987.

31   *The Times*, 28 March 1987.

32   *The Times*, 21 February 1987.

33   *The Times*, 28 March 1987.

34   *The Times*, 30 March 1987.

35   *The Times*, 4 February 1987.

36   Article by Glenys Roberts in *The Times*, 28 March 1987.

37   Article by Simon Barnes in *The Times*, 10 February 1987.

38   *The Times*, 21 February 1987.

39   *Oxford Daily Mail*, 30 March 1987.

40   Gill, *Yanks*, pp. 182–3.

41   Tony Mason (ed.), *Sport in Britain*, Cambridge, 1989: Christopher Dodd, 'Rowing', p. 283.

42   For example, Richard Hoggart in *Uses of Literacy*, London, 1957.

43   For example, Anthony Sampson in *Anatomy of Britain*, London, 1962.

44   Martin Weiner, *English Culture and the Decline of the Industrial Spirit, 1850–1980*, Cambridge, 1981, p. 161.

45   *Guardian*, 13 February 1987.

11 TAMING THE THAMES

1   Fred S. Thacker, *The Thames Highway: A General History*, London, 1914, p. 19.

2   Fred S. Thacker, *The Thames Highway: Locks and Weirs*, London, 1920, p. 22.

3 The first commission, the Oxford–Burcot Commission, was empowered in 1605, but did not construct a pound lock until 1630. See Thacker, *Inland Navigation*, pp. 62–7; see also John Kemplay, *The Thames Locks*, Chipping Camden, 2000, p. 3.

4 The last flash lock, near Kelmscott, was pulled down in 1937. Kemplay, *Locks*, p. 5.

5 'Spring' tides have nothing to do with the season. They occur twice a month.

6 Stow and Pepys both quoted in Stuart Gilbert and Ray Horner, *The Thames Barrier*, London, 1984, p. 3.

7 *Thames Guardian: Journal of the River Thames Society*, spring, 1997, p. 13.

8 See Hilda Grieve, *The Great Tide*, London, 1959, pp. 67–87.

9 Grieve, *Great Tide*, p. 86.

10 Quoted in Grieve, *Great Tide*, p. 149.

11 Quoted in Grieve, *Great Tide*, p. 113.

12 Quoted in Grieve, *Great Tide*, p. 232.

13 Quoted in Grieve, *Great Tide*, p. 233.

14 Ken Wilson, *The Story of the Thames Barrier*, London, 1984, p. 12.

15 Wilson, *Thames Barrier*, p. 18.

16 Docklands Forum, *Docklands – London's Backyard into Front Yard*, London, 1990, p. 13.

17 Quoted in John Carvel, *Citizen Ken*, London, 1987, p. 206.

18 Ken Livingstone, *If Voting Changed Anything, They'd Abolish It*, London, 1987, p. 299.

19 *Paddington Mercury*, 13 April 1984.

20 *Evening Standard*, 12 April 1984.

21 *The Times*, 9 May 1984.

22 *Evening Standard*, 9 May 1984.

23 *Guardian*, 5 November 2003.

24 See http://news.bbc.co.uk/1/hi/uk_politics/3867387.stm. (By the same negotiation David Weeks agreed to pay Westminster Council £44,000: see www.ppmagazine.co.uk/july27.html.)

12 THE THAMES TRANSFORMED

1 For London dockers see John Lovell, *Stevedores and Dockers*, London, 1969, and Jonathan Schneer, *Ben Tillett, Portrait of a Labor Leader*, Urbana Champaign, 1978.

2 For nostalgic evocations of east London life see among many Willilam J. Fishman, *East End 1888*, London, 1988.

3 James Bentley, *East of the City: The London Docklands Story*, London, 1997, p. 46.

4 Sue Brownhill, *Developing London's Docklands*, London, 1990, p. 19.

5 As suggested in the Travers Morgan Report commissioned by Conservative Secretary of State, Peter Walker in 1971. See Janet Foster, *Docklands: Cultures in Conflict, Worlds in Collision*, London, 1999, p. 49.

6   Docklands Joint Committee, *London Docklands Strategic Plan*, London, 1976–: see preface by E. Percy Bell.
7   Michael Heseltine, *Life in the Jungle, My Autobiography*, London, 2000, pp. 211–12.
8   Heseltine, *Life*, p. 213.
9   Quoted in Foster, *Docklands*, p. 63.
10 Quoted in Foster, *Docklands*, p. 84.
11 Quoted in Foster, *Docklands*, p. 71.
12 Quoted in Foster, *Docklands*, p. 82.
13 Heseltine, *Life*, p. 399.
14 Bentley, *East*, p. 58.
15 See *World Architecture*, vol. 87, June 2000, pp. 49–59, and *AA files*, vol. 40, winter 1999, pp. 17–33.
16 Foster, *Docklands*, pp. 119–22.
17 See Andrew Church and Martin Frost, 'The Thames Gateway – an Analysis of the Emergence of a Sub-regional Regeneration Initiative', *Geographical Journal*, vol. 161, part 2, July 1995, p. 204.
18 Heseltine, *Life*, p. 514.
19 'Dockland' by Bernie Steer, quoted in Gillian Rose, 'Local Resistance to the LDDC . . .', in Philip Ogden (ed.), *Update London Dockland: The Challenge of Development*, Cambridge, 1992, p. 39.
20 Quoted in Foster, *Docklands*, p. 287.
21 *The Times*, 30 July 1986.
22 Quoted in Foster, *Docklands*, p. 182.
23 *The Times*, 4 May 1987.
24 See Foster, *Docklands*, pp. 206, 282.
25 Foster, *Docklands*, p. 322.
26 *The Times*, 25 June 1987.
27 Foster, *Docklands*, p. 322. In 1981, 3433 were without jobs in Docklands; in 1996, 4673 were without jobs.
28 *The Times*, 3 August 1989.
29 Ogden, *Update*, p. 34.
30 Bentley, *East*, pp. 58–60.

CONCLUSION: THE THAMES AND THE NATION

1   The Thames is 215 statute miles from the source to the Nore.
2   All information on the funeral procession taken from *Sunday Telegraph*, 31 January 1965; *Daily Telegraph*, 1 February 1965; *Sunday Times*, 31 January 1965; John Lukacs, *Churchill: Visionary, Statesman, Historian*, New Haven, 2002.

Bibliography

COLLECTIONS

Bodleian Library, Oxford University
    John Johnson Collection
    Oxford University Boat Club Papers

Modern Records Centre, Warwick University
    Transport and General Workers' Union Papers

 Henley Rowing Museum
    Archives and Exhibits

Personal
    Oxford University Boat Club President's Notebook in possession of Boris
    Rankov.

DAILY AND WEEKLY NEWSPAPERS

Cherwell
Daily Express
Daily Herald
Daily Telegraph
Evening Standard

Guardian
Lock to Lock Times
Maidenhead Times
Nation
New Statesman and Nation
New Yorker
Oxford Mail
Paddington Mercury
Saturday Review
Sunday Telegraph
Sunday Times
Thames Valley Times
Thames: The Weekly Record of the River
The Times

JOURNALS

Albion
Antiquity
Archaeologia Cantiana
Art and History
Black Art
British Rowing Almanack
Bulletin of the John Rylands Library
Cornhill Magazine
Docklands Magazine
Early Music
Economic History Review
English Literature in Transition
Essex Naturalist
Geographical Journal
Geography
Guildhall Miscellany
History Today
Huntington Library Quarterly
Journal of British Studies
London Journal
Mariner's Mirror
Nautical Magazine
New England Quarterly
Oxford Magazine

Parthenon (Journal of the Incorporated Association of Architects and Surveyors)
Proceedings of the American Philosophical Society
Punch, or the London Charivari
Rowing
Rural History
St. Cuthbert's Magazine
Surrey History
T&GW Record
Thames Guardian: Journal of the River Thames Society

POETRY

Anon.
     'The Character of an English-Man'
Blake, William
     'London'
     Jerusalem: The Emanation of The Giant
     'Why should I care for the men of thames'
Betjeman, Sir John
     'Henley-on-Thames'
Binyon, Laurence
     'Bablock Hythe'
Boas, F.S.
     'Westminster 1941'
Byron, George Gordon Noel
     'Hints from Horace'
Cowley, Abraham
     'A Poem on the Late Civil War'
Cowper, William
     'The Symptoms of Love'
     'The Task'
Denham, Sir John
     'The Thames from Cooper's Hill'
Dryden, John
     Annus Mirabilis, The Year of Wonders, 1666
Dunmore, Helen
     'Hungry Thames Bestiary'
Eliot, T.S.
     The Waste Land
Gray, Thomas,
     'Ode on a Distant Prospect of Eton College'

Hood, Thomas
  'The Turtles A Fable'
  'Bridge of Sighs'
Hughes, John
  'On the Birth-Day of the Right Honourable The Lord Chancellor Parker'
  'July XXIII, MDCCXIX'
Kipling, Rudyard
  'What Say the Reeds at Runnymede?'
Mahon, Derek
  'One of These Nights'
Masefield, John
  'Shopping in Oxford'
Mitchell, Adrian
  'Daydream One'
  'Remember Suez?'
Morris, William
  The Earthly Paradise
  'The Message of the March Wind'
  The Pilgrims of Hope
  'For the Bed at Kelmscott'
Peacock, Thomas Love
  'The Genius of the Thames: A Lyrical Poem in Two Parts'
Pope, Alexander
  'Verses on a Grotto by the River Thames at Twickenham, composed of
     Marbles'
  'Spars and Minerals'
  'Windsor Forest (To the Right Honourable George Lord Lansdown)'
Shelley, Percy Bysshe
  'The Question'
Southey, Robert
  'Ode Written after the King's Visit to Scotland'
Spenser, Edmund
  Prothalamion
Thomson, James
  'Liberty'
Wordsworth, William
  'Composed Upon Westminster Bridge'
  'Lines Written near Richmond upon the Thames at Evening'

BOOKS AND JOURNAL ARTICLES

Abbott, G., *Great Escapes from the Tower of London*, London, 1982.

Adams, George Burton, *The History of England: From the Norman Conquest to the Death of John (1066–1216)*, New York, 1969.

Allen, T.G., and Robinson, M.A., *The Prehistoric Landscape & Iron Age Enclosed Settlement at Mingies Ditch,* Oxford, 1993.

Allen, T.G., Darvill, T.C., Green, L.S., Jones, M.U., *Excavations at Roughground Farm, Lechlade, Gloucestershire: a Prehistoric and Roman Landscape*, Oxford University Committee for Archaeology, 1993.

Allen, Tim, Barton, Nicholas, and Brown, Andrew, *Lithics and Landscape: Archaeological Discoveries on the Thames Water Pipeline at Gatehampton Farm, Goring, Oxfordshire 1985–92*, Oxford University Committee for Archaeology, *1995.*

Anderson, J.R.L., *The Upper Thames*, London, 1970.

Anderson, Patricia, *The Printed Image and the Transformation of Popular Culture, 1790–1860*, Oxford, 1991.

Anon., *A Genuine and Affecting Narrative of Richard Parker's Dying Behavior and Execution . . .,* London, 1797.

Anon., *A True and Particular Account of the Execution of Richard Parker . . .*, London, 1797.

Anon., *The Loss of the Princess Alice . . .*, London, 1878.

Anon., *The Collision, an Allegory*, London, 1878.

Anon., *The Wreck of the Princess Alice on the Thames, September 3, 1878, with a list of the principal calamities which have happened on water during the last 100 years, and the number of lives lost*, London, 1878.

Anon., *Greenwich Palace*, London, 1939.

Anon., *The Life and Extraordinary Adventures of Parker the Delegate and Ringleader of the Mutiny at Sheerness*, London, 1797.

Anon., *News from the Thames; or The Frozen Thames in Tears*, London, 1684.

Arnold, Dana, 'London Bridge and its Symbolic Identity in the Regency Metropolis: the dialectic of civic and national pride', *Art and History*, vol. 22, no. 4, November 1999, pp. 545–55.

Ashton, Nick, Conway, Bernard, and McNabb, John (eds), *Excavations at Barnfield Pit, Swanscombe, 1968–72*, British Museum Occasional Papers, No. 94, London, 1996.

Atterbury Paul (photos by Anthony Haines), *The Thames: From the Source to the Sea*, London, 1998.

Bale, John, *Landscapes of Modern Sport*, Leicester, 1994.

Balston, John, *John Martin, 1789–1854, His Life and Works*, London, 1947.

Banbury, Philip, *Shipbuilders of the Thames and Medway*, Newton Abbot, 1971.

Banks, Leslie, and Stanley, Christopher, *The Thames: A History from the Air*, Oxford, 1990.

Bann, Stephen, *The Clothing of Clio*, Cambridge, 1984.

Barnes, I., Boismier, W.A., Cleal, R.M.J., Fitzpatrick, A.P., and Roberts, M.R., *Early Settlement in Berkshire Mesolithic-Roman Occupation Sites in the Thames and Kennet Valleys*, Salisbury, 1995.

Barnes, I., Butterworth, C., Hawkes, John, Smith, L., *Excavations at Thames Valley Park, Reading, Berkshire, 1986–88*, Nottingham, 1997.

Barrell, John (ed.), *Painting and the Politics of Culture: New Essays on British Art, 1700–1850*, Oxford, 1992.

—— *The Dark Side of the Landscape: The Rural Poor in English Painting, 1730–1840*, Cambridge, 1980.

—— *The Political Theory of Painting from Reynolds to Hazlitt*, London, 1986.

Barrenger, Timothy, '"Our English Thames" and "America's River": Landscape Painting and Narratives of National Identity', unpublished.

—— *The Cole Family: Painters of the English Landscape 1838–1975*, Portsmouth, 1988.

Bates, L.M.. *The Thames on Fire: The Battle of London River 1939–1945*, Lavenham, 1985.

Batts, John, 'American Humor: The Mark of Twain on Jerome K. Jerome', in Wagner-Lawlor, Jennifer (ed.), *The Victorian Comic Spirit*, Aldershot, 2000.

Beaven, Brad, and Griffiths, John, *Mass-Observation and Civilian Morale: Working-Class Communities During the Blitz 1940–41*, Mass-Observation Archive Occasional Paper no. 8, 1998.

Beddard, Robert, 'The London Frost Fair of 1683–84', *Guildhall Miscellany*, vol. IV, no. 2, April 1972, pp. 63–87.

Bekker, Cajus, *The Luftwaffe War Diaries: The German Air Force in World War II*, Edinburgh, 2001.

Belloc, Hilaire, *The Historic Thames*, London 1887.

Bendry, Roy, 'Thames Water on Tap,' *Thames Guardian: Journal of the River Thames Society*, Spring, 1998, pp. 17–20.

Bentley, James, *East of the City: The London Docklands Story*, London, 1997.

Bergeron, David (ed.), *Pageants and Entertainments of Anthony Munday: A Critical Edition*, New York, 1985.

—— (ed.), *Thomas Heywood's Pageants: A Critical Edition*, New York, 1986.

Bermingham, Ann, *Landscape and Ideology: The English Rustic Tradition*, London, 1987.

Bhabha, Homi K, *Nation and Narration*, London, 1990.

Birkhead, Mike, and Perrins, Christopher, *The Mute Swan*, London, 1986.

Blatcher, Margaret, 'Chatham Dockyard and a little-known shipwright, Matthew Baker (1530–1613)', *Archaeologia Cantiana*, vol. CVII, 1989, pp. 155–73.

Bolland, R.R., *Victorians on the Thames*, Tunbridge Wells, 1974.

Boumphrey, Geoffrey, *Down River: A Canoe Tour on the Severn and Thames*, London, 1936.

Bradshaw, Brendan, and Roberts, Peter (eds), *British Consciousness and Identity: The Making of Britain, 1553–1707*, Cambridge, 1998.

Branch-Johnson, W., *The English Prison Hulks*, London, 1957.

Brandon, Peter, and Short, Brian, *The Southeast from AD 1000*, London, 1990.

Branigan, Keith, *Roman Britain, Life in an Imperial Province*, London, 1980.

Bridgeland, D.R., *Quaternary of the Thames*, London, 1994.

Briggs, D.J., Coope, G.R., and Gilbertson, D.D. (eds). *The Chronology and Environmental Framework of Early Man in the Upper Thames Valley, A New Model*, BAR British Series 137, Oxford, 1985.

Brockliss, Laurence, and Eastwood, David (eds), *A Union of Multiple Identities, The British Isles, c.1750–c.1850*, Manchester, 1997.

Broich, John, 'London's and Surrey's "Fight for the River": Politics, Perceptions and the Thames, 1897', *Surrey History*, vol. VI, no. 2, 2000, pp. 75–87.

Broich, John, and Wilson, Roderick, 'Modern Rivers: London's and Tokyo's Remaking of the Thames and Sumida', unpublished.

Brown, D., *An Historical Account of the Late Great Frost . . .*, London, 1684.

Brown, R. Douglas, *The Port of London*, Lavenham, 1978.

Brownhill, Sue, *Developing London's Docklands*, London, 1997.

Brunel, Isambard, *The Life of Isambard Kingdom Brunel, Civil Engineer*, London, 1870.

Bryan, Tim, *Brunel: The Great Engineer*, Shepperton, 1999.

Bryant, Arthur, *Liquid History*, London, 1960.

Burnell, Richard, *Henley Regatta: A Celebration of 150 Years*, London, 1989.

—— 'Hugh Robert Arthur "Jumbo" Edwards', *Dictionary of National Biography*, London, n.d.

—— *One Hundred and Fifty Years of the Oxford and Cambridge Boat Race*, Marlow, 1979.

Burrows, Donald, and Hume, Robert, 'George I, the Haymarket Opera Company and Handel's "Water Music"', *Early Music*, vol. XIX no. 3, August 1991, pp. 322–35.

Burstall, Patricia, *The Golden Age of the Thames*, London, 1981.

Byrne, L.S.R., and Churchill, E.L., *The Eton Book of the River*, Eton, 1935.

Calder, Angus, *The Myth of the Blitz*, London, 1991.

Calhoun, Blue, *The Pastoral Vision of William Morris: The Earthly Paradise*, Athens, Ga., 1975.

Carvel, John, *Citizen Ken*, London, 1987.

Chalfont, Alun, *Montgomery of Alamein*, London, 1976.

Chignell, Robert, *The Life and Paintings of Vicat Cole, R.A.*, Vol. III, London, 1897.

Childe, V. Gordon, *Prehistoric Communities of the British Isles*, London, 1940.

Church, Andrew, and Frost, Martin, 'The Thames Gateway – An Analysis of the Emergence of a Sub-regional Regeneration Initiative', *Geographical Journal*, vol. 161, part 2, July 1995, pp. 198–205.

Cleggs, W. Paul, *Docks and Ports*, Shepperton, 1987.

Clowes, Sir William Laird, 'The French Share in the Mutiny at the Nore', *Cornhill Magazine*, July 1902, pp. 38–52.

Coates, Richard, 'A New Explanation of the Name of London', *Proceedings of the American Philosophical Society*, vol. 96, no. 2, 1998, pp. 214–21.

Coggle, Paul, *Do You Speak Estuary?*, London, 1993.

Coleman, Antony, and Hammond, Antony (eds), *Poetry and Drama, 1570–1770*, London, 1981.

Coleman, D.C., and John, A.H. (eds), *Trade, Government and Economy in Pre-Industrial England: Essays presented to F.J. Fisher*, London, 1976.

Colley, Linda, *Britons: Forging the Nation, 1707–1837*, London, 1994.

—— 'Shakespeare and the Limits of National Culture', Hayes Robinson Lecture Series no. 2, presented at Royal Holloway College, Egham, Surrey, 3 March 1998.

Collingwood, R.G., and Myres, J.N.L., *Roman Britain and the English Settlements*, Oxford, 1975.

Collini, Stefan, Whatmore, Richard, and Young, Brian (eds), *History, Religion and Culture: British Intellectual History 1750–1950*, Cambridge, 2000.

Connolly, Joseph, *Jerome K Jerome, A Critical Biography*, London, 1982.

Conrad, Joseph, *Heart of Darkness and Other Tales*, Oxford, 1990.

Cook, Sir Theodore, *Character and Sportsmanship*, London, 1927.

Corbet, C., *A Frigid Essay Upon Frost Fair*, London, 1740.

Corbet, Charles., *Blanket Fair or the History of Temple Street*, London, 1689.

Cornwall, E.A., London Reform Union: *The River Thames, the Docks and the Port of London, an Address*, Monday, 13 October, 1902.

Cosgrove, Denis, and Daniels, Stephen (eds), *The Iconography of Landscape: Essays on the symbolic representation, design and use of past environments*, Cambridge, 1988.

Cosgrove, Denis, and Petts, Geoffrey (eds), *Water, Engineering and Landscape*, London, 1990.

Cracknell, Basil E., *Canvey Island: The History of a Marshland Community*, Leicester, 1959.

—— *Portrait of London River*, London, 1968.

Crick, Michael, *Michael Heseltine, A Biography*, London, 1997.

Cubett, Geoffrey (ed.), *Imagining Nations*, Manchester, 1998.

Cunningham, Andrew, and Grell, Ole Peter, *Religio Medici: Medicine and Religion in Seventeenth-Century England*, London, 1996.

Cunningham, C., *A Narrative of the Occurrences that took place during the Mutiny at the Nore . . .*, Chatham, 1829.

Currie, Ian, *Frosts, Freezers and Fairs*, Coulsdon, 1996.

Daniels, Stephen, *Fields of Vision: Landscape Imagery and National Identity in England and the United States*, Oxford, 1993.

Darby, H.C. (ed.), *An Historical Geography of England before A.D. 1800*, Cambridge, 1951.

Daunton, Martin, and Reiger, Bernhard (eds), *Meanings of Modernity: Britain from the Late-Victorian Era to World War II*, New York, 2001.

Davis, G., *Frostiana: Or a History of the River Thames in a Frozen State*, London, 1814.

Davis, Godfrey, *The Early Streets, 1603–1660*, Oxford, 1959.

de Jonnès, Moreau (trans. Cyril Hammond), *Adventures in the Revolution and under the Consulate*, London, 1929.

Defoe, Daniel, *A Journal of the Plague Year*, London, 1772.

De-la-Noy, Michael, *Windsor Castle, Past and Present*, London, 1990.

Deutsch, Otto Erich, *Handel, A Documentary Biography*, London, 1955.

Dickens, Charles, *Our Mutual Friend*, London, 1994.
—— *Great Expectations*, London, 1994.
Docklands Development Team, *Help Plan Docklands. Housing*, n.d.
—— *Help Plan Docklands. A Docklands Strategy – Setting the Scene*, n.d.
—— *The Largest Redevelopment Scheme in Europe, London Docklands*, n.d.
Docklands Forum, *Docklands – London's Backyard into Front Yard*, London, 1990.
Docklands Joint Committee, *London Docklands Strategic Plan*, London, 1976.
Dodd, Christopher, *The Oxford & Cambridge Boat Race*, London, 1983.
Dodgson, Campbell, *The Etchings of James McNeill Whistler*, London, 1922.
Doré, Gustave, and Jerrold, Blanchard, *London: a Pilgrimage*, London, 1872.
Drewett, Peter, Rudling, David, and Gardiner, Mark, *The South-East to AD 1000*, London, 1988.
Dugan, James, *The Great Mutiny*, London, 1966.
Dummett, Ann, and Nicol, Andrew, *Subjects, Citizens, Aliens and Others, Nationality and Immigration Law*, London, 1990.
Durant, David N., *Arbella Stuart, A Rival to the Queen*, London, 1978.
Easthope, Antony, *Englishness and National Culture*, London, 1999.
Edwards, H.R.A., *The Way of a Man with a Blade*, London, 1963.
Egerton, Judy, *The British School*, London, 1998.
Emanuel, W.V., *River Thames*, London, n.d.
Evans, John, *The Environment of Early Man in the British Isles*, London, 1975.
Evison, V.I., *The 5th Century Invasions South of the Thames*, London, 1965.
Fagan, H., and Hilton, Rodney, *The English Rising of 1381*, London, 1950.
Faurot, Ruth Marie, *Jerome K. Jerome*, New York, 1974.
Feaver, William, *The Art of John Martin*, Oxford, 1975
Fielding, Henry, *Tom Jones*, London, 1749.
Fielding, Steven, Thompson, Peter, and Tiratsoo, Nick, *'England Arise!' The Labour Party and Popular Politics in 1940s Britain*, Manchester, 1995.
Fishman, William, *East End, 1888*, London, 1988.
FitzGibbon, Constantine, *The Blitz*, London, 1957.
Fleming, Gordon, *The Young Whistler, 1834–66*, London, 1978.
Fosbrooke, Nathaniell, *London's Love to the Royal Prince Henrie . . .*, London, 1610.
Foster, Janet, *Docklands: Cultures in Conflict, Worlds in Collision*, London, 1999.
Fraser, Edward, *Greenwich Royal Hospital and the Royal United Service Museum*, London, n.d.
Freeman, Michael, *Railways and the Victorian Imagination*, New Haven, 1999.
Freethy, Ron, *The Natural History of Rivers*, Lavenham, 1986.
Gage, John, *Turner: Rain, Steam, and Speed*, London, 1972
—— *J.M.W. Turner: 'A Wonderful Range of Mind'*, London, 1987.
Galbraith, V.H., 'Runnymede Revisited', *Proceedings of the American Philosophical Society*, vol. 110, no. 5, 27 October 1966, pp. 306–18.
Gale, Frederick, *Modern English Sports: Their Use and Their Abuse*, London, 1885.
Gedge, Paul, *Thames Journey*, London, 1949.

Gilbert, Stuart, and Horner, Ray, *The Thames Barrier*, London, 1984.

Gill, Alison, *The Yanks at Oxford: The 1987 Boat Race Controversy*, Lewes, 1991.

Gill, Conrad, *The Naval Mutinies of 1797*, Manchester, 1913.

Godolphin, Peter, *London's River: Father Thames*, London, 1949.

Godsal, Major Philip Thomas, *The Storming of London and the Thames Valley Campaign*, London, 1908.

Goldsmith-Carter, George, *The Battle of Britain*, New York, 1974.

Goodburn, Damian, and Milne, Gustave, 'The Early Medieval Port of London, AD 700–1200', *Antiquity*, vol. 64, no. 244, pp. 629–37.

Grahame, Kenneth, *The Wind in the Willows*, Oxford, 1999.

Grant, Alexander, and Stringer, Keith (eds), *Uniting the Kingdom? The Making of British History*, London, 1995.

Grant, Ian, and Maddren, Nicholas, *The City at War*, London, 1975.

Grayson, Anna, *Rock Solid, Britain's Most Ancient Heritage*, London, 1992.

Grieve, Hilda, T*he Great Tide: The story of the 1953 flood disaster in Essex*, London, 1959.

Griffiths, Paul, and Jenner, Mark (eds), *Londinopolis: Essays in the Cultural and Social History of Early Modern London*, London 2000.

Griffiths, Roger, *An Essay to prove that the Jurisdiction and Conservancy of the River Thames &c. is committed to the Lord Mayor of London*, London, 1746.

Grosvenor, J. *The Port of London*, London, 1957.

Guest, Edwin (ed.), *The Wreck of the Princess Alice*, London, 1878.

Hadfield, R.L., 'Convict Hulks of the Thames', *The Nautical Magazine*, vol. 144, July–December 1940, pp. 197–9.

Haill, C.R., *Memoirs of Life of a River Thames Tug*, Gravesend, 1896.

Hainsworth, Roger, and Churches, Christine, *The Anglo-Dutch Naval Wars, 1652–1674*, London, 1998.

Halliday, Stephen, *The Great Stink of London: Sir Joseph Bazalgette and the Cleansing of Victorian London*, Stroud, 1999.

Hamilton, James, *Turner: A Life*, London, 1997.

—— *Turner and the Scientists*, London, 1998.

Harding, D.W., *The Iron Age in the Upper Thames Basin*, Oxford, 1972.

Harper, W.H., *Shakespeare and the Thames*, London, 1888.

Hatts, Leigh, 'Shelley and the Thames', *Thames Guardian: Journal of the River Thames Society*, autumn 1995, pp. 12–13.

Hauser, Kitty, *Stanley Spencer*, London, 2001.

Hawkes, John, and Jenkins, Vince, *The Past in Progress: The Archaeology of the Thames Valley Business Park*, London, 1989.

Headley, Olwen, *Windsor Castle*, London, 1994.

Helgerson, Richard, *Forms of Nationhood: The Elizabethan Writing of England*, Chicago, 1992.

Herbert, A.P., *Light the Lights*, London, 1945.

—— *Independent Member*, London, 1970.

—— *The Thames*, London, 1966.

—— *A.P.H. His Life and Times*, London, 1979.

Heseltine, Michael, *Life in the Jungle, My Autobiography*, London, 2000.

Hibbert, Christopher, *Tower of London*, New York, 1971.

—— *The Court at Windsor*, London, 1982.

Hill, David, *Constable's English Landscape Scenery*, London, 1985.

—— *Turner on the Thames: River Journeys in the Year 1805*, New Haven, 1993.

Hilton, Rodney, *Bond Men Made Free*, London, 1973.

Hobley, Brian, and Milne, Gustave (eds). *Waterfront Archaeology in Britain and Northern Europe*, London, 1981.

Hobsbawm, Eric, and Ranger, Terence (eds), *The Invention of Tradition*, Cambridge, 1983.

Hoggart, Richard, *The Uses of Literacy*, London, 1957.

Holden, Donald, *Whistler Landscapes and Seascapes*, London, 1969.

Hollamby, Ted, Docklands Forum, *Docklands – London's Backyard into Front Yard*, London, 1990.

Hollister, C. Warren, *The Making of England, 55 B.C. to 1399*, Lexington, 1983.

Holmes, Colin (ed.), *Immigrants and Minorities in British Society*, London, 1978.

Holt, J.C., *Magna Carta*, Cambridge, 1991.

Horgan, Paul, *Great River: The Rio Grande in North American History*, New York, 1954.

Howard, Peter, *Landscapes: The Artists' Vision*, London, 1981.

Howarth, William, *Some Particulars Relating to the Ancient and Royal Borough of Greenwich*, Greenwich, 1882.

Hughes, David T., *Sheerness and the Mutiny at the Nore*, Minster-in-Sheppey, 1997.

Humpherus, Henry, *History of the Origin and Progress of the Company of Watermen and Lightermen of the River Thames*, London, 1859.

Hyman, Timothy, and Wright, Patrick (eds), *Stanley Spencer*, London, 2001.

Ingersoll, Ralph, *Report on England*, London, 1941.

Irwin, John, and Herbert, Jocelyn (eds), *Sweete Themmes*, London, 1951.

Ives, E.W., *Anne Boleyn*, Oxford, 1986.

Ives, E.W., Knecht, R.J., and Scarisbrick, J.J. (ed.) *Wealth and Power in Tudor England: Essays presented to S.T. Bindoff*, London, 1978.

James, Henry, *English Hours*, Oxford, 1981.

James, W.M., *The Influence of Sea-Power on the History of the British People*, Cambridge, 1948.

Jarvis, Rupert, C., 'The Metamorphosis of the Port of London,' *The London Journal*, vol. 3, no. 1, 1977, pp. 55–69.

Jenkins, Alan (photos by Derry Brabbs), *The Book of the Thames*, London, 1983.

Jerome, Jerome K., *My Life and Times*, London, 1926.

—— *Three Men in a Boat*, London, 1989.

Johnson, J.P., 'The Paleolithic Period in the Thames Basin', *Essex Naturalist*, vol. 13, no. 3, March 1902, pp. 97–111.

—— 'Paleolithic Implements from Thames Valley, chiefly Ilford and Grays', *Essex Naturalist*, vol. 12, no. 1, January 1901, pp. 53–7.

Jones, R.L., and Keen, D.H., *Pleistocene Environments in the British Isles*, London, 1993.

Kear, Janet, *The Mute Swan*, Aylesbury, 1988.

Keates, Jonathan, *Handel, The Man and His Music*, London, 1985.

Keen, Derek, 'Issues of Water in Medieval London,' unpublished.

—— 'London Bridge and the Identity of the City,' unpublished.

Kelvin, Norman (ed.), *The Collected Letters of William Morris*, Vols. I-III, Princeton, 1984.

Kemplay, John, *The Thames Locks*, Chipping Camden, 2000.

Klingender, Francis, *Art and the Industrial Revolution*, Chatham, 1968.

Lacey, Robert, *Sir Walter Raleigh*, London, 1973.

Lambrick, George, and Robinson, Mark, *Iron Age and Roman Riverside Settlements at Farmoor, Oxfordshire*, Oxford, 1979.

Lampe, David, *The Tunnel*, London, 1963.

Lane, Leonard, *Down the River to the Sea*, London, 1935.

Langford, Paul, *Englishness Identified: Manners and Character, 1650–1850*, Oxford, 2000.

Leeds, E.T., 'Early Settlement in the Upper Thames Basin', *Geography*, no. 82, vol. XIV, part 6, autumn 1928

Leon, Walter, *Thomas Doggett Pictur'd*, London, 1980.

Leopold, Luna B., *Water: A Primer*, San Francisco, 1974.

Linebaugh, Peter, and Rediker, Marcus, *The Many-Headed Hydra: Sailors, Slaves, Commoners and the Hidden History of the Revolutionary Atlantic*, London, 2000.

Livingstone, Ken, *If Voting Changed Anything, They'd Abolish It*, London, 1987.

Lloyd, Christopher, 'New Light on the Mutiny at the Nore', *The Mariner's Mirror*, vol. 46, no. 4, 1960, pp. 286–95.

Loftie, W.J., *Authorised Guide to the Tower of London*, London, 1888.

'London Journalist', *The Wreck of the Princess Alice: or, the appalling Thames disaster with loss of about 700 lives*, London, 1878.

Longmate, Norman, *Defending the Island, Caesar to the Armada*, London, 1989.

Lovejoy, Paul, and Rogers, Nicholas (eds), *Unfree Labour in the Development of the Atlantic World*, London, 1994.

Lovell, John, *Stevedores and Dockers*, London, 1969.

Lowenthal, David, 'British National Identity and the English Landscape', *Rural History: Economy, Society, Culture*, vol. 2, no. 2, October 1991, pp. 205–30.

Luckin, Bill, *Pollution and Control: A Social History of the Thames in the Nineteenth Century*, Bristol, 1986.

Lukacs, John, *Churchill: Visionary, Statesman, Historian*, New Haven, 2002.

MacCaffrey, Wallace, *Elizabeth I*, London, 1993.

MacCarthy, Fiona, *Stanley Spencer: An English Vision*, London, 1998.

—— *William Morris*, London, 1994.

McCave, Fred, *A History of Canvey Island*, Bristol, 1985.

McLean, Rita, *The Downstream Dock: Tilbury, 1886–1986*, Thurrock, 1986.

MacSwiney, Marquis, *Six Came Flying*, Southampton, 1989.

Mandler, Peter, 'Politics and the English Landscape since the First World War,' *Huntington Library Quarterly*, vol. 55, 1992, pp. 459–76.

—— 'Against "Englishness": English Culture and the Limits to Rural Nostalgia, 1850–1940', *Transactions of the Royal Historical Society* Sixth Series, vol. VII, Cambridge, 1997, pp. 155–75.

Mangan, J.A., *The Games Ethic and Imperialism: Aspects of the Diffusion of an Ideal*, London, 1998.

Manwaring, G.E., and Dobrée, Bonamy, *Mutiny: The Floating Republic*, London, 1987.

Markgraf, Carl, 'Jerome K. Jerome, An Annotated Bibliography of Writings about Him', *English Literature in Transition, 1880–1920*, vol. 26, no. 2, 1983, pp. 83–126.

Marsden, Peter, *Ships of the Port of London: First to Eleventh Centuries AD*, London, 1994.

Marshall, Roderick, *William Morris and his Earthly Paradises*, New York, 1981.

Martin, Frank, *Rogues' River: Crime on the River Thames in the Eighteenth Century*, Southampton, 1983.

Mason, Tony (ed.), *Sport in Britain*, Cambridge, 1989.

Mathews, Joseph, J., 'The First Harvard–Oxford Boat Race', *New England Quarterly*, vol. 33, no. 1, March 1960, pp. 74–82.

Mayhew, Henry, and Binny, John, *The Criminal Prisons of London and Scenes of Prison Life*, London, 1862.

Milne, Gustave, *The Port of Roman London*, London, 1985.

Mindell, Jonathan and Ruth, *Bridges over the Thames*, Poole, 1985.

Money, Tony, *Manly & Muscular Diversions*, London, 1997.

Montgomery, Bernard Law, Viscount Montgomery of Alamein, *The Memoirs of Field-Marshal the Viscount Montgomery of Alamein, KG*, London, 1958.

Moorehead, Alan, *Montgomery: A Biography*, London, 1946.

Moran, James, 'Printing on the Thames', *The Black Art*, vol. 2, no. 3, Autumn 1963, pp. 698–72.

Morisawa, Marie, *Streams: Their Dynamics and Morphology*, New York, 1968.

Morris, William, *News from Nowhere*, London, New York, 1966.

Muir, Richard and Nina, *Rivers of Britain*, London, 1986.

'N.A.' *The Life and Extraordinary Adventures of Parker the Delegate and Ringleader of the Mutiny at Sheerness*, London, 1797.

—— *The Trials of Davis, who stiled himself the Captain, and 16 Delegates, (All Seamen belonging to the Sandwich) Who on Thursday last received Sentence of Death, For Mutiny at Sheerness*, London, July 19, 1797.

Neale, J.E., *Queen Elizabeth I*, London, 1952.

Neale, Jonathan, *The Cutlass & the Lash: Mutiny and Discipline in Nelson's Navy*, London, 1986.

Needham, Stuart, *The Passage of the Thames: Holocene Environment and Settlement at Runnymede*, London, 2000.

Nicolson, Adam, *Regeneration: The Story of the Dome*, London, 1999.

Noyes, Alfred, *William Morris*, London, 1908.

Ogden, Philip (ed.), *Update London Dockland: The Challenge of Development*, Cambridge, 1992.

Overman, Michael, *Sir Marc Brunel and the Tunnel*, London, 1971.

Pallister, Anne, *Magna Carta: The Heritage of Liberty*, Oxford, 1971.

Parnell, Geoffrey, *The Tower of London, Past & Present*, London, 1998.

Patin, Sylvie (trans. Maev de la Guardia), *Claude Monet in Great Britain*, Paris, 1994.

Paul Deslandes, '"The Foreign Element": Newcomers and the Rhetoric of Race, Nation, and Empire in "Oxbridge" Undergraduate Culture, 1850–1920', *Journal of British Studies*, vol. 37, no. 1, January 1998, pp. 54–90.

Payne, Christiana, Rosenthal, Michael, and Wilcox, Scott (eds), *Prospects for the Nation: Recent Essays in British Landscape, 1750–1880*, New Haven, 1997.

Payne, John, *Journey up the Thames: William Morris and Modern England*, Nottingham, 2000.

Phillips, Geoffrey, *Thames Crossings*, London, 1981.

Pollard, Michael, *North Sea Surge: The Story of the East Coast Floods of 1953*, Lavenham, 1978.

Poole, Austin Lane, *Domesday Book to Magna Carta*, Oxford, 1993.

Pople, Kenneth, *Stanley Spencer: A Biography*, London, 1991.

Price, Alfred, *Blitz on Britain 1939–45*, London, 2000.

Priestley, J.B., *English Humour*, London 1976.

Pritchett, V.S., 'The Tin-openers', *New Statesman and Nation*, 15 June 1957.

Pugsley, Sir Alfred (ed.), *The Works of Isambard Kingdom Brunel, an Engineering Appreciation*, Bristol, 1976.

Raban, Jonathan, *For Love and Money*, London, 1987.

Rackham, Oliver, *The History of the Countryside*, London, 1986.

Ramsey, Peter, *Tudor Economic Problems*, London, 1963.

Redgrave, Steven (with Nick Townsend), *A Golden Age*, London, 2000.

Reynolds, Susan, *Kingdoms and Communities in Western Europe, 900–1300*, London, 1984.

Reed, David, 'Swan Upping', *Thames Guardian: Journal of the River Thames Society*, summer 1997, pp. 19–21.

Reed, Michael, *The Landscape of Britain: From the beginnings to 1914*, London, 1990.

Reed, Nicholas, *Sisley and the Thames*, London, 1992.

—— *Monet and the Thames*, London, 1998.

Rigden, Reg, *The Floating Prisons of Woolwich and Deptford*, London, 1976.

Roberts, Clayton and David, *A History of England, Prehistory to 1714*, Englewood Cliffs, 1985.

Robbins Landon, H.C., *Handel and his World*, London, 1984.

Robbins, Keith, *Great Britain: Identities, Institutions and the Idea of Britishness*, London, 1998.

Robinson, Duncan, *Stanley Spencer*, Oxford, 1990.

Robinson, John Martin, *Windsor Castle, A Short History*, London, 1996.

Rodner, William, 'Humanity and Nature in the Steamboat Paintings of J.M.W. Turner', *Albion*, vol. 18, no. 3, fall 1986, pp. 455–74.

—— *J.M.W. Turner: Romantic Painter of the Industrial Revolution*, Berkeley, 1997.

Rogers, N.A.M., *The Safeguard of the Sea, A Naval History of Britain, Vol. 1, 660–1649*, London, 1997.

Rogers, Nicholas, *Crowds, Culture and Politics in Georgian Britain*, Oxford, 1998.

Rogers, P.G., *The Dutch in the Medway*, London, 1970.

Rolt., L.T.C., *The Thames, From Mouth to Source*, London, 1951.

—— *Isambard Kingdom Brunel: A Biography*, London, 1957.

Rosenthal, Michael, *British Landscape Painting*, Oxford, 1982.

Ross, Gordon, *The Boat Race: The Story of the First Hundred Races Between Oxford and Cambridge*, London, 1954.

Rowse, A.L., *The Tower of London in the History of the Nation*, London, 1972.

Rubin, Reed, 'Rubin on Rowing,' *Oxford Magazine*, vol. LXXVII, no. 2, 23 October 1958, pp. 32–5.

Ruddock, Alwyn, 'London Capitalists and the Decline of Southampton in the Early Tudor Period,' *The Economic History Review*, Second Series, vol. II, no. 2, pp. 137–51.

Russell, Ronald, *Guide to British Topographical Prints*, London, 1979.

Sampson, Anthony, *Anatomy of Britain*, London, 1962.

Samuel, Raphael (ed.), *Patriotism: The Making and Unmaking of British National Identity*, Vols. I and III, London, 1989.

Schama, Simon, *Landscape and Memory*, New York, 1996.

—— 'The Church of Me', *New Yorker*, 17 February 1997, pp. 51–8.

—— *A History of Britain*, Vol. I, London, 2000.

Schneer, Jonathan, *Ben Tillett: Portrait of a Labor Leader*, Urbana Champaign, 1978.

Sellers, Leonard, *Shot in the Tower*, London, 1997.

Sherwood, W.E., *Oxford Rowing*, Oxford, 1900.

Shetelig, Haakon (ed.), *Viking Antiquities in Great Britain and Ireland*, Oslo, 1940.

Sibly, Job, *The Trial of Richard Parker Complete . . .*, London, 1797.

Simmons, I.G., and Tooley, M.J. (eds), *The Environment in British Prehistory*, London 1981.

Simms, Eric, *A Natural History of Britain and Ireland*, London, 1979.

Simon, Jacob (ed.), *Handel: A Celebration of his Life and Times, 1685–1759*, London, 1986.

Smollett, T.G., *The Expedition of Humphrey Clinker*, London, 1771.

Solkin, David, *Richard Wilson: The Landscape of Reaction*, London, 1983.

Southey, Robert, *Wat Tyler*, Oxford, 1989.

Srigley, Michael, 'The Great Frost Fair of 1683–4', *History Today*, vol. 10, part 12, 1960, pp. 848–55.

Stansky, Peter, *Redesigning the World*, Princeton, 1985.

Starkey, David, *Elizabeth: Apprenticeship*, London, 2000.

Steen, Sara Jayne (ed.), *The Letters of Lady Arbella Stuart*, Oxford, 1994.

Stewart, Gregory, and Trotter, D.A, (eds), *De Mot en mot: Aspects of medieval linguistics, Essays in honour of William Rothwell*, Cardiff, 1997.

Strong, Roy, *The Cult of Elizabeth*, London, 1977.

—— *And When Did You Last See Your Father? The Victorian Painter and British History*, London, 1978.

—— *The Tudor and Stuart Monarchy: Pageantry, Painting, Iconography*, Vol. II, Woodbridge, 1995.

Sutton, Denys, *Nocturne, the Art of James McNeill Whistler*, London, 1963.

—— *James McNeill Whistler: Paintings, Etchings, Pastels & Watercolours*, Aylesbury, 1966.

Tate Gallery, *Stanley Spencer: A Sort of Heaven*, Liverpool, 1992.

Tatham, John. *Aqua Triumphalis . . .*, London, 1662.

Taylor, John Russell, *Cities and Water*, The Gallery West India Quay, London 4–24 September, 1995.

Thames Gateway, *A Summary of the Planning Framework*, London, 1995.

Thacker, Fred. S., *The Stripling Thames, A Book of the river above Oxford*, London, 1909.

—— *The Thames Highway, A General History*, London, 1914.

—— *The Thames Highway. Locks and Weirs*, London, 1920.

Thompson, Edward P., *William Morris*, London, 1976.

Thompson, F.H. (ed.), *Archaeology and Coastal Change*, London, 1980.

Thurston, Gavin, *The Great Thames Disaster*, London, 1965.

Ticehurst, Norman F., *The Mute Swan in England*, London, 1957.

Tinton, Ben, *War Comes to the Docks*, London, 1942.

Todd, Malcolm, *Roman Britain, 55 BC–AD 400*, London, 1981.

Topolski, Daniel, *The Oxford Revival*, London, 1985.

Topolski, Daniel (with Patrick Robinson), *True Blue: The Oxford Boat Race Mutiny*, London, 1989.

Turner, Jane (ed.), *The Dictionary of Art*, vol. 33, New York, 1996.

van Ishoven, Armand, *The Luftwaffe in the Battle of Britain*, New York, 1980.

Van Slyke, Lyman, *Yangtze: Nature, History and the River*, Stanford, 1998.

Vaughan, Adrian, *Isambard Kingdom Brunel, Engineering Knight-Errant*, London, 1991.

Vaux, James Hardy, *Memoirs of James Hardy Vaux, A Swindler and Thief*, London, 1827.

Verona, N.A., *Past Worlds: The Times Atlas of Archaeology*, London, 1988.

Wade, Shamus, O.D., *All the 214 Bridges across the Thames (together with the 17 public tunnels, 12 crossable locks, 5 public ferries, 4 crossable artifacts and 1 ford)*, London, 1995.

Walford, Edward, *Frost Fairs on the Thames*, London, 1886.

Walmisley, Arthur, *The Bridges over the Thames at London*, London, 1880.

Warnicke, Retha M., *The Rise and Fall of Anne Boleyn*, Cambridge, 1989.

Welch, Charles, *History of the Tower Bridge*, London, 1894.

Webb, R.K., *Modern England*, New York, 1980.

Wells, Roger, *Insurrection: The British Experience, 1795–1803*, London, 1983.

Wenke, Robert, J., *Patterns in Prehistory: Humankind's First Three Million Years*, Oxford, 1999.

West, Michael, 'Spenser, Everard Digby and the Renaissance Art of Swimming', *Renaissance Quarterly*, vol. 26, no. 1, 1973, pp. 12–20.

Wheeler, Alwyn, *The Tidal Thames: the History of a River and its Fishes*, London, 1979.

White, Richard, *The Organic Machine*, New York, 1995.

Whitworth, Michael, '"Sweet Thames" and *The Waste Land*'s Allusions', *Essays in Criticism*, vol. XLVIII, no. 1, January 1998, pp. 36–45.

Weiner, Martin, *English Culture and the Decline of the Industrial Spirit, 1950–1980*, Cambridge, 1981.

Wilhide, Elizabeth, *The Millennium Dome*, London, n.d.

Williams, Archibald, *Brunel and After: The Romance of the Great Western Railway*, London, 1925.

Williams, Raymond, *The Country and the City*, London, 1985.

Williams, Sheila, 'A Lord Mayor's Show by John Taylor, the Water Poet', *Bulletin of the John Rylands Library*, vol. 41, no. 2, March 1959, pp. 502–29.

Williams, Stephanie, *Docklands*, London, 1993.

Wilson, David Gordon, *The Making of the Middle Thames*, Bourne End, 1977.

—— *The Victorian Thames*, Dover, NH, 1993.

Wilson, Derek, *The Tower of London*, London, 1989.

Wilson, Jean, *Entertainments for Elizabeth I*, Englewood Cliffs, 1980.

Wilson, Ken, *The Story of the Thames Barrier*, London, 1984.

Wilson, Sheila, *Thames Barrier*, London, 1991.

Wilton, Andrew, *Turner in his Time*, London, 1987.

Wintringham, T.H., *Mutiny: Being a Survey of Mutinies from Spartacus to Invergordon*, London, 1936.

Wohl, Anthony, *Endangered Lives: Public Health in Victorian Britain*, London, 1983.

Wood, Julia K., '"A flowing harmony": Music on the Thames in Restoration London', *Early Music*, vol. XXIII, no. 4, November 1995, pp. 553–70.

Woolf, Virginia, *Orlando*, San Diego, 1973.

Woon, Basil, *Hell Came to London*, London, 1941.

Wright, Patrick, *The River: The Thames in Our Time*, London, 1999.

Young, Alan R., *His Majesty's Royal Ship: A Critical Edition of Thomas Heyood's A True Description of His Majesties Royall Ship (1637)*, New York, 1990.

Ziegler, Philip, *London at War, 1939–45*, London, 2002.

Index

Alfred, King of Wessex 23–4
Anne Boleyn, Queen 46, 58–9, 61

Baldwin, Stanley 196
Baptism, The 191–2
Bazalgette, Joseph 148–9, 154, 159
Beddington 19
Bell Tower 45
Bellamy, Edward 173
Belliqueux 136
Bevin, Ernest 214, 265
bibliography 308–24
Black Death 34
Blake, John 95
Bligh, William 84, 88, 99, 100
Blitz 198–209
Bocking 36
Bondi, Hermann 251
Boudicca, Queen 16
Bray 13
Brentwood 36
Brilliant 98, 107
Britain, Battle of 198
broad gauge 128

Brunel, Isambard Kingdom 124–30, 133
Brunel, Sir Marc Isambard 125
Brunswick 140–2
Buckner, Admiral 95, 110
Burne-Jones, Edward 164–6
Burning of the House of Lords and Commons 131–2
Burns, John 4
Bywell Castle 151–2, *153*

Cambridge-Oxford Boat Race 218–39
Canary Wharf 270–2
Canvey Island 2, 246–9
Caratacus 15
Carline, Hilda 189
Catherine Howard, Queen 46
Catherine of Braganza, Queen 61–2
Chamberlain, Joseph 158, 167
Charles I, King 60
Charles II, King 61–2, 75
cholera 146
Christ in Cookham 192
Christ preaching at Cookham Regatta 192–3

Churchill, Sir Winston 4, 196, 198
    funeral procession 290–1
Clark, Chris 228–37, 239
'Class War' movement 281–2
Claudius, Emperor 15
Clifton suspension bridge 126
Cliveden estate 166, 178
Clyde 90, 94, 98, 99, 100
Cole, George Vicat 67
Conrad, Joseph 18
containerisation 266
Cookham 1914: 180, 182
Cookham Lock 166
Cookham-on-Thames 3, 178–93
Cooling 1
Corresponding Societies 86
cranes dipped in tribute 290
Cromwell, Thomas 59
Culloden 85, 87, 94
Cunningham, Captain 90, 91

D-day invasion 210–16
Danelaw 24–5
Dash, Jack 266
Denham, Sir John 31–2, 67
Dennis, Abraham 152–4
depression LZ 244
diarrhoea 146
Director 88, 90, 94, 106, 109
Disraeli, Benjamin 148, 149
dockers 213–15, 263–9
dockers' strike [1889] 168–70, 264–5
dockland culture 265, 269
Docklands 269
Docklands Light Railway 271
Docklands regeneration, protests
    against 277–85
docks 194–216
Dogs, Isle of 197, 207–8, 270, 272, 273,
    278–81
Doré, Gustave 161
Draper, Charles 251

Dryden, John 67
Dunkirk evacuation 204
Dunkirk, spirit of 213

East End community 283
East India Docks 267
East Thames Corridor 276
Edgar the Peaceable 24–5
Edward the Confessor 25
Edwards, Hugh Robert Arthur
    'Jumbo' 220–7
'effortless superiority' ideal 233
Eliot, T.S. 4
Elizabeth I, Queen 46, 48, 60, 72, 291
Elizabeth II, Queen 258–60
estuary 16
Ethelred the Unready 25
Evelyn, John 61

Fairfax, Sir Thomas 60–1
Falling Radial Gates 252
Faraday, Michael 147, 148
Felixstowe 266
Fighting Temeraire, The 132
filthy river 143–9
frost fairs 69–80
funeral processions
    Queen Elizabeth I 60, 291
    Sir Winston Churchill 290–1

Gallion's Reach 150
Gatehampton Farm 9, 19
General Committee 89, 93–5, 98
George I, King 62–5
Globe Theatre 273
Goebbels, Joseph 207
Goering, Hermann 198
Gondwanaland 4
Graham, Kenneth 191
Great Britain 127
Great Eastern 124
'Great Shield' 125

'Great Stink' 148
Great Western 126
Great Western Railway 124–5,
    127–30, 133–4
Greater London Council 251, 254–6,
    259–60
Grimes, Charlie 223, 226, 227
Gunpowder Plot 53

Hadrian 16
Hammersmith Bridge *219*
Hammersmith Socialist Society 168
Handel, George Frederick 63–5, 259
Hardy, Joseph 107
Harvest Dinner, Kingston Bank 123, 124
Havengore 290–1
Henley Regatta 225
Henry VIII, King 57, 58–9, 61, 144
Herbert, Alan Patrick 202–6, 208,
    211–12, 250, 288
Heseltine, Michael 268, 271–2, 275–6,
    283–4
Hitler, Adolf 198
Howard, Ronnie 222–7, 230
Hurley Lock 166

impressment 84–5
individualism 77–8
Inflexible 88, 91, 94, 98, 99, 108, 110
Ingrebourne, River 247
Isis 98, 107

James I, King [King James VI of
    Scotland] 44, 48, 49
James, Henry 161
Jennings, Humphrey 65
Jerome, Jerome K. 32
John, King 26–7, 29–30
Jubilee Line 271–2

Kelmscott 2–3, 164, 166, 169–70,
    176–7

'kiddles' 240
King's Lynn 245
Kipling, Rudyard 14, 33
Knight, John 106, 107

Labour Party 168
Lady Place 166
Lancaster 97–8
landscape painting 116–18
Lea, River 247
Lechlade 18
Leopard 106, 109
livery companies 65
Livingstone, Ethel 259
Livingstone, Ken 254–61
Lobbenburg, Andy 235
London Bridge 70, 146
London City Airport 271
London County Council 159, 251
London Dockland Development
    Corporation 268, 275
London Docklands Strategic Plan 267
London Eye 273
Looking Backward 173
Lord Mayor of London 58–9
Lord Mayor's processions 65–8
Love among the Nations 191

Magill, John 261
Magna Carta 29–30, 60–1
Maidenhead bridge 3, 128–9, 135
Martin, John 148–9
McDonald, Donald 229–30, 233, 235,
    237
Men with Horses crossing the River 122
Metropolitan Board of Works 149,
    158–9, 167, 251
military significance 21
Millennium Dome 276–7
Millwall Docks 195, 200, 267
Misleading Cases 202
monarchical power 44

Monmouth 106–7
Montagu 106, 108
Montgomery, Bernard Law 214–15
Moonlight, a Study at Millbank 116
More, Sir Thomas 45–6
Morris, William 2–3, 162–77, 193
Mosse, Robert 89, 110
Mulberry harbours 211

Nassau 107, 136
naval corruption 84
Newark Abbey on the Wey 122, 123
News from Nowhere 173–7
Nore mutiny 82, 86, 88–114
Nore, the 81–2
North Sea surge 243–9

'observed paintings' 180, 182
Orlando 76
Oxford UBC 'mutinies'
    1959: 220, 222–7
    1987: 220, 227–37

Paine, Tom 86, 103
Pankhurst, Sir Robert 67
Parker, 'President' Richard 91–112
Peacock, Thomas Love 32, 67
peasants' revolt 35–42
People's Charter for Docklands 284–5
Pepys, Samuel 61–2
Peterloo massacre 137
pillboxes 21
Pitt, William 104–5
Pluto project 211
poets' connections 32
poll tax 1380: 35
Pool of London, The 67
Port Emergency Committee 197
Port of London Authority 197, 265
Porter, Dame Shirley 257, 258–9, 260–1
pound locks 241–2
Preece, Patricia 189

'pressed' men 84–5
Princes in the Tower 44
Princess Alice 149–58, 167
Princess Victoria 245
prison hulks 136–43
promiscuity on ice 76–7
Proserpine 90
Purfleet 247

Queen Mary 244
'quota men' 86

raiding parties 23
Rain, Steam and Speed – The Great Western Railway 125–6, 133–5
Rainham Creek 247, 249
Raleigh, Sir Walter 53–5
Reculver 15, 22
Reichmann, Paul 270–2
Repulse 106–7, 109
Retribution 140–3
Reynolds, Sir Joshua 116
Richard II, King 37–42, 43, 44
Rights of Man, The 86
Rising Sector Gates 251–2
Ritchie, Sir Douglas 197
river and nation 286–91
River Emergency Service 203
River Scene 121
Roding, River 247
Rodney, Edward 49, 51, 52
Roman forts 22
Roman ships 17
Romans 15–20, 22–3
Rossetti, Dante Gabriel 169
Royal Albert Dock 195
Royal Arsenal 142
Royal Docks 195, 249, 267
Royal Naval Thames (Auxiliary) Patrol 204
Royal processions 57–65, 259, 291
Rubin, Reed 222–7

Runnymede 9–14, 29–33

St Katharine's Dock 195, 267
St Thomas' Tower 50–1
San Fiorenzo 91, 94, 100
Sandwich 88–90, 93–5, 99, 108, 110, 112, 136
Sea Palling 245
Seymour, Edward 49
Seymour, Francis 52
Seymour, William 49–53
Sheerness *83*, 84
Sheppey, Isle of 82
sludge boats 159
'smiggins' 141
Smithfield 40
Social Democratic Federation 167
social exclusivity 239
social rank 224–5
social reciprocal obligations 77–8
Socialist League 168
source 2
Spencer, Stanley 3, 178–93
Spithead mutiny 86–8, 93–4
'Starlings' 70–1
stevedores 213–15
stopping up the river 101–5
Stuart, Lady Arbella 48–52
Stukeley, Sir Lewis 54–5
Surrey Commercial Docks 195, 267
Swan Upping at Cookham 182–8
swans 182–5
Swanscombe 6–8
Syon Ferry House 118–20

Tate Modern 273–5
Tatham, John 62
Thackeray, William 135
Thames Barrier 203, 249–54, 258–60, 262
Thames Gateway 275–6
Thames Path 288

Thames tunnel 125
Thatcher, Margaret 238–9, 254–61
Three Men in a Boat 32
Thurrock 247
tides 51–2, 55–6, 287–8
Tilbury 266
Tilbury Dock 247
Tilbury Fort 97–8, 100
Tone, Wolf 86
Topolski, Daniel 228–38, 239
Tower of London 26, 38, 40, 43–56
trade 65–7
Traitor's Gate 45, 56
transformation of England [fictional] 173–7
transportation to Australia 138, 140, 143
Trewsbury 2
Tripcock Point 150–1
Turner, Joseph Mallord William 115–126, 130–5
Tyler, Wat 39–40, 42
typhoid 146

Vaulted Hall, A 126
Vaux, James Hardy 139–43
View of Richmond Hill and Bridge 122
Vikings 22–5

Wallingford 13
War of the Roses 43–4
Ward, Reg 269–70
warehouses 195
wartime lifeline 206
Water Gypsy 203–6
Water Music 62–5, 259
watermen 62, 70, *71*, 77, 156, 185, 225, 234, 275
Waverley, Lord 250
weirs 241
Wessex 23–4
West India Docks 267

West, Benjamin 119

Wey, River 122

White Tower 45

Wiele, Herbert Augustus 151–2

Wind in the Willows 191

Windsor Castle 25, *28*, 29

Woolf, Virginia 76

Words for Battle 65

Wordsworth, William
      161–2